To John Ikenberry,

With my warm
regards

Zalic

The Sciences Po Series in International Relations and Political Economy

Series Editor, Christian Lequesne

This series consists of works emanating from the foremost French researchers from Sciences Po, Paris. Sciences Po was founded in 1872, and is today one of the most prestigious universities for teaching and research in social sciences in France, recognized worldwide.

This series focuses on the transformations of the international arena, in a world where the state, though its sovereignty is questioned, reinvents itself. The series explores the effects on international relations and the world economy of regionalization, globalization (not only of trade and finance but also of culture), and transnational flows at large. This evolution in world affairs sustains a variety of networks from the ideological to the criminal or terrorist. Besides the geopolitical transformations of the globalized planet, the new political economy of the world has a decided impact on its destiny as well, and this series hopes to uncover what that is.

Published by Palgrave Macmillan:

Politics In China: Moving Frontiers
    edited by Françoise Mengin and Jean-Louis Rocca
Tropical Forests, International Jungle: The Underside of Global Ecopolitics
    by Marie-Claude Smouts, translated by Cynthia Schoch
The Political Economy of Emerging Markets: Actors, Institutions and Financial Crises in Latin America
    by Javier Santiso
Cyber China: Reshaping National Identities in the Age of Information
    edited by Françoise Mengin
With Us or Against Us: Studies in Global Anti-Americanism
    edited by Denis Lacorne and Tony Judt
Vietnam's New Order: International Perspectives on the State and Reform in Vietnam
    edited by Stéphanie Balme and Mark Sidel
Equality and Transparency: A Strategic Perspective on Affirmative Action in American Law
    by Daniel Sabbagh, translation by Cynthia Schoch and John Atherton
Moralizing International Relations: Called to Account
    by Ariel Colonomos, translated by Chris Turner
Norms over Force: The Enigma of European Power
    by Zaki Laïdi, translated from the French by Cynthia Schoch
Democracies at War against Terrorism: A Comparative Perspective
    edited by Samy Cohen, translated by John Atherton, Roger Leverdier, Leslie Piquemal, and Cynthia Schoch

Limited Achievements

Obama's Foreign Policy

Zaki Laïdi

Translated by
Carolyn Avery

LIMITED ACHIEVEMENTS
Copyright © Zaki Laïdi, 2012.

All rights reserved.

First published in French in 2010 as *Le monde selon Obama* by
Éditions Stock, Paris, France.

First published in English in 2012 by
PALGRAVE MACMILLAN®
in the United States—a division of St. Martin's Press LLC,
175 Fifth Avenue, New York, NY 10010.

Where this book is distributed in the UK, Europe and the rest of the world,
this is by Palgrave Macmillan, a division of Macmillan Publishers Limited,
registered in England, company number 785998, of Houndmills,
Basingstoke, Hampshire RG21 6XS.

Palgrave Macmillan is the global academic imprint of the above companies
and has companies and representatives throughout the world.

Palgrave® and Macmillan® are registered trademarks in the United States,
the United Kingdom, Europe and other countries.

ISBN: 978–1–137–02085–7

Library of Congress Cataloging-in-Publication Data

Laïdi, Zaki.
[Monde selon Obama. English]
    Limited achievements : Obama's foreign policy / Zaki Laïdi ; translated by
Carolyn Avery.
        p. cm.—(Sciences Po series in international relations and political economy)
        Includes bibliographical references and index.
        ISBN 978–1–137–02085–7 (alk. paper)
        1. Obama, Barack. 2. Obama, Barack—Political and social views.
    3. United States—Foreign relations—2009– 4. United States—Politics and
    government—2009– I. Title.

E907.L3413 2012
973.932092—dc23   2012010432

A catalogue record of the book is available from the British Library.

Design by Newgen Imaging Systems (P) Ltd., Chennai, India.

First edition: September 2012

10 9 8 7 6 5 4 3 2 1

Printed and bound in Great Britain by
CPI Antony Rowe, Chippenham and Eastbourne

To Louise

CONTENTS

TABLES

INTRODUCTION

The election of an American president is unique because it is not important to American citizens alone, given the country's leading global role. It has a systemic effect on all the actors in the international system. However, the scope of this event depends on the personality of the chief executive, the particular political scene in the United States, and the global context. Each of these three factors has been decisive for Barack Obama.

He blazed the trail to the election of the first black president in US history, even though he is biracial, rather than African American. Furthermore, his middle name's Muslim ring—Hussein—did not preclude his being elected in a country that has not yet recovered from the trauma of September 11. At the close of his first term, over a quarter of the American public still believes that the president is Muslim, even though he has repeatedly denied this. To this day, his opponents accuse him of upholding un-American values, which is a way of saying that he is unlike other Americans.[1]

Another decisive factor was that American society entered a period of political doubt with the onset of the 2008 crisis. It has doubted its economic model's ability to deal with the worst crisis since 1929, and with the intensification of economic and strategic competition with emerging countries, especially China, which is closing in on the unipolar moment that has defined the past two decades. Americans also doubted the utility of their military expeditions after an economically ruinous and politically disastrous war in Iraq, and a conflict in Afghanistan that is not likely to yield any better results. The combination of these two factors, which Obama clearly leveraged, naturally led Americans and the rest of the world to raise questions as to whether the United States had the material and political wherewithal to continue shouldering so many responsibilities around the world with increasing difficulty, despite significant political demands for the United States, especially when compared to China.

The final decisive factor was the perception that the structure of the world was changing and that its underlying balance of power was shifting. With the emergence of new powers, the unipolar moment is coming to an end. To address new challenges in the world, such as terrorism, climate change, pandemics, and the possession of nuclear weapons by individuals and no longer just states, an abundance of sophisticated military means does not necessarily suffice. The law of diminishing returns for military power has taken hold.

This observation has an important political corollary that is at the heart of Obama's foreign policy: while the United States cannot solve the world's problems alone, it is not ready to allow any of these to be solved without it, let alone against it. This is the foundation of Obama's policy and the purpose of this book is to verify its validity and effectiveness.

To this end we will begin with the assumption that Obama is inspired by a realist vision of the global order. This vision is rooted in both his personal convictions and the deadlocks created by his predecessor George W. Bush, who was driven by a pronounced messianic ideology. Obama's realism is an ad-hoc realism that reflects twenty-first century constraints and worldviews. Obama is a realist, but not in the Kissinger sense of the term. He is not interested in grand strategies. Bereft of any grand vision, his ambition is to preserve America's great power status and make it acceptable to the rest of the world. Obama no longer wants his country to serve as the world's policeman. However, he has no intention of letting another country displace the United States. His scope of action lies between these two limits. Because he is not driven by a grand design, by the same token he is not willing to take any great risks. Obama is not like Jimmy Carter, who attempted to atone for the Vietnam War after Richard Nixon's presidency. He is also not a "Nixon in China," able to create a watershed in a conflict hampering the United States. This may explain why the five great conflicts he inherited when he came to the White House—Iraq, Afghanistan, Iran, the Israeli-Palestinian conflict, and North Korea—are still not resolved four years after he came to power. Granted, the United States withdrew from Iraq, but at immeasurable political cost compared to the advantage reaped by Iran. The United States will probably also withdraw from Afghanistan in 2014, but it will probably do so before finding a political solution to the country's problems.[2] The Iranian crisis is intensifying, the Israeli-Palestinian conflict is frozen, and China-backed North

Korea is loath to deal with the United States. Does this imply that Obama has a poor foreign-policy record? This is precisely the question that this book will attempt to address while showing that Obama operates within a set of powerful constraints that shape the US system.

The system is first and foremost defined by the gigantic US state apparatus, which is controlled by countless well-organized bureaucracies that are jealous of their prerogatives: the Department of Defense, whose influence, in a paradoxical twist, has grown phenomenally since the end of the Cold War; the Department of State; the 17 intelligence agencies; and the numerous economic and ethnic lobbies, some of which strongly influence the formulation of US foreign policy. Another important player is the US Congress, whose members often have a very narrow view of US interests in the world, and where the positions of the right are increasingly influential. Finally, the president must constantly deal with an equally powerful and partisan media.

The first chapter of this book will highlight the legacy that President Obama inherited from the Bush administration, as every president is constrained by his predecessor's actions. Constraints also include US institutional and bureaucratic politics, the continuity of US interests over time and independent of those in charge, the strengths and weaknesses of US economic power, and the global balance of power. Bush bequeathed considerable constraints to Obama, including:

- Two asymmetrical wars, which by their nature could not and cannot be either completely won or completely lost (Afghanistan and Iraq).
- Two lingering "nuclear conflicts" with no resolution in sight (North Korea and Iran).
- An extremely important regional conflict that is willfully neglected despite rhetoric to the contrary (Israeli-Palestinian conflict).
- A first-rate strategic ally whose unconditional support of American policy in Iraq proved to be domestically costly (Great Britain).
- A former strategic rival (Russia), who has become neither a strategic partner nor a partner resigned to being a fallen power.
- A powerful global popular movement that is increasingly hostile to the United States and that takes a paroxysmal form in the Muslim world.
- A domestic distrust of most multilateral initiatives, including those to which the United States had committed (climate change, disarmament, and international justice).
- A deep hostility from virtually all states to the concept of preemptive war, which was used to justify the Iraq War.

The second chapter will attempt to explain Obama's foreign policy with regard to the interaction between his personality and his way of structuring power in the White House. Foreign policy is not just about ideas but also a series of bureaucratic interactions whose command decisively influences outcomes. Obama clearly chose to concentrate most of the power over foreign policy matters in the White House, even if the experienced bureaucrats who surround him are clearly no foreign-policy visionaries. Hence, perhaps, the mixed performance of an administration that is rather coherent, but not driven by a grand strategy.[3]

The third chapter will provide a detailed analysis of what we consider to be the doctrinal foundation of Obama's foreign policy: realism, not as the term is commonly understood, but as it is defined in international-relations theory. To this end, we will assess Obama's principal foreign policy decisions according to a number of criteria that would likely characterize a realist policy. These metrics are:

- the rejection of messianic ideology in Obama's political discourse
- the emphasis on traditional security issues and on large states irrespective of their domestic political choices
- the ability to gain the support of former adversaries whose support is considered necessary, or to engage with strategic rivals
- replaying Nixon in China: to seek accommodations with real or potential adversaries at the cost of altering relations with one or several allies
- the refusal to militarily engage abroad when such action is deemed contrary to US vital interests, but would save the lives of unprotected populations

The fourth chapter will address what might be the Obama administration's major accomplishment: abandoning the ideology of September 11 in which the Bush administration was entrapped. The repudiation of the war on terror ideology is an important political achievement because it helped to mitigate the negative and very aggressive image that had united a large part of the world against the Bush administration. Of course, this did not make America any more popular throughout the world. Yet its political acceptability is much greater now than it was under the previous administration, even if there are great variations from one country to another. Granted, US counterterrorism policy had already started to change at the end of Bush's second term, but Obama reaped the benefits despite failing to close Guantánamo.

Chapters 6 and 7 will focus on Obama's management of the great asymmetric conflicts he inherited from his predecessor (Iraq and Afghanistan). While these two conflicts theoretically derive from two very different approaches—war of choice and war of necessity—they both underscore how increasingly difficult it is for America to make strategic gains that are commensurate with its military, economic, and political investments in conflicts of this kind.

Chapter 7 will be devoted to the only major issue the Obama administration did not inherit from the Bush administration: the Arab revolutions. These revealed Obama's ability to practice a form of neorealism that eschewed both cynicism, which might have been conducive to nonintervention in Libya as was strongly advised by the Pentagon, and entanglement, which would have hurt America's image in this region. Despite his undeniably skillful management of these developments, his political gain was substantially undermined by his utter inability to change the situation in the Middle East, especially with regard to the Israeli-Palestinian conflict. Obama often appears to have a plan A, but not necessarily a plan B in the event of failure.

Chapter 8 will focus on relations between the United States and Europe, which seems to be the great loser in America's strategic redeployment to Asia. Yet Europe continues to depend on the United States for its security. While the North Atlantic Treaty Organization (NATO) intervention in Libya showed that some European states were willing to use force in a strategic region of the world, it also confirmed that the vast majority of European Union member states were less willing than ever to use force, despite US entreaties that they more actively participate in strategic burden-sharing. The gravity of the economic and financial crisis that is afflicting Europe has overshadowed these strategic issues, however. It has also significantly shown the dramatic reduction in US influence over Europe, when compared to its influence half a century ago. Today the United States can only encourage Europe to make economic and institutional choices to avert a disaster, but it no longer has the resources to impose its preferences. Fifty years ago, the United States could tell Europe that the dollar was its currency but Europe's problem. Europe can now tell the United States that the euro crisis is a European crisis but that in an economically interdependent world it has also become a problem for America.

The book will end with a conclusion that situates Obama's foreign policy in relation to US foreign policy as a whole. It will emphasize three main elements that continue to structure America's power: an extraordinary capacity to punish actors that directly threaten US security, and the power to strategically assure and reassure steadfast allies; an impressive economic and financial attractiveness despite serious internal imbalances; an ability to negotiate arrangements with emerging powers, an equally great inability to manage asymmetric conflicts, and a determination not to let China overtake the United States.

CHAPTER ONE

Legacy

When Barack Obama was inaugurated in January 2009, America's relative position in the world had declined. There was little doubt as to its predominant power, but the social legitimacy of its economic model was now questioned, criticized, and even challenged. The power was still there. However, its foundations had been shaken. In September 2008, the United States had been struck by a terrible and unexpected financial crisis, the shock of which allowed candidate Obama to take the lead over his Republican rival in the presidential race.[1] Aside from damaging the American and then the global economy in a matter of weeks, the subprime crisis called into question the legitimacy of the American financial capitalism and its underlying deregulatory logic dating back to the 1990s. The German finance minister at the time predicted that the United States was going to lose its "superpower status in the global financial system," resulting in the emergence of a multipolar system where the dollar would lose its predominance to the benefit of the euro, yen, and yuan.[2] A British political analyst was even more categorical in his assessment that "the era of American global leadership, reaching back to the Second World War, is over."[3] The governor of the Central Bank of China subtly echoed these statements in March 2009 by contending for the first time that the dollar's role as reserve currency presented more drawbacks than advantages.[4] He then suggested the creation of a new international reserve currency backed by the International Monetary Fund (IMF) and likely to reduce the role of the dollar.[5] Taken together, the critiques highlighted three principal weaknesses in the American system: a blind trust in the market's self-regulating capacity, which Alan Greenspan both theorized and personified as Fed chairman[6]; a financing of the economy based on capturing a significant share of the global savings surplus rather than encouraging domestic household savings, which had become negligible[7]; and the use of this "easy money" to finance a costly foreign policy that had become increasingly militarily aggressive since the Iraq War. From this perspective, the subprime crisis was the product of an economy that was financed through a combination of very low interest rates and ample liquidity.[8] The low interest-rate policy, which stemmed from the American government's financing needs to compensate for lower taxes and to cover new expenditures in the aftermath of September 11, coincided with a huge increase in the savings surplus of Asian countries. Chastened by the financial crisis of the late 1990s, the latter had chosen to shield themselves from the hazards of financial volatility by accumulating trade surpluses. In response to the financial deregulation pushed by the United States in the 1990s, they adopted a mercantilist policy of unprecedented proportions.[9] Asian creditors and American debtors thought they had reached a mutually beneficial arrangement. The Asians saved while the Americans consumed. This calculation was not entirely unfounded as it reflected these societies' preferences, and there is no indication that it has changed much since 2008. Nonetheless, its effects on the American banking system's deregulation, and then on the real economy, were grossly underestimated.[10] Left to their own devices, financial operators used the easy money to take reckless risks.

It is of course an old criticism that America takes advantage of its privileged position in the global financial system to finance its wars and presence in the world. Valery Giscard d'Estaing (not, as is commonly believed, General Charles de Gaulle) was one of the first, in February 1965, to famously denounce the dollar's "exorbitant privilege" in the midst of the Vietnam War.[11] The two issues were indeed related. The United States wanted both to intensify the war in Vietnam and also fund a very ambitious domestic social program. To this end, the government had the choice of either increasing the tax burden on Americans or issuing more dollars to the rest of the world, with the expectation that the European and Japanese Central Banks would hold them under the principle of equivalence between the dollar and gold. Not surprisingly, the second solution was preferred. The Johnson administration's treasury secretary, John Connally, responded to European bewilderment at this request with a phrase that has gone down in history: "The dollar may be our currency, but it's your problem." On countless occasions the United States brandished the threat of withdrawing its strategic umbrella over the Europeans—the Germans to be more exact—or the Japanese to force the implementation of monetary policies that they were not initially willing to carry out.[12]

So there is nothing new here. Rather, the new development is that the 2008 crisis directly affected the United States to a degree that it had not experienced since 1929. The financial capitalism that it had defined received a major blow. Thus the problem was the systemic nature of the 2008 crisis, that is, the scale of its domino effect throughout the capitalist world. Another new aspect of this crisis was that the potentially adversely affected group was no longer limited to longtime partners from the old free world (Europe and Japan), but also included new economic actors that were wealthy, politically ambitious, and much less psychologically dependent on the United States, even though their prosperity did depend on it. The convergence of these elements meant that for the first time since 1945, the United States faced a situation where it could no longer escape its responsibility.[13] It had no country at hand to blame or ostracize, nor did it have any solutions at hand to propose. There was no obvious villain. Also to no avail was the age-old Schmitt reflex, which posits the existence of an enemy as the raison d'être of the political, and on which US power has always fallen back to mark or find its bearings. By necessity, the United States was forced to question itself, to acknowledge the market failures it had brushed aside, and to share the burden of the crisis and the cost of addressing it.

This unprecedented geopolitical development raises questions about the basis for legitimizing American power, even though it would certainly be unwise to draw hasty conclusions from this new reality.

The financial crisis may be considered the first great political challenge that Obama inherited from his predecessor. It is not the only one. Even without the financial crisis, George W. Bush had left a particularly fraught legacy. A quick overview provides compelling evidence. An assessment of America's strategic position in 2008 after eight years under the Bush administration yields the following:

- two instances of asymmetric warfare, which by nature could not and cannot be either completely won or completely lost (Afghanistan and Iraq)
- two lingering "nuclear conflicts" with no resolution in sight (North Korea and Iran)
- an extremely important regional conflict that is willfully neglected despite rhetoric to the contrary (Israeli-Palestinian conflict)

- a first-rate strategic ally whose unconditional support of American policy in Iraq proved to be costly domestically (Great Britain)
- a former strategic rival (Russia) who has become neither a strategic partner nor a partner resigned to being a fallen power
- a powerful global popular movement that is increasingly hostile to the United States and that takes a paroxysmal form in the Muslim world
- a domestic distrust of most multilateral initiatives, including those to which the United States had committed (climate change, disarmament, and international justice)
- deep hostility from virtually all states to the concept of preemptive war, which was used to justify the Iraq War
- a no less marked domestic resistance to the policy of exporting democracy by force

These elements appear as a series of problems and constraints bequeathed to the Obama administration, but they would be incomplete and partial if they did not take into account the beneficiaries of US policy under George W. Bush. After all, a game with losers must also have winners. The latter may have been few, but they carry weight: Israel, India, and to a lesser extent, Central and Eastern European countries. Israel was integrated into a policy of containment vis-à-vis the Muslim-Arab world, toward which distrust reached record proportions after September 11. The result was a loss of incentive to seek a political solution to the Palestinian problem. India had the privileged position of both serving to contain the Islamist extremism purportedly supported by Pakistan, and to provide a subtle counterbalance to an ascending China. Its possession of nuclear weapons was accordingly reinterpreted, thus confirming a major rule in international affairs: the danger of a nuclear weapon is assessed according to the intentions of its possessor. Finally, NATO members in Central and Eastern Europe were valued in terms of containing Russian power, which had reasserted itself at the regional level in the Caucuses and in Ukraine.

These various issues, to which we will return in greater detail, at this point raise an important question. Should we interpret the "Bush doctrine" that Obama inherited as some kind of political accident linked to an over-reaction to September 11? Or, to the contrary, should we interpret it as an extreme expression of the political exuberance that followed the emergence of a unipolar world after 1989? The answer to this question is key to understanding Obama's strategy in the overall framework of American foreign policy.

To address this issue we will review America's thoughts and actions in the world in the decade that preceded September 11, coinciding with the Clinton administration's two terms.

Exuberance through the Market

The Clinton administration is actually not associated to any prominent post–Cold War strategy, as if the "absence of threat permits policy to be capricious."[14] This is hardly surprising. A turning point of such magnitude as the end of the Cold War could not be processed so quickly in a country that had been shaped by a bipolar conflict for close to 50 years. Moreover, at the beginning of the 1990s, the American economy was reeling from a deep recession linked to a major process of deindustrialization, which was portrayed as a disaster for US wealth and power.[15] The economic recession played no small part in George Bush Senior's defeat, despite his First Gulf War victory. Bill Clinton had no international experience and chose to stake his political future on stimulating the American economy at a time when its nature was changing. On the surface, deindustrialization was taking place, but beneath it a new information economy was emerging. And the latter allowed the United States to experience only 16 months of recession between 1984 and 2007, compared to 59 between 1969 and 1983.

It is easy to understand why the Clinton administration was animated by a form of economic optimism that posited the inexorable victory of "market democracy," a new frontier for American policy and diplomacy. This ideology explains the administration's keen interest to ratify a free-trade agreement with Canada and Mexico, create the World Trade Organization (WTO), open Asian financial markets under strong pressure from Wall Street, and prepare for Chinese accession to the WTO. Clinton's principal foreign-policy adviser, Anthony Lake, formalized the political aspect of this strategy, which sought to expand market democracy. The goal was no longer to contain communism, but to expand the benefits of market democracy to the rest of the world without giving the idea a specific operational content.[16] Indeed, of the six conflicts that confronted the Clinton administration (Middle East, Iraq, Korea, Rwanda, Somalia, Bosnia and Kosovo), none naturally lent itself to forming a market democracy.[17]

This vagueness had no notable consequences. The levers of American action and influence did not lie in the hands of American diplomacy so much as in the hands of shock-therapy theorists who sought to convert Central and Eastern Europe and Russia to the market economy at an astounding pace. Shock therapy—introduced by American economist Jeffrey Sachs—was underpinned by the basic idea that social change can occur quickly, and even immediately, so long as political elites are determined to make it happen. The shock is cloaked in therapeutic virtue suggesting that the more brutal the shock, the more effective it is. Therefore, it is important to focus on the production of shock, which has two ingredients: simultaneous reforms and rapid execution. The reforms must be simultaneous due to the systemic nature of an economy. Sachs tells us that structural reform only makes sense if it can take place within a new and effective pricing system, which is at the heart of everything. It is this system that allows for the transition to a convertible currency, protection from hyperinflation risks, and the Darwinian selection of state-owned companies that are able to survive.[18] This was nothing more than the implementation of a form of market Leninism. It may have been a very peculiar Leninism, but it was one in which certain Central and Eastern European elites could easily recognize themselves.[19] "There is a race against time in taking the final step of transforming the state's property into private property. If this step is too long delayed, Poland's macroeconomic successes to date could still be reversed."[20]

Shock therapy was further echoed by what was beginning to be called the "Washington consensus." Coined by John Williamson in the spring of 1989 to describe economic reform policies in Latin America, the Washington consensus was also a master plan. Unlike Sachs's shock therapy, it emphasized the coherence of reforms more than the necessity of implementing them at an accelerated pace. Like shock therapy, though, it embraced the bedrock principal that only a large array of coherent reforms can produce real and immediate results: fiscal discipline, public expenditure reductions, interest-rate liberalization, competitive exchange rates, trade liberalization, deregulation, and protection of property rights.[21] This vision of social change, in no way masterminded by the White House, was perfectly aligned with American interests.

Incidentally, top US diplomat Warren Christopher was in favor of making market opening the cornerstone of American diplomacy. And if this policy happened to fall short or appear inappropriate, the United States would first resort to sanctions, which have the advantage of being coercive without any of the drawbacks of the use of force.[22] Clinton's approach to Iraq illustrated this fallback position: a regime deemed beyond reform was sanctioned, but no preparations were made for a military confrontation, even though the Clinton administration was the first to officially state the possibility of overthrowing the Iraqi regime.[23]

While this approach was significantly flawed in its failure to really address the problem in Iraq, it did assuage the anxiety of an American public that is loath to undertake any military operation abroad. Nevertheless, and contrary to what Saddam Hussein may have believed during the First Gulf War, aversion to the use of force could not be considered an inviolable principal of American foreign policy. The famous Powell doctrine had sought to reconcile American aversion to war with an American obligation to militarily intervene if necessary. It defined three criteria for any military intervention: a specific goal, a crushing military superiority to minimize risk, and an exit strategy to avoid any risk of entanglement.[24] Yet the Clinton administration's first military operation, in Somalia, did not meet these criteria. At first, it was supposed to be a humanitarian and basic police operation in a failing state. Unfortunately, instead of ensuring overequipped American forces the upper hand, the operation backfired when armed Somali bands shot down two American helicopters, killing 18 GIs. For the first time, the United States experienced asymmetric warfare, where vastly superior means do not guarantee a desired outcome.[25] The media fallout from this failure consolidated the Clinton administration's almost intuitive approach: make every effort to avoid military intervention in civil conflicts in which the United States has no vested interests. This rendered moot any political proselytizing on human rights and democracy, for example.[26] Clinton's optimism was based on the conviction that the new momentum of market democracy was so strong that America would not need to put in much effort to realize it. Consequently, the administration cavalierly brushed aside any concerns and demands from states that had trouble adapting to this new imperative ("market democracy"). The idea that Russia might be deeply wounded by its loss of great-power status does not seem to have particularly troubled the administration. Yet international reality reflects social reality, and status is crucial to identity. When an actor is not satisfied with its social position, it has three options: mobility, competition, or distinction.[27] Mobility is the appropriation of the values and practices of dominant social groups with the intention of joining them. This is clearly what Boris Yeltsin tried to do in the first years of his leadership, largely by following the recommendations of shock-therapy theorists. The results were hardly convincing. The capitalism in five hundred days that liberal Russian economists dreamed of did not come to fruition. It was the state rather than the economy that was privatized.

Competition is the second available option for a dissatisfied state. It consists of catching up or surpassing the dominant group in the area where the latter asserts its superiority. China opted for this strategy in the mid-1990s by developing its economic power. It was also the choice that tsarist Russia made in the middle of the nineteenth century during the Crimean War with Great Britain and France. By affirming suzerainty over Orthodox sites and believers in the Ottoman Empire, Russia was pursuing a purely symbolic goal: to obtain great power status in a region of the world where France had obtained recognition of its authority over the Christians in Palestine. Russia was at the time a great rival of Great Britain and could not forgo comparable privileges. It became a matter of honor, that is, status.[28] A military conflict ensued, and Russia lost. In the wake of the Cold War, which Russia also lost, Moscow was only left with the third option: to acquire a higher status by expressing its own voice instead of imitating the dominant actors.[29] Vladimir Putin obviously chose this path as Russian grievances against America deepened. The Clinton administration had but limited awareness of all this.[30] It refused to let Moscow into the Western club so long as it had not completed its economic reforms. Moscow did not take well to the feeling of being subjected to the ultimate judgment of the West in order to one day become a part of it. The resentment swelled in 1994 with the beginning of the process of NATO enlargement to former Central and Eastern European countries. Yevgeny Primakov, who had succeeded Andrei Kozyrev as head of Russian diplomacy after the latter was deemed too slavish, embarked with few means on a long process of political realignment premised on Russia's recovery of great-power status.[31] After belatedly becoming aware of Russia's dissatisfaction, Clinton sought to temper it by admitting Moscow into the Group of 7 (G7). But the cooptation was only a partial one. Russia was generously offered a place within the Group of 8 (G8), which is considered a political forum, while it was left out of the G7, which focuses on purely economic concerns.

Exuberance through War

The United States entered the twenty-first century in exceptionally favorable circumstances. It was the leading economic power, the leading military power, and as a result of this rare combination, the leading political power. The United States thus combined material wealth with coercive power and ideological domination. It was the age of the unipolar world, characterized by the existence of an actor with no rival and no coalition of actors able to overtake its leadership for lack of means or will.[32] This era has often been compared to the one that Great Britain experienced at the end of the nineteenth century and that Arnold Toynbee described: "Here we are on top of the world, and we have arrived at this peak to stay there forever. There is, of course, a thing called history, but history is something unpleasant that happens to other people. We are comfortably outside all of that I am sure."[33]

However, the comparison of these two countries is not fully satisfactory. American power in the twenty-first century is far superior to that of Great Britain at its height. Great Britain may have been the world's leading economic power in 1870, but its competition was not far behind. The United States was already very close, while Germany was committed to taking the lead. On the eve of the First World War, the global power hierarchy had already shifted. The United States had taken the lead (32 percent of global gross national product [GNP]), followed by Germany (14.8 percent) and Great Britain (13.6 percent).[34] At the time, the United States fully benefited from its demographic potential, which in the long run continues to be the key element of power. This dynamic may turn against the United States with the rise of China and India, provided that these two countries pursue their economic development smoothly. Yet even if their rise fully materializes, the scenario is 20 to 30 years away in China's case. Were China to become the world's leading economic power in 2050, America's unchallenged domination over the global economy would have lasted at least one century, while Great Britain's was only a quarter century.[35] Militarily, the contrast between the United States of the twenty-first century and Great Britain of the nineteenth century is even starker. At the peak of its power, Great Britain was never more than a great naval power. Its land capabilities remained limited. Otto von Bismarck was known to mock Great Britain by saying that if it ever dared to invade Germany, Berlin's police force would suffice to stop it.[36] The United States has no similar constraints. Its supremacy permeates all areas of power, be it land, air, naval, or nuclear. US military expenditures account for 50 percent of known global expenditures, or more than the next 14 top military powers combined.[37]

We will return to this later to explain how the United States has been able to delay the infamous *overstretch*, that is, the moment when a state's external commitments far exceed its ability to finance them.[38] At this point we need to explore why the United States suddenly moved from a form of exuberance through the market under the Clinton administration to exuberance through war under the Bush administration. International-affairs experts are in disagreement over this point.

Some argue that a state with such a strong position will naturally be inclined to preserve the status quo by consolidating, or preventing the erosion of its position. The Clinton administration implicitly adopted this perspective, as the world seemed to be moving in a direction that was favorable to US interests. Others claim that hegemony allows a dominant actor to capitalize on its position by reshaping the rules of the game to its advantage.[39]

History tells us which argument prevailed. The Bush administration proved to have revisionist plans. It tried to change the way in which the international system operates by emphasizing the principal of pre-emptive war and its political corollary: regime change. New concepts or ideas are never as novel as they claim to be. The Vietnam War could have been considered a preemptive war in the sense that it sought to prevent a Communist takeover of the Indo-Chinese peninsula.[40] The United States has historically used force to remove political regimes it did not favor: Iran, Guatemala, Chile, Panama, Grenada, and so on. The main innovation of the Bush doctrine deals with two critical points: it claims to be a legitimate norm for action in international affairs, but then goes on to claim that force can be used in response to both imminent and potential threats:

> Deterrence based only upon the threat of retaliation is less likely to work against leaders of rogue states more willing to take risks, gambling with the lives of their people, and the wealth of their nations [...]. The greater the threat, the greater is the risk of inaction—and the more compelling the case for taking anticipatory action to defend ourselves, even if uncertainty remains as to the time and place of the enemy's attack. To forestall or prevent such hostile acts by our adversaries, the United States will, if necessary, act preemptively.[41]

This policy shift can be explained by September 11, when the United States was attacked on its soil for the first time since Pearl Harbor in December 1941. America responded with force not only to avenge the affront, but also to signal to the world that it was not going to renounce its primacy in the international system.[42] From this perspective, one can reasonably assume that any American head of state would have most likely responded to September 11 with a military operation in Afghanistan, where the protectors and commanders of the attack on Manhattan's twin towers had taken refuge. It is unclear whether any administration other than that of Bush would have gone beyond the

Afghani operation. One might reasonably doubt it. September 11 can explain a lot of things, but it cannot explain everything. From the beginning, it was politically framed to justify subsequent choices that had nothing to do with the attack itself. The attack was connected to an American neoconservative vision of the world that predated September 11. Without September 11, the neoconservatives probably never would have succeeded in implementing their ideas, but without the neoconservatives' political influence, US choices probably would have been different. The ideological influence of the neoconservatives is key to understanding the Bush administration's policies for two reasons: first, it is based on a radicalized vision of the world with messianic and virulent streaks that break from the traditional premises of Republican ideology as defined by Henry Kissinger; second, for the first time in American political history, political forces that had traditionally focused on domestic policy issues became extremely interested in international policy issues, especially with regard to the Middle East. Neoconservative ideology offers a Manichean interpretation of the world that identifies an evil enemy destined for destruction.[43] At its core is a prophetic dualism that divides the world into two camps and sees no end to the division until one camp utterly defeats the other. As a result, there can be no compromise. Neutrality is seen as delusion, and negotiation is equated with capitulation.[44] In these circumstances, war comes as no surprise. Its moral justification trumps any other considerations, including legal ones.

The idea of preemptive war is based on a relatively simple principle, but its consequences are incalculable. It consists of eliminating any threat before it can even really form. Of course, threat prevention is part of the international society's codes, practices, and obligations. The Bush doctrine's novelty was that it cited the inadequacy and inapplicability of deterrence as the reason for the preemptive use of force. It is predicated on the existence of new global actors (terrorist groups, rogue states) that do not respect the rules of the game and that use unconventional means, such as Weapons of Mass Destruction (WMDs), to circumvent US military superiority. Two civilian planes crashing into the towers perfectly illustrate this new form of threat to the United States on its own territory. The idea of responding differently to actors using different means was and remains acceptable, even if the fight against terrorism always presents moral and political dilemmas: should terrorism be fought with the same means that it uses? The Bush doctrine raised a much more serious issue by linking the source of the threat to a specific actor (Iraq) at the outset, without proving that the latter constituted a real threat to US security, nor that it was at the root of the attack that founded a new international practice. Hence the temptation to apply the doctrine to any international political situation the United States deems unsatisfactory. This risk is precisely why so many states in addition to Iraq rejected it. The trauma of September 11 became politically traumatic for a large number of states as they worried about the indiscriminate use of preemptive war. Rightly or wrongly, states like Brazil and Turkey continue, more than ten years later, to point to the excesses of the preemptive war in Iraq to oppose sanctions against Iran.[45] They view sanctions as a step toward war so long as the negotiation route has not been exhausted.

Preemptive war may have been shaped by September 11, but its doctrinal foundations were laid long before. They originated with the nuclear doctrine defined in the 1960s and 1970s. Reflecting a deep mistrust of arms control and deterrence, it called for achieving strategic superiority to give the United States a first-strike advantage over the Union of Soviet Socialist Republics (USSR). The goal was to destroy the opponent before it might attempt to attack or retaliate. This was the foundation of preemptive war, and its principal theorist was Albert Wohlstetter, University of Chicago colleague of philosopher Leo Strauss. His epigones, Paul Wolfowitz and Richard Perle, later became the intellectual fathers of the Iraq War. When one reads the strategist Wohlstetter's works, it is easy to understand how an analogy might have been drawn between theses developed in the context of the Cold War and of nuclear deterrence against the USSR, and the post–Cold War neoconservative determination to overthrow the Iraqi regime. Wohlstetter's key insight was to anticipate the wide range of challenges that would arise from growing nuclear proliferation and the danger it would represent for US security, independent of any Soviet attack:

> By the late 1980s several nations might be capable of delivering nuclear weapons against the continental U.S. As a result, we may find it desirable to allocate offensive forces to target third country nuclear forces (e.g., those of India) and to build up air defense and civil defense systems and possibly ABMs [anti-ballistic missiles] to cope with these additional nuclear threats.[46]

Wohlstetter significantly overestimated the potential number of nuclear powers on the horizon at the end of the 1980s. However, in the mid-1970s he had already identified the possession of nuclear weapons by terrorist groups as a possible risk:

> All responsible governments (by definition) have an interest in keeping nuclear weapons out of their hands. And all such governments will have a strong incentive to retaliate against irresponsible governments that make weapons available to extra-governmental groups.[47]

It is quite obvious how these contentions—and they are perfectly tenable—could be made again 20 years later by epigones who were more concerned about ideology than strategy. It was sufficient to replace "nuclear weapon" with "weapon of mass destruction" and postulate, without proof, the existence of a direct relationship between an "irresponsible government" (Iraq) and terrorist groups (Al Qaeda) to fulfill Wohlstetter's prophesy. Wolfowitz had no difficulty doing exactly this the day after September 11 when he advocated to preemptively attack Iraq and overthrow its regime, because of the risk that WMDs might be transferred to terrorist groups.[48] The idea that this risk was limited, improbable, and unverifiable had little traction in the context of September 11. Such reservations were all countered with the retort: "What could be less likely than terrorists flying airplanes into the World Trade Center and the Pentagon?"[49] The temptation is great to politically abuse the argument that an extraordinary event can change everything and overturn the assessment criteria of the international order. By insisting that September 11 had changed everything, the Bush administration allowed itself to in turn change everything in its retaliation. The shell-shocked American public generally accepted this line of reasoning. It was not until 2006 that the public began to slowly acknowledge that the September 11 attacks were not attributable to Saddam Hussein's regime.[50] In the history of American foreign policy, the recourse to preemptive war is an undeniable break with preceding administrations, including that of Ronald Reagan, who had rejected such an approach. For instance, America condemned Israel when it used this argument to justify its military attack on the Iraqi nuclear facility in Osirak in 1981. The corollary of preemptive war is an aversion to all international regulation based on universal norms that are enforceable against any state. Hence the appeal of militant unilateralism that is characterized by a withdrawal from any multilateral arrangement that might limit the US scope of action. At the heart of the theory of preemptive war is a vision of America above the laws of the world and determined to decisively strike those who provoke it. The Bush doctrine cannot be fully understood without referring to another influence: the evangelical Christians who significantly contributed to electing George W. Bush, and for whom September 11 deeply resonated as a form of deliverance:

> For many believers in biblical prophecy, the Bush Administration's go-it-alone foreign policy, hands-off attitude toward the Israeli-Palestinian conflict, and proposed war on Iraq are not simply actions in the national self-interest or an extension of the war on terrorism, but part of an unfolding divine plan.[51]

Evangelical Christians subscribe to a literal interpretation of the Bible: they believe that Palestinian territory belongs to Israel, and saw the war in the Middle East as heralding "the imminent return of Christ."[52] Unconditional support for the Israeli state is thus a pillar of the evangelical political agenda, which is also fueled by a strong abhorrence of Islam. The famous Reverend Pat Robertson portrayed Islam as a "bloody, brutal type of religion," while his colleague Jerry Falwell called the prophet Muhammad a terrorist.[53] Granted, the American public's support for the state of Israel extends well beyond evangelicals. Public-opinion polls nonetheless show that support is strongest among evangelicals.[54] By attacking Iraq, which was portrayed as the sponsor of the September 11 attacks and the bitter enemy of the state of Israel, the Bush administration was able to convince this constituency of the coherence of its approach. By occupying Iraq, the United States hoped to achieve five goals: avenge the affront of September 11, liberate a people from oppression, overthrow a regime hostile to Israel, contribute to the emergence of democracy in the Arab world, and facilitate the resolution of the Israeli-Palestinian conflict. These arguments had the advantage of being both mutually enhancing—war ultimately leads to peace—and independently viable so that if one fell, as in a game of skittles, the others would remain standing. This is why democracy promotion was swiftly brought to the forefront as soon as the weapons-of-mass-destruction argument collapsed.

CHAPTER TWO

White House Tight Rope

Like most of his predecessors—except perhaps George Bush Senior, who directed the Central Intelligence Agency (CIA) and the American liaison office in Beijing—Barack Obama had little time to familiarize himself with international issues before he assumed the presidency. This is hardly surprising. In the United States, as in most democratic countries, political careers are first and foremost built from the ground up. Following stints as a community organizer and attorney in Chicago, Obama entered politics through the narrowest of doors: local politics. In 1997, he was elected to the Illinois Senate. In 2000, he had a failed run for the House of Representatives, the lower chamber of the US Congress. Nonetheless, through exceptional circumstances and remarkable willpower, he managed to get elected senator from Illinois in November 2004. A few months earlier, he had gained national visibility for the first time when he addressed the 2004 Democratic Convention.

Obama's Personal Equation

Throughout his meteoric career that remarkably brought him from the Illinois General Assembly to the White House in less than ten years, Obama barely commented on international affairs. The Iraq War was an exception, but it was then as much a domestic policy issue as a foreign policy one. In October 2002, as the Bush administration was gearing up for Iraq, Obama was invited to participate in an antiwar protest. The content of his carefully prepared address sheds light on both his convictions and political talent. On the one hand, he condemned the war as an attempt by "armchair, weekend warriors [...] to distract us from corporate scandals and a stock market that has just gone through the worst month since the Great Depression."[1] However, he carefully avoided the appearance of being a pacifist, stating at the outset that he "[doesn't] oppose all wars."[2] In a patriotic America that had just been traumatized by September 11, this was not a fortuitous choice. The black and liberal white electorates strongly opposed the war, but Obama was already looking further ahead. He instinctively felt that his blackness and two names, of which the second has a patently Muslim ring (Hussein), might raise suspicions about his patriotism. It is well established that black Americans are overwhelmingly Democratic and traditionally loath to pursue an expansionist foreign policy. It is also clear that, compared with the rest of the American population, their expression of patriotic fervor after September 11 was less spontaneous.[3] Obama's advisers feared that in the aftermath of September 11 the hardening of American public opinion might hurt his political prospects.[4] After he took office as a US senator in 2004, Obama became involved in international issues, especially disarmament.[5] However, his time in the Senate was too short to give him the requisite experience in international policy. He did express his opposition to the surge in Iraq that was recommended by his future colleague, General David Petraeus, but this was probably to remain consistent with his initial opposition to the war. In January 2007, he proposed the *Iraq War De-Escalation Act*, which would have reversed the troop surge and redeployed US troops to Afghanistan and other locations.[6]

There was nothing in Obama's career to suggest he was ready to address international political issues, but everything in his personal story did. As the son of a Kenyan father who had immigrated to the United States to pursue graduate studies, he could not ignore Africa, which meant more to him than to most African Americans. Africa did not hark back to distant ancestors, but to his father. Obama was the son of a highly educated African father and an atypical American mother, with whom he lived on the margins of America: first Honolulu, and then Indonesia. As a result, when he began his studies at Occidental College in Los Angeles, Obama was both completely American by education and cultural references, and outside of mainstream America. He was an unusual black because he did not share in the trauma of slavery.[7] He was also unusual with regard to white America, as he had lived on the territorial periphery. This outsider aspect might have been a political liability. Obama's genius was his ability to transform it into an asset.[8]

How might Obama's personal journey influence the direction of American foreign policy? This question should be answered with caution.

More than George W. Bush or even Hillary Clinton, Barack Obama is better able to understand and sense how the rest of the world perceives American policy and how the United States can be arrogant—a flaw that few great powers fail to display. More and better than any other American president, he is sensitive to the sin of American-centrism of which his country is often accused. Obama's subtle answer to a question about his views on American exceptionalism provides an excellent illustration of his search for equilibrium between his commitment to maintaining American leadership in the world and his recognition of the limits of American power:

> "—[C]ould I ask you whether you subscribe, as many of your predecessors have, to the school of 'American exceptionalism' that sees America as uniquely qualified to lead the world, or do you have a slightly different philosophy?
> —Obama: I believe in American exceptionalism, just as I suspect that the Brits believe in British exceptionalism and the Greeks believe in Greek exceptionalism. (...) Now, the fact that I am very proud of my country and I think that we've got a whole lot to offer the world does not lessen my interest in recognizing the value and wonderful qualities of other countries, or recognizing that we're not always going to be right, or that other people may have good ideas, or that in order for us to work collectively, all parties have to compromise and that includes us."[9]

In Chicago, prior to his election, Obama showed a certain interest in the Israeli-Palestinian conflict through his close personal relationship with an American university professor of Palestinian descent, Rashid Khalidi. This relationship drew criticism from political opponents during the 2008 presidential campaign, forcing him to downplay it and break off all contact with Khalidi since then.[10] The new American head of state's personal views must therefore be taken into account politically to understand his subsequent choices. Their influence can hardly be overestimated with regard to the permanence of constraints on a state's external conduct. Obama never thought that his international popularity would change the political behavior of US partners: "In Europe, people believe in our plan for Afghanistan, but their politics are still such that it's hard for leaders to want to send more troops into Afghanistan. That's not going to change because I'm popular in Europe or leaders think that I've been respectful towards them."[11]

Upon taking office Obama moreover ensured that his foreign counterparts would not try to take advantage of his global appeal by claiming a personal rapport with him. This is a sign of both an independent temperament and a concern that his peers might use his popularity for their own ends. For example, one of his first moves was to end the videoconferences that his predecessor had held every two weeks with the Afghan president. Besides the fact that they were not conducive to making real progress on the issues, they appeared as a form of manipulation of US policy. Indeed, President Hamid Karzai leveraged his privileged relationship with President Bush to evade, for instance, the pressure from the American embassy in Kabul to fight corruption. George W. Bush maintained an almost affectionate relationship with his Afghan counterpart that his successor clearly ended.[12] Obama is careful to have no personal animosity or conflict with his counterparts, while ensuring that he does not cultivate personal relationships that might hamper his discretion or scope for action. He would like to be everyone's friend, and thus nobody's in particular. The domestically weak Gordon Brown and Nicolas Sarkozy did their utmost to become his closest allies. The former sought to retain the special relationship that his country has with Washington, while the latter intended to subtly take over Britain's position to the benefit of France. Both utterly failed in their endeavors,[13] and both have realized it. Sarkozy learned his lesson when he found out that Obama was opposed to a formal agreement with France whereby the two countries would refrain from spying on each other, along the lines of the informal agreement between the Americans and the British.[14] Britain underwent a similar, but probably more painful experience given the historically close Anglo-American relations. As a Conservative, though, David Cameron understood that an excessively systematic alignment with American policy, as had been the case under Tony Blair, was detrimental to British interests.[15] In the aftermath of the Iraqi fiasco, Great Britain now wanted to avoid appearing subservient to the United States, even if it does not have a European equivalent to its relationship with the United States. It is nonetheless noteworthy that since the beginning of the Arab Spring, Britain's relationship with France has become central to British policy on a number of issues, including the Palestinian issue. With regard to the recognition of a Palestinian state by the United Nations (UN), London's position seems closer to the position of Paris than to that of Washington.[16]

In reality, in the United States as elsewhere, a state's external action is generally quite impervious to political discontinuities. Obama readily concedes this: "States are like big tankers, they're not like speedboats. You can't just whip them around and go in a new direction. Instead you've got to slowly move it and then eventually you end up in a very different place."[17]

Over time, US interests in the world have remained relatively stable: guarantee the security of its territory; sustain an open international economic system; ensure that the international rules and attendant world order remain compatible with US interests and values; and maintain the privileges that the United States has acquired over half a century of global supremacy, despite a relative erosion of its means. The priority for a new administration is most often either to pursue successful policies and reverse previous decisions, or to address unforeseen situations: the Soviet invasion of Afghanistan for Carter, the USSR's profound transformation for Reagan, the invasion of Kuwait for George H. W. Bush, and September 11 for his son.

Obama and the NSC

At the heart of the organization, initiation, and coordination of American foreign policy lies the National Security Council (NSC), which was founded in 1947 at the beginning of the Cold War and directly connected to the president of the United States. According to the *National Security Act* that created it, the NSC's function is "to advise the President with respect to the integration of domestic, foreign, and military policies relating to the national security so as to enable the military services and the other departments and agencies of the Government to cooperate more effectively in matters involving the national security."[18] This council, created at the same time as the CIA and the Joint Chiefs of Staff, currently comprises 20 members, including the president, the vice president, the secretaries of state, defense, energy, and homeland security, as well as the chairman of the Joint Chiefs of Staff, the director of the CIA, the director of National Intelligence, the national security adviser and his deputy, the Homeland Security adviser, and the White House chief of staff. Over the decades this body has changed profoundly, reflecting changes in foreign policy and the issues involved. The NSC initially focused on politico-military issues in the context of the Cold War, but its responsibilities gradually expanded to cover all diplomatic matters, economic and technological issues, and in the past ten years, challenges in the fight against terrorism. The security field's growth has been accompanied by a strengthening of the White House's decision-making process to the detriment of the State Department, which has clearly lost its monopoly over international relations, as have its counterparts in all the other countries of the world. Hence the growing importance of the NSC's coordination and arbitration roles in a country where a remarkable number of actors are involved in defining and conducting foreign policy: the State Department, the Defense Department, the Treasury Department, the numerous information agencies, and Congress, let alone the powerful economic and financial lobbies that play a considerable role in trade policy, for example. Furthermore, given that each important actor contains autonomous subgroups (the Special Forces or the Marines in the military, to take just one example) and that strong rivalries exist among the institutions, the White House has great leeway to arbitrate. The limitless expansion of the NSC's responsibilities has led American presidents to look for other sources of analysis, especially in the economic field. Thus, Bill Clinton created the National Economic Council in 1993.[19] Obama significantly diversified his sources of influence by appointing powerful advisers for energy and climate change, and for science and technology.[20]

As terrorism issues became more salient, Obama merged the Homeland Security Council with the NSC to eliminate the artificial distinction between domestic security and foreign security.[21] However, contrary to what his first National Security adviser, James Jones, had initially claimed, the NSC's responsibilities have not substantially increased.[22] In fact, Obama has only added three new members to the NSC: the energy secretary, the homeland security secretary, and the US ambassador to the United Nations.

The NSC, the head of state's principal support agency for foreign-policy decision making, comprises three levels: the president's advisers (Principals Committee), the advisers' deputies (Deputies Committee), and the Interagency Policy Committees. The Principals Committee alone brings together not only the NSC's full members but also the secretaries of energy, treasury, and homeland security, the attorney general, the White House chief of staff, the US ambassador to the United Nations, the director of national intelligence, the chairman of the Joint Chiefs of Staff, and the director of the Office of Management and Budget. This bureaucratic apparatus existed well before Obama came to the White House, but it was centralized so as to prevent the development of parallel channels of intervention and influence outside of the White House, as was the case under the Bush administration.

The NSC's role varies with the selected national security adviser and his relationship with the president of the United States. Of the 16 advisers who have held this position since 1947, only five particularly distinguished themselves: McGeorge Bundy under John F. Kennedy, Henry Kissinger under Richard Nixon, Zbigniew Brzezinski under Jimmy Carter, Brent Scowcroft under George H. W. Bush, and Sandy Berger under Clinton.[23] These men succeeded in establishing themselves because they shared three assets: a knowledge of international policy, a close relationship with the American president, and a personal ability to lead all of the actors involved in American foreign policy. Obama's initial pick for this position was unexpected and eventually proved to be unwise. He appointed James Jones, a former commandant of the Marine Corps who had led the NATO's military forces, but who was not familiar with Washington's bureaucratic intricacies, which he was even less willing to master.[24] Moreover, he did not have a close rapport with President Obama, whom he hardly knew before taking this key position. Several hypotheses have been put forward to explain this choice. They deserve a closer look because they show how Obama understood and structured his power. The most plausible hypothesis is that Obama was wary of an overly powerful adviser who might interpose himself between Obama and the top five political figures involved in foreign policy: the vice president, the secretary of state, the secretary of defense, the director of the CIA, and the chairman of the Joint Chiefs of Staff. He seemed confident enough that he could make sense of American foreign-policy options without a guru or mastermind.[25] This explains why solid candidates for the national security adviser position such as Susan Rice and John Steinberg were dismissed.[26] The selection was also apparently driven by the American president's desire to have an adviser who could reassure the military establishment over the important military decisions Obama knew he would have to make (withdrawal from Iraq, commitments in Afghanistan, reduction in military expenditures). He had to prove to the military that he was not a dove. The selection of a technically qualified but politically unsavvy national security adviser was encouraged by Obama's immediate political entourage, especially by Rahm Emanuel, the first White House chief of staff, and Tom Donilon, who served as deputy to Jones before succeeding him in 2010. It would therefore appear that Obama's team marginalized Jones from the outset. For his part, Jones did not do anything to truly assert himself at the White House. His successor, who had previously served in the White House under Jimmy Carter and at the State Department when Bill Clinton was president, shows a much better grasp of the political circuits of the federal government and the Democratic Party. That does not make him a strategist of international politics, far from it.[27] His priority is purportedly to ensure that

President Obama's foreign policy decisions incur minimal risk with regard to domestic politics. More specifically, the priority is to prevent any international initiative from standing in the way of Obama's reelection in 2012. A number of Obama's recent decisions, especially since the Republican victory in the November 2010 elections, have been made on this basis: the abandonment of any prospect of concluding a multilateral agreement under the Doha round of the WTO; the jettisoning of any Middle East policy that might impede Israel in one way or another; the end of any bold strategy to fight climate change, and this despite a promising start on the latter two issues. None of these developments are surprising since these are three areas where, as will be discussed below, domestic political constraints are key. By contrast, on other matters such as Libya where the domestic stakes were lower, Obama did not hesitate to take risks against the advice of Donilon for caution, that is, inaction.[28]

Clinton, Biden, and Gates: The Guardians of Continuity

While the appointment of Jones proved to be a mistake, that of Hillary Clinton was enlightened. It was not an obvious decision to appoint a former rival with such a strong personality to head the State Department. Kissinger, the master of power relations, saw this as a sign of political courage for which President Obama should receive credit: "To appoint a very strong personality to a prominent cabinet position requires a great deal of courage."[29] Above all, the decision was clever. It allowed Obama to immediately neutralize a potential opponent and use her international notoriety to help American diplomacy. The principal risk was that Clinton might use her strategic position to attempt to regain the upper hand over the president by defending hard-line positions, such as the one she adopted against Iran during the presidential campaign.[30] But this risk did not materialize. Clinton has demonstrated great loyalty to Obama.

Moreover, the White House immediately set out to carefully define the State Department's role. It had initially thought to place Donilon by Clinton's side, but then settled on John Steinberg, on the advice of Steinberg's close colleague, Donilon.[31] Clinton's favored pick for the number-two position, Richard Holbrooke, was brushed aside. That being said, it is very difficult to assess Clinton's real influence on Obama's foreign policy for several reasons. The White House has at every opportunity conveyed the message that she has a great influence on the decision-making process.[32] By the State Department count she had taken part in 600 meetings at the White House and visited 95 countries.[33] However, the outside talk is that she is a loyal soldier.[34] These two assessments are not necessarily contradictory. The first one recognizes the fact that American foreign policy is increasingly scattered and that the State Department is only one actor among others in this area. It is present everywhere, but wherever it is present it must share its regal powers with other public and private actors. For example, in all situations of war, the State Department's influence is much weaker by design than that of the Department of Defense and the CIA. The now-deceased Holbrooke provided the best insight into this reality. When he was appointed special envoy to Afghanistan and Pakistan at the request of Clinton, to whom he was very close, he was immediately met with strong opposition from the American generals on the ground, who obviously did not make much of him. He related "a dramatic story of a fractured relationship between the State Department and the White House."[35] The military considered Afghanistan to be its war, and it was certainly determined not to relinquish any of its power on this matter.[36] The real challenge for any secretary of state is to identify issues that are likely to increase his or her relevance to the administration.[37] Since the Arab revolutions, Clinton seems to have politically set her sights on social networks and public diplomacy, especially in Pakistan, where the United States has a very poor image.[38] Another reason it is difficult to gauge Clinton's added value is that since 2009 she has not expressed any political differences with the American president on the right course of action.[39] On the most sensitive issues such as Iraq, Afghanistan, Pakistan, Iran, and the Middle East, her positions are generally in line with those of the president and Defense Secretary Robert Gates, with whom she maintained excellent relations.

It is fair to say that since 2009, the Obama administration has shown much greater internal cohesion than the Bush administration. And Obama is probably one of the most hands-on foreign policy presidents since Nixon. This cohesion can be structurally explained by the fact that the principal foreign-policy actors have all come to recognize the limits of American foreign policy: its politically and economically costly unilateralism and its excessive tendency to use force. The need to act in greater concert with the rest of the world at a time when the United States is saddled with considerable financial constraints has attenuated ideological divides on foreign policy even while American society has become highly polarized over domestic policy issues. Hence the similar thrust of Gates's reference to the militarization of American foreign policy[40] and the chairman of the Joint Chiefs of Staff's statement that the debt is the most significant threat to US security.[41] This greater cohesion can also be explained by the simultaneously authoritarian and consensual way in which Obama conducts foreign policy. There is wide room for debate and discussion before a decision is taken. However, there is no room for any actor outside of the White House to take initiatives that have not received prior approval, or that might hinder the administration's objectives. Obama's concern about remaining in charge of the process and of the decision in the face of well-structured interest groups was clearly demonstrated in his first major foreign-policy decision: America's future presence in Afghanistan. Indeed, when Obama began the process of redefining the US mission in this country in the spring of 2009, he was confronted with a military establishment that favored a long commitment without deadlines as well as a significant eighty-thousand-troop increase in American forces.[42] The three principal American military leaders, Admiral Mike McMullen and Generals Petraeus and Stanley McChrystal, did not hesitate to attempt to force the new president's hand by clearly expressing their preferences to the media and Congress. For this, they received a veiled warning from the defense secretary and the president's national security advisor.[43] The first options presented to the president called for the deployment of forty-five thousand troops over a period of 21 months, even though the surge in Iraq had been completed in less than 6 months.[44] This deliberately drawn-out timetable allowed the military men to show that only a long-term commitment was workable.[45] Obama ultimately adopted the bulk of the recommendations in McChrystal's report, but he only authorized the deployment of thirty thousand additional troops to be completed by the end of 2010. He also insisted that the military agree to two safeguards against entanglement: a withdrawal that would be phased in beginning in July 2011, and a commitment not to occupy any new Afghan territory unless Afghan forces had committed to subsequently taking over the occupation.[46] By the summer of 2010, the prospects of holding to a withdrawal timetable beginning in July 2011 appeared increasingly dim given the lack of compelling results on either the military or political fronts. The situation rekindled tensions between the White House and General Petraeus, at that time the commander of US forces in Afghanistan.[47] Nonetheless, the Obama Plan substantially adhered to the tenets of the COIN (counterinsurgency) doctrine, which draws on a combination of military and civilian tools and drastically restricts the conditions under which combat troops can use force.[48]

Afghanistan is not the only issue where the White House has sought to assert its leadership. During the Iranian Spring in 2009, it appears to have fiercely opposed the initiative of a State Department expert in social networking who has since become the head of *Google Ideas.* He had "e-mailed the social-networking site Twitter with an unusual request: delay scheduled maintenance of its global network, which would have cut off service while Iranians were using Twitter to swap information and inform the outside world about the mushrooming protests around Teheran."[49] At the time, the Obama administration was pursuing a policy of openness toward the Iranian regime in an attempt to extract concessions on the nuclear issue, and therefore did not want to provoke the regime.[50] During the Arab Spring, the White House firmly corrected the statements of a former ambassador to Cairo who favored Hosni Mubarak (see chapter 7). It is not known whether Hillary Clinton endorsed these statements, but the tone of a speech she made at the time in Munich suggests that she at least partly did. Regardless, the White House's point of view prevailed in the end. The White House thus jealously guards the decision-making process. The resulting cohesion is also due to another factor: Obama has not addressed any important issue by taking risks that might give rise to strong disagreements within the administration. Cohesion has been achieved at the price of foregoing boldness.

Before 2009, Vice President Joe Biden served as senator between 1972 and 2008. This to say that he plays a key intermediary role between the White House and Congress, where his powerful network of relations largely transcends party boundaries. In his long tenure as chairman of the Senate Foreign Affairs Committee, Biden adopted varying positions, which were rarely original but never extreme. Like Clinton, he did not hesitate to support the Iraq war for fear of breaking the national consensus around September 11, or of being accused of "lacking patriotism" in future presidential campaigns that he and Clinton were already contemplating. He subsequently regretted his initial choice and called for a rapid withdrawal.[51] He was also very skeptical of increasing troops in Afghanistan, because he thought the priority in the region should be to fight Al Qaeda and therefore focus on antiterrorism rather than counterinsurgency.[52] Finally, Biden has favored a policy of strong support for Israel, to the point of coming close to defending Israel during the Gaza flotilla incident.[53] Yet two months earlier, Israeli authorities had humiliated him by granting permission to build new units in a West Bank settlement as Biden was arriving in Israel to call for a freeze.[54]

Robert Gates, who served as defense secretary until June 2011, when Leon Panetta succeeded him, further illustrates American policy continuity. Gates was the only member of the Bush administration who was retained by the Obama administration. Moreover, in a historically unprecedented development in US politics, he was retained in the same position. After entering the CIA in 1966, he worked his way through the ranks to become the agency's director under President Bush Senior. A moderate Republican, Gates was appointed by George W. Bush in 2006 to replace Defense Secretary Donald Rumsfeld, who was widely discredited for his handling of Iraq. Despite its significant contribution to militarizing American foreign policy, the Bush administration had paradoxically irked many in the military establishment, which felt marginalized by the very political Defense Secretary Rumsfeld, who had sought to be the president's only discussion partner on defense issues. Gates was tasked with remedying this situation. Gates was convinced that the United States had gone too far in militarizing its foreign policy and called for shifting certain activities from the Department of Defense to the Department of State.[55] This has allowed for integration between two traditionally rival departments for the first time in a long while. The integration can be attributed to both the personalities of their respective heads and the constraints on American foreign policy. It appears that Gates has made it a priority to reverse a number of previously made decisions favoring exceptionally costly military programs of doubtful utility.[56] He has emphasized the crushing military superiority of the United States in the world—one that he implicitly regards as almost unnecessary.[57] In addition to calling for the US military to adapt to new forms of war, he also officially lamented that the funding of civilian activities had been crowded out by military priorities. This is not a point one expects a Defense Secretary to make.[58] What is more, the chairman of the Joint Chiefs of Staff shares this perspective.[59] Gates does not buy into the idea that every defense secretary should increase the power of his administration by arguing for a greater budget. In Congress he has had to spar with senators from states that depend on revenue from military bases. Gates may have good intentions, but that does not mean they have been effectively put into practice. In constant dollars the current American military budget is the largest in history. And while Gates deplores inadequate programs, he has not argued for a reduction in the defense budget, a huge task that will inevitably fall to his successor.[60]

As US ambassador to the United Nations, Susan Rice is officially a member of the US government. Among the ten senior American officials who help to define foreign policy, she is probably one of the few to combine well-established professionalism with early allegiance to Barack Obama.[61] Her position as assistant secretary of state for African Affairs under the Clinton administration was certainly a political promotion. Her previous positions place her with the other officials, at the center of the political spectrum. While she did not fail to criticize the Bush administration, during her tenure in African Affairs she distinguished herself by taking very strong positions, for instance, against the Sudanese regime. She does not appear to have been opposed to the Clinton administration's decision in 1998 to bomb a factory in Sudan that was mistakenly believed to produce chemical products for Al Qaeda.[62] She participated in the talks that led Washington to request that the Khartoum government expel Osama Bin Laden, who then found refuge in Afghanistan. Her hostility toward the Sudanese government continued even after she left the American government. In 2006, she stated her support for a possible use of force against the Sudanese regime in Darfur, even in the absence of legitimacy conferred by the UN Security Council.[63] In 2011, she strongly argued in favor of recognizing South Sudan as an independent state. She holds an important position in the Obama camp because the United Nations is where the United States is, trying to regain its international legitimacy in order to justify and defend its strategic choices, especially with regard to Iran. However, she has experienced America's struggle to recast its position on a number of issues such as the Israeli-Palestinian conflict.

The new head of counterterrorism, John Brennan, also plays an essential role on the new American foreign-policy team. Originally considered for director of the CIA, where he had served as deputy executive director, he was appointed chief counterterrorism adviser after it became clear that the Senate might block his confirmation.[64] Like Gates, Brennan is a pure product of the CIA, for which he served as station chief in Saudi Arabia in the 1980s. His path also underscores the continuity in American policy. Indeed, Brennan was deeply involved in implementing the Bush administration's counterterrorism strategy. However, he quickly became aware of the operational and political limits of the "war on terror" ideology. In 2006 he gave an interview that foreshadowed, almost word for word, Obama's future doctrinal choices on combating terrorism. He did not support the use of the war on terror concept, which he considered overly bellicose and overly focused on the problem's consequences rather than its causes. He criticized the Bush administration for having reduced American foreign policy to combating terrorism, suggesting that it may have overplayed the terrorism card: "We've used the blunt force of the United States government to address the post-9/11 terrorist threat. Unfortunately, we've used the blunt force of the government, in some respects, to perpetuate the threat."[65]

He was also worried about the deteriorating image of the United States in the Arab world, where it is increasingly seen as an occupier. Finally, with regard to Iran he advocated a change of tack by proposing to end the war rhetoric, engage in direct dialogue with Tehran, push for the political integration of Hezbollah into the Lebanese government, and take into account Iran's regional interests.[66] President Obama initially adopted this position, but then abandoned it for lack of significant results.

The Internal Constraints of Foreign Policy

One cannot survey the new players in American foreign policy without mentioning the decisive role of Congress. The United States has a presidential system in which Congress plays an important role, as several well-known and long-standing procedures show: the confirmation of senior political officials for positions proposed by the head of state, the ratification of treaties, and the vote on the budget and therefore on civilian- and military-aid programs. In all these areas, the US Congress can draw on a wealth of autonomous expertise and impressive legislative tools to easily block any executive initiative that does not gain its approval. Congress's role is even more important now that the Democrats only have a very slim majority in the Senate and a minority in the House of Representatives since the November 2010 elections. Due to the Republican Party's radicalization and deep internal divisions, which prevent it from adopting a common position, the practice of a bipartisan foreign policy has become very difficult if not impossible. The Strategic Arms Reduction Treaty (START) agreement with Moscow was only narrowly ratified. Obama's attempt to reactivate the Comprehensive Nuclear-Test-Ban Treaty (CTBT), which would ban nuclear tests, now seems unlikely to be ratified.[67]

Congress largely focuses on domestic policy issues, but the interaction between domestic policy and foreign policy has never been so great. The wars in Iraq and Afghanistan have for over a decade now been issues in which the distinction between domestic and foreign policy does not make much sense given the importance of US engagement in these countries. These are not the only examples. The issues of terrorism, climate change, trade, and military expenditures have such great domestic implications that they can hardly be discussed as foreign-policy topics alone. Moreover, in light of the close ties between the United States and Israel, Congress is particularly interested in the settlement of the Israeli-Palestinian conflict. What Congressional interest in the Israeli-Palestinian conflict actually means, thanks to AIPAC's outstanding work, is alignment with the most hard-line Israeli positions.

At first, Obama thought he only had to express unconditional political support for Israel's security to pursue a more balanced policy, including a settlement freeze in the West Bank. To keep his options open, Obama did not appoint Dennis Ross to the White House. While he was an old hand on the Israeli-Palestinian issue across US administrations, his very close ties to Netanyahu might have limited Obama's room for maneuver. Instead, Ross was appointed to the State Department to handle Iran, and Obama assigned the Israeli-Palestinian issue to George Mitchell, the tireless mediator in the Irish conflict and a proponent of a settlement freeze as the first step in an Israeli-Palestinian settlement. Mitchell thought he could count on support from the White House, State Department, and his Congressional connections to advance the peace process. He had not factored in the determination of Ross, who apparently, according to the Israeli newspaper *Haaretz*, seriously undermined him: "He has whispered in the ear of U.S. President Barack Obama, maintained a secret and direct channel with Prime Minister Benjamin Netanyahu and his envoy Isaac Molho, and undermined U.S. Mideast envoy George Mitchell."[68] Ross was soon brought into the White House to resume his long-held policy: deal directly with the Israeli prime minister by marginalizing the State Department and of course Mitchell, with whom he had a terrible relationship, and whose vision of a settlement was anathema to his. *Haaretz* reported "the two refused to speak to one another, partly over Ross' tendency to hold talks with Israeli officials behind Mitchell's back."[69]

Therefore, even if Netanyahu had tense relations with Obama, he knew that he could counter Obama through key intermediaries in the Congress, AIPAC, and even within the White House. Obama was cognizant of this power relationship, which steadily deteriorated, especially after the midterm elections in 2010. He therefore chose not to rock the internal bureaucratic boat and simply reaffirmed his willingness to remain involved in the conflict despite the stalled negotiations. Such was the goal of his May 2011 speech on the Arab Spring and the Israeli-Palestinian conflict, wherein the inclusion of references to the Israeli-Palestinian conflict provoked a debate in the US administration.[70] Informed of these plans, Netanyahu traveled to Washington to meet the president and address Congress and AIPAC in order to counter Obama.[71] The White House sensed a trap and ensured that the president would speak before Netanyahu's arrival, demonstrating the extent to which Israeli domestic policy is embedded in US domestic policy.[72] In his speech of May 19, 2011, Obama developed the argument for a settlement of the conflict whereby "the borders of Israel and Palestine should be based on the 1967 lines with mutually agreed swaps."[73] Although the speech did not mention the issues of Jerusalem and refugee return in an effort not to alienate Netanyahu, Obama's statement sparked the Israeli prime minister's "rage."[74] In an official statement made before his trip to Washington he had declared he "expects to hear a reaffirmation from President Obama of US commitments made to Israel in 2004, which were overwhelmingly supported by both Houses of Congress. Among other things, those commitments relate to Israel not having to withdraw to the 1967 lines which are both indefensible and which would leave major Israeli population centers in Judea and Samaria beyond those lines."[75] Netanyahu was right about the guarantees given to Israel by Obama's predecessors on the delimitation of borders. However, the prime minister's almost threatening tone seemed so harsh that several influential members of the American Jewish community such as Jeffrey Goldberg were disturbed.[76]

With the support of Congress and AIPAC, Netanyahu arrived at the White House in a position of strength and confronted Obama, before whom he publicly declared: "While Israel is prepared to make generous compromises for peace, it cannot go back to the 1967 lines, because these lines are indefensible; because they don't take into account certain changes that have taken place on the ground, demographic changes that have taken place over the past 44 years."[77] Obama took a hit, but two days later when he in turn addressed the AIPAC assembly, he strongly qualified his previous position under the pretext of clarifying it, and even used Netanyahu's terms: "let me reaffirm what '1967 lines with mutually agreed swaps' means. [...] The parties themselves—Israelis and Palestinians—will negotiate a border that is different than the one that existed on June 4, 1967. *It allows the parties themselves to account for the changes that have taken place over the last 44 years.*"[78]

This last phrase is precisely the one Netanyahu used to criticize Obama's call for a return to the 1967 borders. It convinced everyone that Obama had set aside a Middle East settlement until the next presidential elections. By April 2011, Mitchell had quietly resigned from his position as Special Envoy for Middle East Peace, after refusing to return to the region beginning in December 2010. In August 2011, Barack Obama appointed Dan Schapiro ambassador to Tel Aviv; according to the Israeli newspaper *Haaretz*, Schapiro's primary task was not to "promote peace between Israeli and Palestinian leaders, but between Obama and American Jewish leaders..."[79]

Congress is, by extension, closely following all of the issues in this region (Iran, Turkey). As a result, the dramatic deterioration of relations between Israel and Turkey immediately caused Congress to significantly reevaluate Turkey's role in the Middle East.[80] Turkey's distancing from the United States led Congress to mete out punishment, even if this did not align with the administration's objectives and interests. It can be speculated that Brazil's independent stand from the United States on sanctions against Iran will not escape the notice of American legislators either. All this imposes real political constraints on Obama's policies, especially since, for the most part, Congress has a strong sovereignist tendency when it comes to international policy issues: a distrust of multilateral processes, a reluctance to facilitate a multilateral trade agreement at the WTO, little receptivity to the expectations and points of view of US partners, and an appetite for sanctions against those who thwart America. Congressional sentiment on nuclear and human-rights issues and the settlement of the Israeli-Palestinian conflict is also out of tune with President Obama's approach. Finally, because it is a sounding board for the public that elects it, Congress can sometimes suddenly retract in response to public opinion. For example, there was initially a broad consensus over Afghanistan due to the terrorist factor. This consensus has since frayed, even within the Democratic Party, because the war's objectives are unclear.[81] In some circles of the Left, Obama's excessive caution is the subject of much discussion and even criticism. But this caution is not only a matter of temperament. In a system as complex as the American system, the multiplicity of actors and interests is such that he must closely navigate the many pitfalls before him. Of all the recent foreign policy initiatives in which Congressional approval was explicitly required, only the START agreement with Russia had any likelihood of passing Congress. Even on this rare issue that still has bipartisan support, the Obama administration was forced not only to provide additional guarantees on the treaty itself, but also to propose a nuclear weapons modernization program.[82] The problem is that the modernization of nukes seems to violate the obligations enshrined in the Non Proliferation Treaty (NPT) and fuels the nuclear ambitions of have-not nations.[83]

With regard to climate change, Obama had made commitments in Copenhagen to reduce greenhouse gas emissions by 17 percent by 2020, but here again the administration is hampered. Since the November 2010 elections, Obama has virtually ceased raising the issue, even though three months earlier he had declared that he would not tolerate inaction in this area. Moreover, at the domestic level he has adopted a series of measures that work against fighting climate change.[84] In stark contrast with his promises made in 2008, he has opened new federal lands for drilling, signaled a desire to approve the Keystone XL oil pipelinefor Canada, and trumpeted rises in oil and gas production. Under Obama's administration, imports from OPEC (Organization of the Petroleum Exporting Countries) countries have been reduced by 20 percent.[85] Hence the sharp criticism from former Vice President Al Gore, who has become the most authoritative voice on global warming:

> President Obama has thus far failed to use the bully pulpit to make the case for bold action on climate change. After successfully passing his green stimulus package, he did nothing to defend it when Congress decimated its funding. After the House passed cap and trade, he did little to make passage in the Senate a priority. (...) He has also called for a massive expansion of oil drilling in the United States, apparently in an effort to defuse criticism from those who argue speciously that "drill, baby, drill" is the answer to our growing dependence on foreign oil.[86]

Another area that is significantly constrained by domestic politics is trade policy. In the summer of 2008, the multilateral WTO negotiations were on the verge of completion when they met American and Indian opposition with regard to agricultural products. These differences could have been overcome since the issue was more symbolic than real. The fact remains that this blockage has considerably reduced the chances of concluding the Doha Round. Since taking office, Obama has not focused much on trade issues for obvious domestic political reasons. Indeed, a good part of his base is composed of blue-collar workers, often AFL–CIO union members, who are employed in sectors of the old economy: steel, textiles, and automobiles. These sectors have not sufficiently restructured and employees understandably fear that market liberalization will threaten their jobs, especially since the social safety net in the United States is much weaker than in Europe. Not all share this viewpoint, however:

> America's president is captive to the country's labor unions, who buy the false narrative that trade with poor countries is increasing

the ranks of the poor in the US by driving down wages. In fact, however, there is plenty of evidence for the rival narrative that rapid and deep labor-saving technological change is what is putting pressure on wages, and that imports of cheap labor-intensive goods that US workers consume are actually offsetting that distress.

The root of the problem is actually that the least competitive sectors of the US economy are highly unionized, while the most competitive ones, particularly the services, are not. The result is an imbalance in interest representation and the creation of a political discourse that is far removed from reality. Obama has completely bought into the idea that unemployment is partly linked to outsourcing and therefore that "we have a great opportunity to bring manufacturing back."[87] Yet it is commonly agreed that this discourse bears absolutely no relation to economic reality, because the jobs going abroad will not return to the United States. Industrial employment is declining because industry has become more competitive. Since 1979 the American economy has lost eight million manufacturing jobs. At the same time industrial value added increased by two-thirds. In other words, worker productivity has tripled since 1979, meaning it is now possible to better produce much more with many fewer people.[88] But Obama knows very well that this truth is extremely difficult to sell, especially in an election year.

What is more profitable electorally is to develop a rhetoric that is both critical of the WTO, whose multilateral framework is no longer deemed conducive to advancing US interests, and supportive of regional economic agreements with an anti-China bias, such as the Trans-Pacific Partnership (TPP): "The US's decision to walk away from the Doha Round is a reflection of a deeper dissatisfaction with the WTO process itself. India, Brazil and China in particular are the centre of this dissatisfaction."[89]

The TPP does not offer significant value added to the American economy given that the United States has already signed free-trade agreements with most of this partnership's member states.[90] However, it is of great political import. By portraying the TPP as open to all, the United States is seeking to attract Japan in order to better force China to accede to US demands or be excluded from this partnership: "The texts for this agreement are heavily focused on services trade liberalisation especially on financial services, strong protection for intellectual property rights and rights of cross-border data flow, a key preoccupation for US financial service providers in the region who have come up against regulation on data movement that have required them to decentralize data storage in each jurisdiction rather than through regional hubs."[91] The message being sent to Beijing is clear: if you would like to join this vast Trans-Pacific market, you will have to accept disciplines that you refused to accept in a multilateral setting like the WTO. "The real target of such reforms is China, the hope being that a successful trade deal across the Asia-Pacific region would serve as a powerful inducement for Beijing to reform China's own powerful entrenched state-owned enterprises."[92] For Obama, defending employment and containing China are two sides of the same policy.

There is also another very powerful protectionist lobby in the United States: the agricultural lobby that is represented by the infamous Farm Bureau. While the Bureau has not traditionally been a part of the Democratic Party's constituency, it has a disproportionate influence on the US Congress, which ultimately ratifies international trade agreements. Of course, the administration and the Congress always play a negotiating game in these matters, but Obama does not believe he can gain any political advantage from trade. This is all the more true as the public and its representatives view trade through the prism of US trade relations with China. Like Japan in the 1980s, China is blamed for many ills: it undervalues its currency, destroys jobs, does not respect intellectual property rights, does not have high environmental standards, and makes it difficult for US investors by giving preference to domestic investors. The US Congress's uphill battle to ratify bilateral trade agreements with countries as small as Panama and Colombia underscores just how unpopular global trade and the opening of markets have become. They are even more so because the economic forces that favor a greater opening, such as the industries of the new economy, are not well organized and are politically closer to the Republican Party anyway. The challenges that confront Obama in his exercise of power grow by the day. In this area, as in others, he has no desire to take significant political risks. His multilateralism clearly ends at the gates of the WTO.

Fragments of a Pragmatic Doctrine

The Obama administration has clearly sought to lend a degree of cohesion to its actions by formalizing a number of principles, which Clinton has best conveyed. Her first major speech, given in July 2009, provided several very interesting clues as to how the Obama administration thinks about the US position in the global system. First, she stated unequivocally that the United States is determined to continue exercising its leadership: "The question is not whether our nation can or should lead, but how it will lead in the 21st century."[93] At the same time, she well understands that the United States no longer has the means to ensure this, either because it does not have the resources to do so, or because growing interdependence makes it difficult to exercise leadership alone.[94] In this twofold reality she sees the following lesson: "For just as no nation can meet these challenges alone, no challenge can be met without America."[95] That is: America cannot do anything by itself, but nothing will happen without it, let alone against it.

On this basis, how to create a political architecture that is likely to attain its objective? The first way would be to acknowledge the existence of a multipolar world where the United States's partners will collectively address the problems of an interdependent world. But this was not Clinton's answer. She recognized the interdependence of the issues, but rejected the idea of multipolarity in favor of partnerships: "We will lead by inducing greater cooperation among a greater number of actors and reducing competition, tilting the balance away from a multi-polar world and toward a multi-partner world."[96] Is there a difference? Certainly. In a multipolar world all the actors are supposed to be of equal power and therefore would be able to deal with the United States as equals. The United States has no interest in promoting such an approach. For the United States, to be recognized as an influential player must be deserved, so long as it is the one providing this recognition. In exchange for the recognition that it is willing to concede to a certain number of actors as US strategic partners, these actors are encouraged and forced to provide a solution to a problem that the United States cannot resolve alone: "We will offer a place at the table to any nation, group, or citizen willing to shoulder a fair share of the burden."[97] The issues that thus need to be addressed include: nuclear proliferation, the fight against terrorism, burden-sharing for wars conducted in the interest of several nations and not just the United States, the reduction in financial imbalances, the fight against various forms of trafficking, market access, and so on. It is therefore in the interest of the United States to find credible and effective partners, though it might not rely on the same set of partners for each issue. The insistence on partnerships is very important, because the United States is seeking to prevent the classical collective-action problem of free riding: "We believe this approach will advance our interests by uniting diverse partners around common concerns. It will make it more difficult for others to abdicate their responsibilities or abuse their power."[98]

When the world was dominated by a relatively limited number of actors that lived separately from one another, collective-action problems were less acute. Today the international situation is different. There are both many more actors competing at the international level and an increasing number of influential and powerful actors. Rich and developed countries like the United States are still ahead, but their lead is decreasing. How to ensure that a community's joint problems do not result in some of its members evading their attendant obligations while continuing to benefit from the issue's resolution by others? This is the problem of free riding.

This major issue cannot be addressed without revisiting the pioneering thesis of Mancur Olson, who in 1965 published a famous book that discussed the dilemma of collective action, even though his thesis did not particularly apply to states. Olson's hypothesis was relatively simple.[99] He posited that for a group composed of many individuals, any collective action incurs costs in order to achieve a satisfactory outcome for all. For example, students sharing an apartment will have to take the time, each in turn, to clean this apartment so that it remains neat. Each student taken separately would naturally prefer to walk into a clean bathroom than a dirty one, even if he would egotistically like even more to enter a neat room that he did not have to clean. At any level, the collective-action problem thus consists of ensuring that everyone contributes fairly to resolving a problem through an individual contribution. International society functions in a similar way. There are a number of public goods at the international level that benefit the international community as a whole. However, it is obvious that contributions from different members of this community to protecting the public good vary widely. The most problematic actors are large states, and specifically emerging countries that benefit greatly from the international system's stability and many of its global public goods, but do not participate in proportion to their means, at least according to the United States. The argument is that states need to contribute to the cost of protecting global public goods in accordance with their means or derived benefits. How to compensate for allowing the Europeans to benefit from the US military guarantee and the security it provides them? How to avoid that the Chinese benefit from the opening of African markets without increasing their public aid, which the West has largely provided to Africa thus far? How to prevent Russia from saddling the United States with the sole responsibility for combating nuclear proliferation even though it is also threatened by this problem? How to ensure that China does not keep its currency undervalued while it benefits from open access to the American market? Here are some concrete illustrations of the dilemmas that collective action raises for American diplomacy.

Olson proposed two ways to overcome collective-action dilemmas. The first is to have a benefactor. One actor within a group pays for all the others in order to solve a problem. This generosity costs the benefactor, but the incurred cost is much lower than that of not solving the problem. In other words, even though the United States has guaranteed Europe's security for the past 50 years without real compensation, it continued to offer the guarantee because it knew that failure to do so would have jeopardized its own security. US security played out on the borders of Europe.

It is precisely this kind of situation that is unsustainable for the United States today given its diminishing financial means. It can no longer play the role of benefactor in Olson's sense of the term. Another solution remains: what Olson called *selective incentive*.[100] To ensure participation of all, and especially of the most important members, particular advantages can be granted. India might be promised support in its bid to become a permanent member of the Security Council in exchange for Indian support in a number of areas. This approach is selective, though, enabling the United States to select the relevant partner(s) for each issue. There is no abstract appeal to good will or open invitation to the power table. The title of partner is only bestowed on those who can concretely help the United States. These partnerships are of very different natures. Some are clearly aimed at deterring other actors from acting against US interests: "Not everybody in the world wishes us well or shares our values and interests. (...). In those cases, our partnerships can become power coalitions to constrain or deter those negative actions."[101] This is the case, for instance, with the P5 plus 1 with regard to Iran, or the Six-Party Talks with regard to North Korea. These two examples alone demonstrate that the partners are not always the same even though the issue is one: nuclear proliferation. The Russians and the Chinese are included in both groups because their ability to influence North Korea is deemed significant and perhaps decisive. By contrast, the Europeans are excluded because their influence over North Korea is deemed weak or insignificant. With regard to Iran, the role of the Europeans is considered to be decisive, but not that of the Japanese, who are not part of the group. American policy could not have a more realist vision.

CHAPTER THREE

No More Monsters to Destroy?

All foreign policy is part of one or several traditions, and the United States is the country where references to these traditions most abound. US diplomatic history is full of references to these traditions, which often become doctrines: Monroe's Doctrine with its Polk, Ohney, and Roosevelt corollaries, Manifest Destiny, the Open Door Policy, President Wilson's Fourteen Points, Acheson's doctrine, Nixon's doctrine, Reagan's doctrine, and Clinton's doctrine.[1] Every president claims, or is identified with a foreign-policy doctrine. Barack Obama is no exception. As described below, however, he challenged attempts to define his policy with regard to the Arab Spring. This is the crux of the problem. The press and academic circles often use the term "doctrine" to mean guidelines, which can be more or less strict. What is sometimes pompously called the Clinton doctrine, based on the idea of "democratic enlargement," was in fact but a bureaucratic exercise to theorize US foreign policy after the end of the Cold War, even though the term doctrine is probably not the most appropriate to describe a fundamentally pragmatic, post–Cold War policy.[2] These doctrines often serve to give formal coherence to tentative policies, but also to rationalize policies and constraints. The Nixon doctrine was nothing more than a means to prepare the United States for a withdrawal from Vietnam by emphasizing that it was time for the Vietnamese to take responsibility for their security. This does not mean that these doctrines have no importance or that they are all equivalent. The Monroe Doctrine has profoundly influenced US foreign policy even though it did not have the meaning that is often attributed to it. President Wilson's Fourteen Points also strongly influenced US choices. This is even truer for the *containment* doctrine that George Kennan admirably defined in 1947 and that guided US foreign policy for a long time.

Obama's foreign policy cannot be understood without situating it in relation to various doctrinal strands. To this end, two parameters should be considered. The first is an assessment of US policy with regard to its willingness or propensity to actively engage in world affairs. This places US policy on a scale ranging from isolationism to expansionism. The second is an interpretation of US policy trade-offs between the preservation of its closest and most narrow national interests (realism) and the promotion of values beyond its borders (messianic liberalism). These traditions overlap while remaining separate. Realism and isolationism are not one and the same, and neither are interventionism and messianic liberalism. The Vietnam War, for example, was not really motivated by messianic politics. Rather, it was the byproduct of Cold War thinking following the Cuban crisis. Washington wanted to show Moscow that it would not be allowed to gain ground in Asia. The resulting military escalation was more attributable to entanglement than a predetermined strategy. In fact, Lyndon Johnson, who became responsible for this disaster after Kennedy, was politically much closer to the realists than to the messianic internationalists.[3] Not all realists are opposed to military action (Johnson, Nixon, Bush Senior), and not all idealists are militarists (Carter). Moreover, there are realist wars and more messianic ones. The First Gulf War in 1991 was of the former nature, while the second was of the latter. In a review of the monumental biography of Kennan, one of the greatest influences on US foreign policy during the Cold War, Henry Kissinger, who is identified with the most traditional realists, aptly reminds us that

> stable orders require elements of both power and morality. In a world without equilibrium, the stronger will encounter no restraint, and the weak will find no means of vindication. At the same time, if there is no commitment to the essential justice of existing arrangements, constant challenges or else a crusading attempt to impose value systems are inevitable.[4]

Political actors must navigate many constraints and many legacies. Obama cannot escape these limitations. Before delving into the debate over the traditions of US foreign policy in order to better understand Obama's policy, one notion needs to be dismissed: the alleged alternation between isolationism and expansionism.

An Unlikely Isolationism

Many US foreign-policy observers and analysts see America alternating between phases when it turns inwards and disengages from the world, and phases when, to the contrary, it takes action, which is sometimes benevolent and sometimes aggressive.[5] One might expect that after the messianic excesses of George W. Bush, the United States would retreat from the world. But this hypothesis is unlikely because the United States has never really been isolationist, at least since the end of the nineteenth century. The American author Walter McDougall has brilliantly shown that since the 1898 Spanish-American War, the United States has definitively moved from the Old Testament era to the New Testament era.[6] In the Old Testament era, America determined it could be a promised land of freedom so long as it recognized its limits and left the rest of the world out. The New Testament phase, which began with the Spanish-American War over Cuba, was driven by a crusading spirit and aspirations to bring salvation to a world ravaged by revolution and war.[7] American messianic beliefs took on a religious dimension and took aim at weakening Europe's position in the world, especially in Latin America. This power dynamic based on a religious messianic vision was a source of nervous amusement for Otto von Bismarck, who remarked, "God has a special providence for fools, drunks, and the United States of America."[8] The Spanish-American War thereby led the United States to occupy the Philippines in order to further weaken Spain. Indeed, beginning with this war in Cuba, US interest in global affairs intensified. It progressed in lockstep with America's transformation into the world's leading economic power. At this point, the United States definitively gained the upper hand over Europe in the American hemisphere.

Barely two years after the war against Spain, the United States sent five thousand troops to fight in the Boxer Rebellion in China. In 1904, the Roosevelt corollary to the Monroe Doctrine established the US right to intervene throughout the American hemisphere. In 1905, Theodore Roosevelt brokered the settlement of the conflict between Japan and Russia, earning him the Nobel Peace Prize. That same year, Woodrow Wilson, who would become famous by the end of the First World War, did not hesitate to say, "I suppose that in our hearts we know that we shall rule the world."[9]

Subsequently, the United States has militarily intervened in the two World Wars, Korea, Vietnam, Kuwait, Kosovo, and finally Iraq, not to mention countless ad-hoc interventions—direct and indirect, open and clandestine—to remove leaders hostile to its interests and replace them with more malleable regimes.

The isolationist label is generally attached to the Monroe Doctrine, the US Senate's refusal to ratify the treaty to create the League of Nations, and America's initial neutrality during the Second World War. Yet none of these historical examples prove their point. The Monroe Doctrine was by no means an isolationist doctrine. To the contrary, it aimed to scale back the European presence on the American continent at a time when the US territorial conquest was still far from complete.

One must recognize that in 1823, America's strategic position was quite modest. Great Britain was expanding in Latin America, as demonstrated by its occupation of the Falkland Islands in 1833, while Spain was still very present. Meanwhile, America's territorial boundaries were not yet set since Texas, New Mexico, and California were not part of the republic. US territorial expansion had just started, and it was only in 1830 that the famous *Indian Removal Act* was enacted to displace Native Americans to the west of the Mississippi.

In fact, the greatest constant in US foreign policy is not isolationism but rather the desire to avoid binding commitments when US interests were not at stake. This constant did not, however, prevent the United States from alternating between realist and messianic approaches, and between pragmatism and messianic idealism.[10]

The refusal to ratify the Treaty of Versailles was also not an expression of isolationism. The disagreement between US president Wilson and Senator Henry Cabot Lodge was not over US participation in European security, but over the appropriate framework for engagement. Wilson believed that a multilateral arrangement was best because he was confident that the United States would fully dominate it. Cabot Lodge was more skeptical and preferred to see the United States forge bilateral ties with the large European states rather than tie its hands through arrangements it might not fully control.[11] Wilson had in a way foreshadowed the United Nations, while Cabot Lodge was envisioning the NATO. These mistakenly labeled isolationists were in fact unilateralists or bilateralists.

Franklin Roosevelt's decision not to intervene in the Second World War until the Japanese attack on Pearl Harbor was more tactical than strategic. The *Neutrality Act* of September 5, 1939, was accompanied by the lifting of the arms embargo. It was followed, in March 1941, by the *Lend-Lease Act*, which allowed the United States to sell, lend, or donate war material that its allies needed. The vision for rebuilding a postwar world order was in fact outlined in January 1941, before the Pearl

Harbor attack.[12] As a Congressional report has pointed out, since its creation the United States has formally declared war on foreign countries 11 times.[13] Furthermore, since 1798 many military interventions have taken place without a formal declaration of war but with Congressional authorization. The latter include the Vietnam War, the First Gulf War, the intervention in Afghanistan, and the 2003 Iraq War.[14] The 1973 Goldwater report estimated that between 1798 and 1972 the United States conducted 199 foreign military operations without a declaration of war.[15] One of the very first US military interventions took place in 1801 in what is today Libya: "A few marines landed (...) to raise a force against Tripoli in an effort to free the crew of the *Philadelphia*. Tripoli declared war but not the United States, although Congress authorized US military action by statute."[16] The latest US intervention also ironically took place in Libya.[17]

The Vietnamese debacle was interpreted as both a symbol of US decline and the beginning of inevitable isolationism, but it had neither of these consequences. The president most closely identified with the post-Vietnam and supposedly isolationist America is Jimmy Carter, without whom the Camp David accords between Israel and Egypt would never have been signed. Carter also called for a significant military buildup after the Soviet invasion of Afghanistan in December 1979. Even the end of the Cold War, which was expected to put an end to the international political and military overexposure of the United States, did nothing of the sort, although the United States did massively cut back its presence in Europe and, accordingly, its military expenditures in constant dollars. The First Gulf War, which broke out after the balance of power between Iran and Iraq tipped, led the United States to militarily intervene to liberate Kuwait. This paved the way for a military return to the Middle East ten years after losing Iran. Once this objective was achieved, the United States did not disengage, however. To the contrary, it chose to establish a long-term presence by playing the card of double containment—of Iraq and of Iran—to protect the petro-monarchies and Israel. The US presence in the region fueled an Islamist anti-Americanism that distorted this reality and gave birth to Al Qaeda. The latter found sanctuary in Sudan before creating its base in Afghanistan. President George W. Bush did not come into office with grand strategic designs and was not particularly interested in strengthening US engagement with the world. He nonetheless had to respond in Afghanistan and he made the ideological decision to invade Iraq. This latter war, the so-called "war of choice," is the one that Obama challenged. However, as described later, repudiating the war of choice gave way to justifying the war of necessity (Afghanistan).[18] Richard Haass, who coined the distinction between these two types of war,[19] disputes the validity of this characterization of Afghanistan: "Afghanistan evolved from a war of necessity into a costly and futile war of choice early in 2009 when the Obama administration sharply increased force levels and elected to target the resurgent Taliban and not just al-Qaeda."[20] He also used a realist rationale to condemn the US intervention in Libya, though his arguments appear questionable.[21] In fact, there has been a "scissors" effect between the wars in Iraq and Afghanistan. The deployment of US troops in Iraq culminated in the November 2007 surge, before beginning to decrease at the start of 2009, the year Obama took office. The Obama administration then decided to bolster its presence in Afghanistan by increasing US troops from 68,000 in November 2009 to 98,000 in September 2010, reaching 102,000 at the end of 2011.[22]

Consequently, the cost of the wars, which had fallen in the Obama administration's first year when compared to Bush's last year ($144 billion as opposed to $185 billion), increased again in 2010 and reached $165 billion at the end of 2011 (see table 3.1).[23] With the definitive withdrawal of US troops from Iraq, the cost of the wars should fall back to $131 billion.[24] This figure remains extraordinarily high, given that the cost of war totaled $34 billion in 2002. In 2008, at the end of Bush's term, 180,100 American soldiers were deployed in Iraq and Afghanistan. Since the complete withdrawal of US troops from Iraq in December 2011, deployment has been limited to Afghanistan, where troop levels do not exceed 100,000. The reduction is significant in comparison to the 190,000 troops deployed across the two battlegrounds at the end of 2007. It is also relative, however: in December 2002, there were only 9,700 soldiers in these two countries. Furthermore, 40,000 US soldiers remain deployed in the region. It is important to understand that even with the reduction in US troop levels abroad, America's base military budget remains incredibly high, and there are no signs it will fall. In 2012, the last year of Obama's first term, the budget is forecast to reach $553 billion, compared to $480 billion in 2008.[25] Due to financial pressures, especially since 2008, the US defense budget is projected to fall by $400 billion in 12 years. This is a very modest figure, as Robert Gates explained to Congress:

> What's being proposed by the President is nothing close to the dramatic cuts of the past. For example, defense spending in constant dollars declined by roughly a third between 1985 and 1998.

What's being considered today, assuming all $400 billion comes from DOD [Department of Defense] over 12 years, corresponds to a projected reduction of about 5 percent in constant dollars—or slightly less than keeping pace with inflation.[26]

The objective here is not to judge the relevance of strategic decisions. Rather it is to emphasize that isolationism is an extremely powerful and constant sentiment or line of thought in the United States that is expressed today in certain elements of the Tea Party led by Ron Raul, though he firmly rejects the isolationist label.[27] But a widespread public perception does not constitute a strategy.[28] Moreover, it is difficult to pinpoint the concrete characteristics of an isolationist policy. For example, it might be considered isolationist to withdraw from international agreements or refuse to sign new agreements. Yet this criterion is not relevant. The George W. Bush administration was one of the most active US administrations in this area. However, its approach stemmed more from unilateralism than from isolationism. These two concepts are far from synonymous. While the United States often aspires to embrace or return to isolationism, the scope of its engagements precludes this from happening. The United States cannot afford to be isolationist. Hence it rarely has been isolationist since becoming the most powerful actor in the world: "Between the defeat of Napoleon in 1815 and the Soviet demise, great powers were involved in wars on average one every six years. Since it became the sole superpower, the United States has been at war for more than half the time, or twelve out of twenty two years."[29]

Table 3.1 Boots on the ground, costs of war and military budget, 2008–2011

	2008	*2009*	*2010*	*2011*
War Costs/Overseas Contingency Operations (in billions of dollars)	187.1	145.8	129.6	159.3
Military Budget/ DOD Appropriations (in millions of dollars)	606.5	513.2	530.8	548.9
Average Monthly Boots on the Ground in Afghanistan and Iraq	187.900	186.300	151.800	106.200

Source: Adapted from Amy Belasco, "Troop Levels in the Afghan and Iraq Wars, FY2001–FY2012: Cost and Other Potential," *CRS*, July 2, 2009, http://www.fas.org/sgp/crs/natsec/R40682.pdf; Pat Towell, "Defense: FY2011 Authorization and Appropriations," *CRS*, September 17, 2010, http://assets.opencrs.com/rpts /R41254_20100917.pdf; and from numbers released by the Department of Defense (DOD) on its website.

This does not mean that the United States acts all of the time and everywhere. It also does not mean that the United States never fails to act or intervene. But its failure to act is often deliberate for two reasons. First, like all actors, the United States needs to prioritize—a task whose difficulty is compounded by America's economic problems.[30] Second, the cost of a politico-military action is sometimes deemed too high in relation to other US interests, or for what it is worth. The United States must constantly contend with inward-looking domestic forces, but it always eventually finds good reasons to take a keen interest in world affairs. To this end, the United States has a hierarchy of strategies. It ranges from *offshore balancing*, which, like isolationism, does not require a priori international commitments, but prescribes intervention abroad to prevent the rise of peer competitors, to *offensive dominance*, which involves a sustained effort by the unipole to directly control substantial areas of the world. Between them lies selective engagement in areas of strategic interest.[31]

Is Obama a Realist?

The question is how the United States proceeds with these strategies. This is where the second explanatory parameter for US foreign policy comes into play: to what extent is the policy realist or messianic? This debate is not new. In a famous speech, John Quincy Adams highlighted the fine line, for a country like the United States, between the belief in universal principles and the risk of wanting to spread them throughout the world:

> America has, in the lapse of nearly half a century, without a single exception, respected the independence of other nations while asserting and maintaining her own. (...) Wherever the standard of freedom and Independence has been or shall be unfurled, there will her heart, her benedictions and her prayers be. But she goes not abroad, in search of monsters to destroy. She well knows that by once enlisting under other banners than her own, were they even the banners of foreign independence, she would involve herself beyond the power of extrication, in all the wars of interest and intrigue, of individual avarice, envy, and ambition, which assume the colors and usurp the standard of freedom. (...) She might become the dictatress of the world. She would be no longer the ruler of her own spirit."[32]

Upon taking office, Obama refused to choose between strict realism, which would necessarily be cynical, and messianic ideology, of the corrupting kind he had fought under the Bush administration: "Within America, there has long been a tension between those who describe themselves as realists or idealists—a tension that suggests a stark choice between the narrow pursuit of interests or an endless campaign to impose our values around the world. I reject these choices."[33] This did not stop his very close aide Rahm Emanuel, now mayor of Chicago, from saying, "If you had to put him in a category, he's probably more realpolitik, like Bush 41."[34]

Various actors have made claims about realism, but it is worth recalling briefly what this concept means, before discussing how it can be verified as an operational policy framework. These are not one and the same.

We will not review the theories of realism, which have given rise to an abundant literature.[35] The analysis here will be limited to reviewing the central tenets linking the theories of realism that may be relevant to understanding the specific conduct of an actor, such as the United States. In essence, the theory of realism is based on four general assumptions.[36] The first is that the world is anarchic, meaning it is not based on a principle of order that one state could use to protect itself from another. The second is that states are the central and key actors in the global game. The third is that power politics take precedence over any set of rules and norms governing the international community. Finally, realism is generally pessimistic about the prospects for eliminating conflict and war.[37] It is also skeptical about the pursuit of moral objectives in international relations.[38] Such pursuits are not deemed to be inevitable, but rather likely. Of course, the realist school includes many strands and substrands of thought that diverge on essential issues. It is important to understand, however, that theories are only conceptual frameworks. Political actors most often completely disregard the admonitions of the theoreticians of international relations. The most famous of them, Kenneth Waltz, has argued that theoretical development and foreign-policy analysis are two different enterprises that are disconnected from one another.[39] Steve Walt, one of the best US foreign-policy experts, lamented the growing gap between conceptualization, which is confined to academic circles, and diplomatic practice, which substantially diverges from the former.[40] Does this render nugatory an interpretive framework for the foreign policy of the Obama administration? No, provided we develop an analytical grid to relate the general assumptions of realism to the effective conduct of US foreign policy.

In this perspective, we propose five criteria to evaluate Obama's realism:

- the rejection of messianic ideology in political discourse
- the emphasis on traditional security issues and on large states irrespective of their domestic political choices
- the ability to gain the support of former adversaries whose support is considered necessary, or to engage with strategic rivals
- replaying Nixon in China: to seek accommodations with real or potential adversaries at the cost of altering relations with one or several allies
- the refusal to militarily engage abroad when such action is deemed contrary to US vital interests, but would save the lives of unprotected populations

This is but an analytical framework. However, it is better to try to measure or evaluate Obama's realism in terms of verifiable and comparable criteria than to do so on the basis of favorable or unfavorable bias.

The Rejection of Messianic Ideology in Political Discourse

This criterion can only be evaluated comparatively. A comparison of Obama's discourse with that of Bush is very instructive in this regard. A selection of the terms for which there is a disparity in use between the two presidents shows that the gap is highest for the terms *liberty* and *democracy*. These are the two political terms that Bush used most in his speeches, whereas they rank very low for Obama. The contexts in which the Bush and Obama used these words are also very different.

For example, Bush often used the term liberty in charged phrases, such as: "spread liberty," "promote liberty," "expand liberty," "believe in liberty," "live in a free society," and "in the free world." Obama discusses liberty very differently. He mentions "religious liberty," "freedom of movement," and "freedom of expression," and seems to have banned the use of the term *free world*, which is a legacy of the Cold War that is too closely associated with the idea of the West against the rest.[41] Bush was thus highly ideological with these terms, which he used abundantly. Obama uses them much less, and when he does, he places them in context precisely to avoid giving them an ideological slant. Similarly, Obama has virtually never used the term *free world* that is associated with the West, nor the term *war on terror*, while Bush widely

Table 3.2 Discourse on democracy and liberty

	George Bush	Barack Obama
Democracy	Ranked 1st[*] (Used 7 times as much as Obama)	Ranked 10th[*]
Liberty[**]	Ranked 2nd[*] (Used 7 times as much as Obama)	Ranked 12th[*]

[*] The rank refers to the term's position in relation to the 25 political terms that were selected from George Bush's speeches between 2005 and 2009, and Barack Obama's between 2009 and June 2010. The term "democracy," for example, is quantitatively the term Bush used most in his speeches, while it is ranked tenth in Obama's speeches. When we say that Bush used the terms "democracy" and "liberty" seven times as much as Obama, the reference base includes all the speeches. The figures have been rounded. The sources and methodology used in these calculations are explained in the annex.

[**] Includes the terms "liberty" and "freedom."

used both. On this first criterion, there is no doubt as to Obama's realist turn. It is expressed in his reaffirmation of the principle whereby it is not for the United States to impose its political system on the world. Moreover, Obama reaffirmed this in speeches in Cairo, Moscow, and Shanghai. These three cities were not selected by chance: it is in the Muslim world, Russia, and China that the Bush administration's messianic democracy met with strong resistance. Obama therefore asserted in Moscow that "America cannot and should not seek to impose any system of government on any other country, nor would we presume to choose which party or individual should run a country. And we haven't always done what we should have on that front."[42]

Obama's realism is also reflected in his recognizing that a considerable number of international security issues of particular importance to the United States are very weakly correlated with the political nature of existing regimes. Certainly, if North Korea were a democracy, there probably would be no nuclear issue. But this interpretation cannot be generalized. For a long time, the Israeli-Palestinian conflict was depicted as a conflict pitting the Israeli democracy against nondemocratic Arab regimes. However, since the victory of Hamas in 2005, it has become apparent that democratic elections generally brought victory to the Islamists, a development that could only mitigate the West's infatuation with such processes. Furthermore, the Bush administration's argument that the establishment of democracy in Iraq would have a ripple effect on the democratization of other Arab countries and on the settlement of the Arab-Israeli conflict, proved to be completely unfounded.[43]

The Middle East is not the only region of the world where the question of democracy turned out to be separable from security issues. In Pakistan, for instance, the fear of seeing nuclear arms fall into the hands of Islamists is independent of the nature of the Pakistani regime. It can even be assumed that the military is a better bulwark against this threat than the civilians. Finally, the Afghan crisis has shown that democracy can become meaningless if it does not incorporate such critical elements as strong state building to ensure the security of citizens, the close-to-normal functioning of society without the use of violence, and the establishment of a minimal rule of law to reduce corruption, which foreign aid has only aggravated. The fact that Hamid Karzai was able to get reelected in Afghanistan despite the steadily worsening situation is a testament to the enormous gap between an ideological vision of the world positing democracy as the best system, and an infinitely more complex international reality where democracy can only flourish if the national question has been resolved.[44]

Even in Iran's case, the nuclear conflict can neither be conceived nor resolved by reference to the dictatorial nature of the Tehran regime, since even the fiercest domestic opponents of the regime are committed to pursuing a civilian nuclear program at the very least. The Obama administration has refrained from linking the nature of the Iranian regime to its position on the nuclear issue. For example, the administration was careful not to politically exploit the Iranian election rigging in 2009 because it did not want to jeopardize the settlement proposal it was then preparing: "Just when Obama seemed to have fallen a step behind events, he emerged from his silence to do what no politician in our time could have managed: emphasize American respect for Iranian sovereignty and yet, in measured terms, make it clear that the U.S. cannot be indifferent to the tragedy unfolding in Iran."[45]

Of course, the administration has since been disappointed by the lack of response from Iran to its overtures. Yet even as US discourse toward Iran has hardened, it has refrained from ideological or bellicose rhetoric.

The Emphasis on Traditional Security Issues and on Large States Irrespective of Their Domestic Political Choices

This second criterion also shows a marked change between Bush and Obama. Classic realist terms appear much more frequently in Obama's speeches, particularly the terms *security* and *nuclear*. They are Obama's most used terms, while they are ranked fifth and sixth for Bush.

The most dramatic difference relates to the NPT. This is hardly surprising. Despite Bush's warnings about WMDs, his administration believed that proliferation was inevitable. Simply, there were "good proliferators" and "bad proliferators," against which little could be done anyway.[46] The administration itself weakened antiproliferation measures by signing a nuclear-cooperation agreement with India that reversed the 1992 Nuclear Suppliers Group's (NSG) provision to forbid any agreement with a country that is not a signatory to the NPT and does not submit to International Atomic Energy Agency (IAEA) controls.[47] Furthermore, by signing a nuclear agreement with India, a nonsignatory to the NPT, the United States was sending the wrong signal to other nonsignatory countries. Given that the Bush administration had made the political choice to wage preemptive wars, it had little interest in strengthening classical deterrence. Its objective was not to deter its opponents from attacking the United States so much as to attack them before they could attack the United States. Through the war against terror the Bush administration saw its opponents as inherently irrational actors. Moreover, the 2001 U.S. Nuclear Posture Review envisioned a role for nuclear weapons that went beyond deterrence. Most importantly, it indicated that nuclear weapons might "discourage attacks by frustrating enemy attack plans and the like."[48] This blurred the line between conventional weapons and nuclear weapons by endowing the latter with an offensive potential, rather than simply a deterrent one.

Obama sought to break with this approach by returning to a classic policy of arms reduction without affecting US nuclear security. The analysis comparing the speeches of Obama and Bush clearly confirms this.

Table 3.3 Nuclear discourse

Nuclear	Used 2 times *more* by Obama than by Bush
NPT Non Proliferation Treaty	Used 9 times *more* by Obama than by Bush
WMD Weapons of Mass destruction	Used 3.5 times *less* by Obama than by Bush

Table 3.4 Russia's place in US discourse

Obama: Ranked 4th after the three crisis countries (Afghanistan, Iran, Iraq), almost equal with China.

Bush: Ranked 8th, behind Iraq, Afghanistan, India, Israel, North Korea, and Lebanon.

As a logical consequence of this return to realism, Russia was res-urrected in US discourse. The Bush administration had relegated it to the back burner (8th rank) as relations between the two countries deteriorated at the beginning of the 2000s. Russia has since returned to the forefront, and ranks the same as China, right after the three crisis countries—Afghanistan, Iraq, and Iran.

Obama made his most eloquent case for realism since taking office during the Nobel Peace Prize award ceremony. This was no coinci-dence. He wanted to show the world that his arrival in power did not herald America's embrace of an irenic vision of the international system. In a space dedicated to honoring men of peace (the Nobel Academy), he wanted to show that the man of peace was not a pacifist and that he should not be relied on to disarm America:

> Make no mistake: Evil does exist in the world. A non-violent movement could not have halted Hitler's armies. Negotiations cannot convince al Qaeda's leaders to lay down their arms. To say that force may sometimes be necessary is not a call to cynicism—it is a recognition of history; the imperfections of man and the limits of reason. I raise this point, I begin with this point because in many countries there is a deep ambivalence about military action today, no matter what the cause. And at times, this is joined by a reflex-ive suspicion of America, the world's sole military superpower. But the world must remember that it was not simply international institutions—not just treaties and declarations—that brought stability to a post–World War II world. Whatever mistakes we have made, the plain fact is this: the United States of America has helped underwrite global security for more than six decades with the blood of our citizens and the strength of our arms.[49]

According to John Ikenberry, Obama wanted to underscore that the United States was not abandoning its "hegemonic duties."[50] Yet he understood, in a profoundly realist way, that a foreign policy cannot consist of a series of extravagant, brief, and Manichean battles based on exaggerated fears, grandiose promises, and shaky doctrine, but rather the exercise of responsibility, based on limited power and knowledge in situations of radical uncertainty.[51] This message was clearly welcomed by a number of governments who interpreted it in the most restrictive way possible. In July 2010, when Hillary Clinton urged the Vietnamese leadership to pursue its reforms and protect basic rights and liberties, Vietnam's prime minister recalled President Obama's argument that it is up to each nation to choose its own way and that human rights cannot be imposed from outside.[52]

The Ability to Obtain the Support of Actors Deemed Necessary to the Attainment of Certain Strategic Objectives

A realist actor is able to organize its objectives into a hierarchy. In view of this, it should demonstrate the ability to build a relationship with actors with whom it might have strong disagreements on certain issues, but with whom an accommodation is considered essential to achieving priority objectives. This is the thrust of the Obama administration's famous reset with Russia, whose relations with the United States had been deteriorating since the beginning of the Iraq War: "Distancing ourselves from nuclear engagement with Russia would greatly reduce our knowledge of what is happening in Russia, hinder our ability to consult with Moscow in a timely manner on nuclear and national security issues, further strain our own defense resources, weaken our non-proliferation diplomacy worldwide, and, potentially, heighten arms competition."[53] The deterioration culminated in 2007 in Munich, where Vladimir Putin publicly delivered a full-scale attack on US policy, which he accused of seeking to dominate the world in all areas through unilateral action.[54] A year later, the Russian-Georgian war exacerbated tension between the two countries, as Moscow accused Washington of encouraging Georgian leaders to go to war.[55] Relations between the two countries continued to deteriorate through the end of Bush's presidency, as evidenced when then–Defense Secretary Gates announced the launch of a new generation of nuclear weapons. This announcement was immediately followed by a Russian decision to develop 70 new nuclear warheads.[56] By reaching a new Strategic Arms Reduction Treaty (START) with Moscow in 2010, Washington clearly expressed its desire to renew relations with Moscow on the basis of a realistic partnership. This allowed the United States to set an example in terms of arms reduction, and to obtain Moscow's support in dealing with Tehran. The START agreement will bring the American nuclear arsenal down from 5,113 to 1,550 warheads, translating into a 30 percent reduction in the arsenals of both countries, which control 90 percent of global nuclear weapons.[57] Apart from the fact that this target will not be reached until 2017, the agreement still leaves the United States an impressive arsenal. The United States does not need more than 311 nuclear warheads to keep its deterrence intact.[58] In other words, even a 90 percent reduction in the US nuclear arsenal would not make a dent in its deterrence. The relationship with Moscow is key to facilitating a broader nuclear-arms reduction without jeopardizing American security. The 2010 Nuclear Posture Review makes no secret of this:

> By reducing the role and numbers of U.S. nuclear weapons—meeting our NPT Article VI obligation to make progress toward nuclear disarmament—we can put ourselves in a much stronger position to persuade our NPT partners to join with us in adopting the measures needed to reinvigorate the non-proliferation regime and secure nuclear materials worldwide.[59]

To this end, Washington has symbolically recognized that its nuclear arsenal's *fundamental* role is to deter its opponents from attacking it.[60] In reality, this claim is more ambiguous than it may seem. If the Obama administration had really wanted to assert that it would only use nuclear weapons for deterrence purposes, it would have indicated in the white paper that the *only objective* of nuclear arms is to deter adversaries. There is an important difference between stating that the *fundamental* role of nuclear arms is to deter adversaries, and stating that this is the *only* objective. To consider nuclear arms as principally aimed at deterring does not preclude their use for other purposes in exceptional cases. Conversely, to consider they are *exclusively* aimed at ensuring nuclear deterrence would, by definition, preclude their use for any other purpose. Hence the clever phrasing, as summarized in the white paper: "The fundamental role of U.S. nuclear weapons is to deter nuclear attacks on the United States and its allies and our goal is to make deterring nuclear attacks the sole purpose of nuclear weapons."[61]

That is, the United States aspires to limiting the use of nuclear arms to the sole purpose of deterring, while giving it discretion in the matter. This ambiguity reappears in the affirmation of a second objective, known in jargon as *negative assurance*: to commit to never using nuclear weapons against non-nuclear countries, even if they attacked the United States with chemical or biological weapons. The latter part is the novelty of the Obama administration's nuclear doctrine.[62] This commitment is far from being unconditional, however. It remains subject to compliance with the NPT and "non-proliferation requirements." Here again, the United States would like to leave room for discretion on this formal principal, particularly in the event of a North Korean chemical attack against South Korea.[63] The crux of the matter is how these obligations will be defined, and more importantly, what institutions will be responsible for monitoring compliance: the United States, the Security Council, or the IAEA?[64] Finally, even in the theoretical event of an attack against the United States with chemical or biological weapons, the white paper makes it clear that while the United States fully respects its obligations under the NPT and Additional Protocols: "Given the catastrophic potential of biological weapons and the rapid pace of bio-technology development, the United States reserves the right to make any adjustment in the assurance that may be warranted by the evolution and proliferation of the biological weapons threat and U.S. capacities to counter that threat."[65]

Even if the extent of the Obama administration's changes to US nuclear doctrine is relatively limited, the administration's concern about increasing the symbolic value of its negative assurances is no less real, especially when compared to those offered by the Bush administration.[66]

The change may be modest, but it has allowed the Obama administration to more easily address its second priority in this area: to strengthen the NPT's authority. Indeed, during the 8th NPT Review Conference held in New York in 2010, the United States agreed that a conference be convened in 2012 focusing on the denuclearization of the Middle East. Despite its reservations about the part of the final declaration calling for Israel to join the NPT and accept control over its nuclear facilities, the United States did not block it. The objective was to prevent a politically costly failure less than a year after the Prague speech and five years after a similar conference that had ended in failure.[67] It appears that the United States went so far as to ensure that India and Pakistan would not be singled out in the appeal to join the NPT; this must have infuriated Israel, which was mentioned by name.[68] However, it cannot be ruled out that the United States may have reached a tacit agreement with a number of affected countries, such as Egypt, to endorse plans for the conference on Middle Eastern disarmament.[69] Indeed, the United States expressed reservations right after the conference about the final declaration's singling out of Israeli obligations without referring to Iran's violation of NPT obligations.[70] In the end, everyone gained something. The Indians and Pakistanis were not singled out; the Israelis were covered by the reservations that the United States expressed after the conference; finally, Egypt and the Arab Gulf countries saw their initiative approved, at least in theory. This symbolic result nevertheless has little practical significance. Four nuclear powers (India, Pakistan, North Korea, and Israel) are still not parties to the NPT. Meanwhile, the CTBT has still not been ratified by the United States, Israel, India, China, and Pakistan. The prospect of a regional conference in the Middle East on nuclear disarmament seems more illusory than ever. Even in the area of nuclear security, progress remains very modest because the harmonization of standards constantly runs up against state resistance to forfeiting any political sovereignty.[71]

> *Replaying Nixon in China: To Seek Accommodations with*
> *Real and Potential Adversaries Or to Redefine*
> *Relations with One Or Several Allies*

Since 2009, the Obama administration has faced six issues affecting its national security: the fight against Islamist terrorism, the war against the Taliban in Afghanistan, the stabilization of Iraq, the containment of Iran, the settlement of the Israeli-Palestinian conflict, and the Korean nuclear crisis. Without getting into the details of these conflicts, which will be analyzed later, it appears that conflict mitigation or resolution has entailed seeking accommodations with adversaries (Iran), difficult partners (Pakistan), or close strategic allies whose political conduct can hamper US policy (Israel). In the realist tradition, accommodations involve strategic arrangements whereby one accedes to certain requests from partners in exchange for significant concessions. Strategic arrangements are fundamentally about exchanging insecurity for security. The renowned American author Charles Kupchan has written a remarkable book about the diplomatic processes through which an enemy becomes a friend.[72] The most famous example of realist strategy in US foreign policy over the past 50 years is obviously Nixon's trip to China. The political recognition of Beijing came at a cost, and the victim was Taiwan. However, in relation to the USSR, the strategic gain was substantial.

In the current diplomatic context, the United States is not facing a situation that is comparable to the one it experienced with China. Rather, it has to deal with asymmetric configurations that are very different from each other. They are asymmetric in two respects. First, the countries involved are less powerful than the United States. Second, political power is fragile, divided, or fragmented in these countries. There are three states, however, with which the United States maintains very different relations, but which share the common feature of pursuing policies that hinder US strategic interests. These three states are Iran (enemy), Pakistan (frenemy),[73] and Israel (friend). It may seem surprising to mention these three countries in one breath, since their relations with the United States fundamentally differ. Yet these states share one important feature. They are highly influential at the regional level; they have great autonomy of action, even in relation to the United States; and their conduct comes in the way of US strategy to varying but substantial degrees. Iran is clearly a political opponent of the United

States. But it does not directly threaten the United States given its military inferiority. On the other hand, it threatens the security of US regional allies such as the Gulf countries and Israel. The lack of consensus over the facts about the Iranian nuclear program is the subject of much debate that is reminiscent of the debates that surrounded the evaluation of the Iraqi threat under Saddam Hussein.[74]

The Pakistani case is very different from the Iranian one since Pakistan is officially a US ally. It is in a very particular situation, as it is both a vital US ally in the war in Afghanistan and a serious obstacle to America's Afghan strategy because, as discussed later, part of the Pakistani political-military elite supports the hardest opponents of the Kabul regime. Pakistan fully deserves to be designated as a frenemy.

The third case, Israel, is completely different from the two preceding ones because Israel is probably America's closest ally in the world. But, in view of the hostility toward Israeli policy in the region and, more generally, throughout the Arab and Muslim world, Israel automatically comes in the way of US strategy, especially since Obama's presidency, which is seeking to reconcile with the Arab and Muslim world. This was the meaning of the US army's mission briefing, which was sent to the Middle East at the request of General David Petraeus, who was seeking an expansion of Central Command (CENTCOM) to include the Israeli-Palestinian conflict; the White House refused: "The briefers reported that there was a growing perception among Arab leaders that the U.S. was incapable of standing up to Israel, that CENTCOM's mostly Arab constituency was losing faith in American promises, that Israeli intransigence on the Israeli-Palestinian conflict was jeopardizing U.S. standing in the region."[75]

Because of the fundamental differences in the situations of these three states, the kind of arrangement that the United States is likely to reach with each one will inevitably be different. What is asked of an ally is not comparable to what is requested of an adversary. However, in all three cases the goal is to affect the conduct of these actors in a way that will make it more compatible with America's global strategic interests. The United States expects the following: for Iran to cease threatening the Arab states in the region and Israel, for Pakistan to cease undermining Afghanistan's stability, and for Israel to make substantial concessions and pave the way for the creation of a Palestinian state, which is an indispensable prerequisite to America's rehabilitation in the Arab world. Since Obama has taken office, his diplomatic strategy has sought to influence the conduct of these three actors. The United States has made overtures to Tehran, has tried to be more attentive to

Pakistani and Afghan interests with regard to India in particular, and has requested that Israel freeze settlements in the West Bank. Almost four years into the Obama administration, however, it clearly appears that very little has changed vis-à-vis these three countries. On all three fronts, US efforts have ended in failure, although not through the fault of the United States alone. The Iranian regime is too divided to be in a position to engage constructively in a dialogue with Washington on the nuclear issue, especially since it is in the opposite position on the domestic front, where moderate opponents are accusing the current regime of seeking agreement with the Americans. The sanctions have made life difficult for Tehran, but have not changed its stance:

> Sanctions have imposed heavy financial and political costs on the Islamic Republic, but they have not convinced Iranian leaders that their interests would be better served by relinquishing their nuclear ambitions, abandoning their other reckless policies, or even opening a serious dialogue with Washington.[76]

In the absence of tangible results in the course of 2012, the prospect of a military intervention against Iran will become increasingly likely. Furthermore, the US public is ready to support it, contrary to certain beliefs. The Pakistani regime is also deeply divided, but between civilians and the military. Since the death of Osama Bin Laden, it has fallen back into a vicious cycle of mistrust with the United States. After an American air strike killed 26 Pakistani soldiers near the Afghan border in November 2011, Pakistan closed the supply routes into Afghanistan, boycotted a conference in Germany on the future of Afghanistan, and forced the United States to shut its drone operations at a base in southwestern Pakistan.[77] In essence, Pakistan has lost hope of seeing Washington help it meet its principal, if not unique objective: to improve its power position vis-à-vis Delhi. It is true that this is a peripheral concern for the United States. As for Israel, it has refused to yield to US demands for a settlement freeze because in the short term, the status quo is in its favor. Also, a settlement freeze would lead to the breakup of the government coalition. Finally, Benjamin Netanyahu has significant political support in the United States to counteract any attempt by Obama to cross him. Ultimately, in these three areas, Obama faces a situation that is just as uncomfortable as his predecessor's at the end of his presidency. What do these failures reveal about Obama's realism? The answer is mixed. The ability to conclude an agreement with difficult adversaries or partners obviously depends on their willingness to reach a new political arrangement with the United States. But it also implies that the United States has a credible alternative to offer or impose on them. What is striking about Obama is the potential goodwill he initially shows. This contrasts with his lack of determination to see his policies through past the obstacles, especially when they have domestic political implications. For example, Congress is fundamentally pro-Israeli and anti-Iranian. It has a more ambivalent attitude toward Pakistan. It will probably become more hostile to this country as soon as US troops withdraw from Afghanistan, especially if the political situation continues to deteriorate. Obama often has a plan A, but rarely has a plan B. When the Iranians snubbed his overtures, he reverted to a policy of sanctions, which are set to further tighten under pressure from Congress. Even if this forceful strategy is likely to hamper the implementation of an Iranian nuclear program, it is doubtful that the Tehran regime will back down, unless the logic of sanctions leads, as it did in the Iraqi case, to the logic of war and its all too familiar consequences. With regard to Pakistan, the deterioration in relations is striking. The two countries find themselves in the same situation they were in on the eve of September 11. The relationship is one of deep mutual distrust. With Israel, however, relations are better. The improvement is entirely due to the Obama administration's decision to no longer pressure the Israeli government in any significant way. The reasons for this excessive prudence owe much to the personality of Obama, who only takes calculated risks. But there is more to it than that. The fact of the matter is that on many issues, such as Iran, Israel, or Pakistan, the pursuit of realism would come up against powerful domestic constraints or would call too much into question. In the US political climate, it would be virtually impossible to venture that a nuclear Iran might not necessarily threaten US vital interests. Similarly, the issue of Israeli nuclear weapons cannot be raised, since the American political establishment sides so closely with Israel, regardless of its policies and their cost to US regional policy. The crux of the conundrum with regard to Israel is not the extent of US support granted to this extraordinary state that is heir to survivors of the Holocaust. Rather it is why any public debate on the subject is virtually impossible, even though at the highest levels of American power in the White House, Department of Defense, State Department, and the CIA many are concerned about either too unconditional support for the Jewish state, or the absence of reciprocity, while the United States takes political and strategic risks to support Israel. Indeed, before leaving his position former Defense Secretary Gates lamented that "Netanyahu is not only ungrateful, but also endangering his country by refusing to grapple with Israel's growing isolation and with the demographic challenges it faces if it keeps control of the West Bank."[78] As it often the case in the United States, such comments are only made when an official has stepped down or is about to do so. Furthermore, they are never made publicly. Thus US policy toward Israel continues to be a fundamental taboo in US foreign policy. This simple fact precludes any realistic reassessment of US policy in the region. Here, Obama is not, or does not have the means to be, a realist.

The Refusal to Engage Militarily Abroad When Such Action Is Deemed Contrary to US Vital Interests, But Would Save the Lives of Unprotected Populations

As will be discussed later, Obama has not reduced US military commitments in the world. He did withdraw US troops from Iraq, but that was just following through with his predecessor's choice. On the other hand, he decided to increase the US presence in Afghanistan, with a view of tilting the playing field against the Taliban. Counterinsurgency was the official doctrine. But in reality, counterterrorism, which was initially rejected, was massively employed. More than two thousand night raids against the Taliban have been conducted in the last three years. And the day Bin Laden was killed, 12 similar operations were conducted at the borders between Afghanistan and Pakistan.[79] More recently, Obama decided to shift American forces in Asia in order to balance China. Air and naval power, which are key in Asia, are preserved at the expense of the army. The navy will retain its 11 air carriers and will invest in littoral combat vessels, high-speed ships made for operations close to shore. Disappointed by US performance in the Great Middle East, Obama wants to develop power projection in Asia. This is fully consistent with a realist vision as long as it aims at preventing Chinese expansion in Asia and not denying its ability to control its own maritime approaches.[80] Yet the US engagement in Libya shows that Obama's realism does not ignore certain moral dilemmas (see chapter 8). Against the advice of the Pentagon, he clearly took a political risk to prevent a bloodbath in Benghazi that might have been held against him, even though Libya is not part of America's strategic perimeter. Because Obama is essentially not an ideologue, he appears to be a realist. However, the realism of the twenty-first century is not the same as that of Hans Morgenthau or Kissinger. The role of nonstate actors and the undeniable diffusion of transnational values make it difficult to practice a cold or cynical realism. Obama is first and foremost a realist by default.

CHAPTER FOUR

Repudiating the Ideology of September 11

The United States was only attacked on its territory three times in its history. The first time was in August 1814 when the British burned down the White House and the Capitol. The second was on December 7, 1941, when the Japanese bombed the naval base of Pearl Harbor. The last was on September 11, 2001, when Islamist terrorists on board two airliners targeted the twin towers of the World Trade Center in New York. In all three cases the United States responded to the attacks by confronting and attempting to contain and control the sources of danger, rather than by distancing itself from them.

> Americans, in contrast, have generally responded to threats—and particularly to surprise attacks—by taking the offensive, by becoming more conspicuous, by confronting, neutralizing, and if possible overwhelming the sources of danger rather than fleeing from them. Expansion, we have assumed, is the path to security.[1]

The attack of 1814 did not provoke an immediate response, but a few years later it led to the famous Monroe Doctrine of 1823. The doctrine was in reality inspired by John Quincy Adams, who could not conceive of US influence in the world independent of its humanist moral values. Even then, however, Adams saw the potential risks and abuses of a messianic drift. Texas was not yet American, and Adams was already worried about America using its power without moderation in the name of its values. If US policy shifted from the defense of liberty to the use of force, "it might become the world's dictator."[2] It was only 1821 . . .

After 1814, the United States started to think of itself as a great hemispheric power. After 1941, it became the leader of the Western world by gaining the upper hand over Europe, which had so vexed it throughout the nineteenth century. In the aftermath of September 11, American ambitions swelled. Lacking any strategic rival, the United States sought to assert its supremacy in the world by preventing the emergence of any potential rival and justifying its pursuit of this objective by underscoring the undeniable blow it had just suffered. This is why September 11 not only simply gave rise to a strategy for combating terrorism, but to a real ideology: the ideology of September 11.

An ideology refers to a set of ideas and representations, but also to an interpretation of the world that is hailed as the truth, interlinking all events and assigning a common meaning to them. America did everything to create a new world narrative beginning with September 11, to ensure that any reading of the world open with this watershed, and to bring the rest of the world around to admitting the pertinence and legitimacy of this turning point. The 2002 white paper on security (National Security Strategy) significantly states that "the events of September 11, 2001, fundamentally changed the context for relations between the United States and other main centers of global power, and opened vast, new opportunities."[3]

This message has a double meaning: to clearly indicate to the other powers that the grievous injury inflicted on the United States should not be interpreted as a sign of weakness and vulnerability, and to propose a new narrative of the world justified by September 11, allowing the United States to unabashedly secure its hegemony in the world:

> America has, and intends to keep, military strengths beyond challenge—thereby making the destabilizing arms races of other eras pointless, and limiting rivalries to trade and other pursuits of peace.[4]

The Ideological Impasses of September 11

In the end, the Bush administration's proposed narrative of the world floundered for three main reasons.

The first is that, from the outset, the "war on terror" was not framed as a political struggle, but as an ideological and military crusade. It is extremely difficult to measure results within such a framework given the sheer number of parameters involved. In Afghanistan, the first months of American intervention following the September 11 attacks were deemed successful: the Taliban regime was overthrown and Al Qaeda was expulsed, while Kabul saw a new regime headed by President Hamid Karzai. Seven years later, the situation is very different. The Taliban who were rightly viewed as inseparable allies of Al Qaeda are now considered part of the political solution to the Afghan conflict. The very idea of a victory in Afghanistan has also been abandoned simply because no actor, including the United States of course, can give a meaning to this word. According to the colorful phrase of a Russian general, winning in Afghanistan is not like planting the Soviet flag on the Reichstag in ruins.[5] In 2005, General Richard Myers, former chairman of the Joint Chiefs of Staff, moreover confided "that he had objected to the use of the term 'war on terrorism' before, because if you call it a war, then you think of people in uniform as being the solution. The solution is more diplomatic, more economic, more political than it is military."[6]

The paradox is that in December 2001, when the United States faced the real possibility of stopping or eliminating the head of Al Qaeda in Afghanistan, it refused to commit the military resources needed to do so. There are now a considerable number of first-hand accounts suggesting that in December 2001, US Special Forces had clearly identified the physical presence of Osama Bin Laden in the caves of Tora Bora. Despite the Special Forces' repeated calls for reinforcements that would have allowed them to either stop him or cut off his retreat to tribal zones, US military headquarters and the Secretary of Defense outright refused this option. The refusal was attributable to several factors: the maintenance of unchanged strategic policies based on the idea that US military operations should only mobilize a very limited number of people on the ground; the refusal to take the risk of seeing an operation lead to military losses that had until then remained insignificant; the political concern about conducting a risky military operation just as Karzai was arriving in Kabul; and finally, the reluctance to commit additional troops to Afghanistan at a time when the decision to intervene in Iraq had actually already been taken.[7]

The second reason for failure is that the war on terror denied any political rationale to terrorism, which was reduced to an undifferentiated set of actors whose only motivation was the desire to destroy the values embodied by the United States. And since one cannot compromise on values, this left no room for discussion or negotiation. A whole discourse was built around the idea of the enemy as a demon, a barbarian, and an inhuman "other," thus making any violence directed toward it acceptable and even proportionate in the eyes of the public.[8]

However, the most serious available studies show, for instance, that 95 percent of terrorist attacks conducted throughout the world between 1980 and 2004 were of an irredentist nature in the sense that they aimed to reclaim a Muslim territory that was occupied by non-Muslims. According to University of Chicago professor Robert Pape, who authored this particular study, it is important to understand the challenges and motivations of terrorism to effectively combat it, rather than stick to religious or cultural interpretations such as jihad or martyrdom, which can be poorly operational in assessing terrorists' tactical choices: all suicide attacks share a common tactical objective, which is to force democracies—through violence—to withdraw their armies from territories that the terrorists perceive as belonging to their homeland: "Suicide terrorist campaigns are directed at gaining control of what the terrorists see as their national homeland, and specifically at ejecting foreign forces from that territory."[9] Indeed, even from a cursory observation of the initial motivations of groups as diverse as the Lebanese Hezbollah, the Palestinian Hamas, the Pakistani Laskhar e Taiba, and the Somali Shabab, it is clear that the starting point for their action is rooted in their desire to recover what they rightly or wrongly consider as foreign-occupied territory: South Lebanon for Hezbollah, Palestine for Hamas, and Kashmir for the Laskhar e Taiba.

Territorial claims are not the only terrorist motivation. Terrorist or insurgent groups, between which there is often a very porous border, are also purveyors of social services that states do not satisfactorily provide out of carelessness or choice, for instance to punish a part of the population that is considered hostile to the established government. An example of the latter are the Sunnis in Eastern Iraq after 2003. Accordingly, one of the most effective ways to combat terrorism is to closely evaluate the population's needs, which the terrorists exploit to their advantage. This is the conclusion that General David Petraeus came to when combating the insurgency in Iraq, before extending his reasoning and analysis to the Afghan situation. A large part of his counterinsurgency theory is dedicated to studying how the insurgency offers the population better services in villages or tribal groupings, to learn how to better fight terrorism on its own turf.[10] He also emphasizes the importance of taking into account the particularity of each local situation.[11] This approach seems to refute the principles of the war on terror, even though General Petraeus was paradoxically George Bush's favorite general and the crafter of the famous *surge* in Iraq.[12]

The question of whether terrorists are rational political actors may seem purely abstract. Yet this debate actually has extremely important concrete implications. There is now talk of a possible dialogue with the Taliban so long as they break with Al Qaeda, whereas this option was initially completely ruled out due to the very strong links between the Taliban and Bin Laden. This would tend to prove that the United States recognizes the political rationality of their behavior, to the point of considering discussions with them that are likely to lead to a political solution.[13] What applies to the Taliban in Afghanistan also obviously applies to Hamas in Gaza, which has never been linked to Al Qaeda.[14]

The final reason for America's failure under George Bush is that even in Muslim societies where Islamic terrorism is broadly rejected and where political democracy is ardently sought, the ideology of September 11 had the paradoxical consequence of making it more difficult for these societies to embrace the democratic project, which seemed to be imposed from the outside. Furthermore, it very quickly became clear that the fight against terrorism entailed collaboration with repressive regimes whose efficiency was inversely related to democratic performance.[15] Another key obstacle is linked to the importance of the Palestinian issue in the Arab imagination. The Bush administration tried to justify its commitment in Iraq by invoking a virtuous circle that would lead Arab countries from authoritarianism to democracy and from democracy to a natural dialogue with Israel: "When the terrorists would have been wiped out, scattered and discredited... We will see that the old and serious conflicts can be resolved in a reasonable way with good will and based on the principle of mutual security. I see a peaceful world after the war on terror and with courage and unity we are building this world together."[16]

But to the extent that the Palestinian problem remains a national one, it is difficult to see how a transition to democracy could magically facilitate the resolution of this conflict. The implausibility of this reasoning, which was consciously developed by the neoconservatives, was confirmed during the Palestinian elections. The obvious lack of democracy within the Palestinian Authority of Yasser Arafat was at first presented to Washington as a major obstacle to the pursuit of peace. The complication arose when democratic elections were organized in the Palestinian territories and Hamas largely won. Washington was then dismayed to discover that legitimization through the ballot box could fail to solve the problem at hand, and even worse, aggravate it in the sense that the United States wanted to see the emergence of a Palestinian partner that would be acceptable to Israel. Here again, the ideology of September 11 sidetracked the United States from the task of every state: to find concrete solutions to problems that are primarily political.

The Repudiation of the "War on Terror"

Barack Obama's abandonment of any reference to the concept of a "war on terror" shows his desire to return to a more political rather than ideological management of terrorism, and his concern not to play into the hands of Islamists who purposefully seek to globalize their fight in order to transform it into a global jihad. This break is more significant still, because even if the concept of war on terror has been abandoned, the need to fight against terrorism has not disappeared. Simply, instead of sticking to a very general and ideological discourse on terrorism, the Obama administration prefers to focus on the specific terrorist actors that it wants to fight. This explains why, in 18 months in office, Obama has referred to Al Qaeda much more than George Bush did throughout his second term.

President Obama's adviser for homeland security and counterterrorism, John Brennan, provided the most explicit and official justification for jettisoning the "war on terror" concept:

> Our enemy is not "terrorism" because terrorism is but a tactic. Our enemy is not "terror" because terror is a state of mind and as Americans we refuse to live in fear. Nor do we describe our enemy as "jihadists" or "Islamists" because jihad is a holy struggle, a legitimate tenant of Islam, meaning to purify oneself or one's community, and there is nothing holy or legitimate or Islamic about murdering innocent men, women and children. Indeed, characterizing our adversaries this way would actually be counterproductive. It would play into the false perception that they are religious leaders defending a holy cause, when in fact they are nothing more than murderers, including the murder of thousands upon thousands of Muslims. This is why Muslim leaders around the world have spoken out—forcefully, and often at great risk to their own lives—to reject al Qaeda and violent extremism. And frankly, their condemnations often do not get the recognition they deserve, including from the media. (...) The United States of America is at war. We are at war against al Qaeda and its terrorist affiliates .[17] (See table 4.1)

This message is very important. It attempts to dissociate the war against terrorism from a war against Islam to avoid conferring religious legitimacy on a terrorist movement, and especially to avoid lending credence to the idea of a US fight against the Muslim world. This was also the

Table 4.1   Discourse on terrorism*

	Bush	Obama
"war on terror"	72	0
"Al Qaeda"	104	155

* These figures measure references to these terms in the speeches of George Bush during his second term, and of Barack Obama since he took office. The sources and methodology are explained in the annex.

primary meaning of the message that Obama delivered himself during his famous Cairo speech, in June 2009: "I've come here to Cairo to seek a new beginning between the United States and Muslims around the world, one based on mutual interest and mutual respect, and one based upon the truth that America and Islam are not exclusive and need not be in competition."[18] This political task is a long-term process that will not be able to change perceptions overnight. Indeed, a public-opinion poll conducted throughout the Arab world in November 2011 reveals that Arabs believe that the weakening of the Muslim world is one of US policy's three priorities in the Middle East, after controlling oil and protecting Israel.[19] Combating terrorism is relegated to the sixth rank among American concerns in the region, as if it was implicitly considered to be a pretext.[20] It does not matter whether these perceptions have any basis. From the US standpoint, what matters is to reverse them. The Obama administration has unquestionably started to do this. However, the structural perception of America's role in the region remains very negative.[21]

Obama's policy therefore aims to fight Islamist terrorism—if necessary, using force—by specifically attacking the actors who thwart its interests, whether these actors are in Afghanistan, Yemen, or Somalia. By doing so, the policy heeds the recommendation of many terrorism sociologists who have deplored the globalization of the war against terrorism and advocated for cutting the links between Islam and individual local contexts.[22] In other words, even if terrorist groups in Yemen, Somalia, Iraq, Afghanistan, and Mali claim to be part of Al Qaeda, that does not mean that they do the bidding of those orchestrating action from the caves of Tora Bora without regard for local dynamics. This is especially so because virtually all terrorism analysts consider Al Qaeda to be a political signature that local terrorist groups more or less formally claim to gain legitimacy, rather than to take orders.[23] The very term "Al Qaeda," which means "the base" in Arabic, evokes a social network of terror rather than a corporal institution modeled after the Comintern. Al Qaeda in the narrow sense of the term has actually lost considerable operational capacity, even in Afghanistan, after waves of attacks from the United States.

> Al Qaida is no longer the same organization we faced on September 11, 2001. In many ways, it has been decimated and constricted in its capabilities, with the core elements of the organization on the ropes. Al Qaida's senior leadership is being methodically destroyed, its primary safe haven is being undermined, its ideology is being rejected within Muslim communities around the world, and its strategy has yet to produce the results promised.[24]

Symbolically, the death of Bin Laden in May 2011, resulting from a secret US military operation in Pakistan, not only confirmed Obama's ability be a war leader, but also turned the page on September 11. It furthermore validated a political rather than ideological counterterrorism strategy.

Yet nothing has been solved. The core has undeniably weakened, but the reconstitution of Islamic terrorism is an equally undeniable development. Al Qaeda is a network of terrorist movements that share a flexible but complementary affiliation—hence the extremely contradictory assessments of its influence. In some respects, Al Qaeda may seem very weak if Islamist terrorism is considered as a pyramid structure. In others, it may seem very strong if it is considered as a network structure, where all the actors are both important and interdependent. Affiliate members include Al Qaeda in the Maghreb (AQIM), in the Arabian Peninsula (AQAP), and in Iraq (AQI). Additionally, several autonomous movements share political and operational synergies with Al Qaeda: the Taliban in Afghanistan; the Pakistani Taliban (Tehrik i Taliban Pakistan), the Shabab in Somalia, the Islamic Jihad Union (IJU) and the Islamic Movement of Uzbekistan (IMU) in Central Asia; Ansar el Sunna and Ansar el Islam in Iraq; Laskhar e Taiba in Kashmir; and Harakat i Islami in Bangladesh.[25] Regardless of the chosen hypothesis, what matters is to recognize that this terrorist association can only be analyzed with reference to the local conditions that enable it.

The challenge is to no longer think of terrorism as an incurable condition, but rather as a problem that calls for political treatment, using the whole gamut of available means. The war-on-terror strategy failed in part because globalizing the issues served the cause of Al Qaeda, which seeks to exploit and shift the local dynamics of the Chechens, the Uighurs, the Islamic Uzbek movement, the Algerian Salafists, and many others, to reframe them in an international context.[26]

It is therefore important to deconstruct the fight against terrorism and offload its overgeneralized emotive and ideological character.

The Bush administration did the exact opposite by stating in the official National Security Strategy of 2006 that "the struggle against militant Islamic radicalism is the great ideological conflict of the early years of the 21st century."[27] Its vision of terrorism, modeled on Israel's vision, contributed to radicalizing American policy; this was precisely Al Qaeda's goal. As a result, the United States was rejected throughout the Muslim world, even in the areas that were most hostile to Islamic terrorists. The Bush administration clearly failed to win the sympathy of moderate Muslims, as attested by the results of a public opinion study showing that 73 percent of Indonesians, 73 percent of Pakistanis, 92 percent of Egyptians, and 78 percent of Moroccans were convinced, to varying degrees, of US designs to undermine Islam.[28]

The Permanence of American Objectives

The Obama administration has evidently sought to reevaluate US counterterrorism strategy. In fact many shifts already occurred under the Bush administration due to operational, legislative (Congress), and legal (Supreme Court) constraints.[29] Yet the need to fight terrorism remains constant and has even expanded to new areas, such as Yemen, for instance. America's primary concern is to prevent new attacks on its soil from Al Qaeda. The United States must also now take account of the emergence of homegrown terrorism, which was initially difficult to accept, probably because it challenged the reassuring idea that American Muslims were much better integrated than those in Europe.[30] Since 2009, the United States has reassessed the situation in light of the increase in terrorist incidents in the United States that directly implicate American citizens more or less directly tied to terrorist networks or radical preachers. Finally, the United States needs to adapt to the fluidity and geographic mobility of terrorist hotbeds, which are increasingly emerging in Yemen and Somalia.[31] While a change in discourse is apparent, political practice is not necessarily any different.

Obama fears that in the event of a terrorist attack, Republican opponents and the televised media determined not to let anything slip, will interpret his new discourse against terrorism as a sign of softness.[32] He has therefore chosen prudence. The choices that he has made since taking office have been carefully weighed. He requested an end to interrogations using torture and authorized the publication of CIA memorandums on terrorist interrogation. He also renounced his predecessor's exorbitant prerogative, which granted the commander in chief of American troops the power to unilaterally violate the law. Moreover, in 2010, when a panel of the US Court of Appeals for the DC Circuit "ruled that the president's authority to detain was not bound by the laws of war, the Obama Administration took the extraordinary step of arguing that the court had granted it too much power. It argued to the full court that the president's authority is indeed constrained by the laws of war."[33] On the other hand, he has neither found an alternative that would allow him to close down Guantánamo,[34] nor has he ended expulsions of former Guantánamo detainees to their country of origin despite the release of 600 of the 775 detainees, nor has he abandoned the use of military commissions to judge Guantánamo detainees under the *Military Commission Act* of 2006, despite his pledge to revoke it.[35] Like the previous administration, the Obama administration claims only to transfer detainees after ensuring that destination governments will not harm them. But it is hard to imagine how regimes that routinely engage in torture will, as if by magic, renounce it to satisfy official US requirements.[36] Furthermore, Obama did not repudiate the Patriot Act or the surveillance system implemented after September 11:

> Most disturbing, from the standpoint of resurrecting the rule of law, the administration has refused to confront honestly the nation's past wrongs. As President Obama entered office, he sought to make a clean break with his predecessor. But at the same time, he has insisted that we look forward, not back. (...) The administration has sought to derail efforts in Spain to investigate US responsibility for torture of Spanish citizens held at Guantánamo. And President Obama continues to oppose even a high-level commission to investigate and report on the nation's departure from the rule of law and descent into torture, abduction, and disappearances.[37]

In addition, the administrative structure of counterterrorism has not been challenged, and virtually all of its leading officials, who were nominated by the previous administration, have remained in place.[38]

It is interesting to note how a state's continuities and discontinuities transcend people and partisan divides. On terrorism, for example, it is

Table 4.2 The antiterrorist system from Bush to Obama

	Bush 2001–2006	Bush 2007–2008	Obama
Guantánamo	open	Limited efforts to close	Limited efforts to close / political and judiciary obstacles to closure *
Military commissions	no	Attempts to set up failed	Beginning
"Black Sites"	yes	Detainees transferred	Most, but not all, closed
Habeas Corpus rights	yes	Limited, as per Supreme Court**	Limited, as per Supreme Court**
Indefinite detention	yes	yes	yes, but limited
Enhanced interrogation	yes	no	no
State secrets	yes	yes	yes
Patriot Act provisions	yes	yes	yes
Warrantless Wiretapping	yes	yes	yes
Targeted Assassination	yes	yes	yes
Drones	yes	yes	yes, expanded***
Extraordinary renditions	yes	yes	yes
National Security Letters (FISA)	yes	yes	yes, restricted

* Congressional refusal to vote for closing the prison in 2009; problems transferring detainees to their country of origin or a host country.
** Habeas corpus applies to Guantánamo detainees (see supra note 31).
*** Drone strikes increased from 35 strikes in 2008 to 118 strikes in 2010.
Source: Adapted from Marc Lynch, *Rhetoric and Reality: Countering Terrorism in the Age of Obama*, June 2010, http://www.cnas.org/node/4545.

striking to see the leaders of Bush's team change course while at the same time new leaders, who had been critical of the previous administration, now endorse its choices. Thus, Brennan, the aforementioned source of the new approach to fighting terrorism, was one of the supporters of "enhanced" interrogation techniques at the CIA during the dark years of the war on terror.[39] His name was removed from the list of candidates to head the CIA due to fears that Congress would block his nomination.[40] Inversely, former CIA director Leon Panetta had vehemently condemned the antiterrorist methods of the Bush administration, but after taking the helm of the CIA he opposed attempts to hold his agents accountable.[41]

CHAPTER FIVE

Back from Baghdad

When he started campaigning in 2007, Barack Obama reiterated his strong opposition to the Iraq War, which had by then degenerated into a violent and bloody civil war that the United States was struggling to control. His engagement with the issue had three advantages: to emphasize the consistency of his positions, since he had opposed the war since 2002; to differentiate himself from his rival Hillary Clinton, who had supported George W. Bush in this matter without careful consideration; and to create a wedge between him and his Republican rivals who were burdened by the legacy of Bush. This is when he developed his famous tale of two wars: war of choice (Iraq) and war of necessity (Afghanistan).[1] The clever distinction was designed to convince the American public that a withdrawal from Iraq would not be costly because it did not respond to any strategic necessity, while the fight against those responsible for the September 11 attacks— Al Qaeda—justified an increased commitment in Afghanistan.[2]

Obama had just arrived in office when he requested a thorough assessment of American policy in Iraq. Less than a month later, he announced its conclusions, which garnered widespread agreement because they were expected: withdrawal of combat troops on August 31, 2010, and total withdrawal of American forces in December 2011.[3]

If Obama was able to define an exit strategy from Iraq in less than a month, even though this was the most important American military intervention since the Vietnam War, it is simply because the military and political conditions for the withdrawal had been negotiated by his predecessor just before he left. In January 2009, the Obama administration started to work on implementing the two agreements signed between the United States and Iraq in November 2008: the

Strategic Framework Agreement, which defined the terms of cooperation between the two countries, and the *Security Agreement*, which set out the terms for the withdrawal of American forces and for military cooperation between the two states. The latter agreement came into effect on January 1, 2009. It was the last major foreign policy action of the Bush administration, which thus symbolically brought closure to the Iraqi issue that it had deliberately opened by invading the country in March 2003.

The Iraqis agreed to the conditions because they understood how they could benefit from the Bush administration's desire to end this matter on a successful note, be it only symbolic.[4]

Yet the war that dominated American and international foreign policy for more than six years (2002–2006) has all but been forgotten. US attention has shifted to Afghanistan and Pakistan as if this war had never happened, as if there were no lessons to be drawn from it, and as if the divide between war of choice and war of necessity was as great as it was officially portrayed.[5] This short political memory is probably the first great lesson of the Iraq War. It undoubtedly derives from the material and political superpower of the United States, which for the first time in its history had to deal with two politico–military conflicts one after another: Iraq and Afghanistan. Simply withdrawing from Iraq is no trivial operation, however. It involves the repatriation of 128,000 troops and 119,000 civilian contractors, let alone the 3.3 million pieces of military equipment worth the colossal sum of $45.8 billion.[6] This in addition to all the projects launched since 2003 for which funding is no longer guaranteed as the United States seeks to financially disengage from Iraq. This conflict alone has cost the United States $784 billion in constant dollars since 2003.[7] At the same time, one hundred thousand soldiers were deployed for operations in Afghanistan at the end of 2010, as if the United States were now destined to always be at war in the Middle East. No country in the world can intervene simultaneously in this way on such a broad scale.

There is a current tendency to consider Iraq as some kind of political error that is attributable to the neoconservatives. The latter may be overwhelmingly responsible, but nothing could be more irresponsible than to forgo learning the deep lessons from this conflict. The reasons for intervention aside, it raises a number of fundamental questions that have inevitably arisen again in Afghanistan, and that have faced the United States since the end of the Cold War: What is the purpose of military operations in complex and segmented societies, where the state is often weak but nationalism remains very strong?[8] What is America's strategic interest in militarily intervening in societies where it knows it cannot stay indefinitely and where the elites will eventually have to free themselves from their American chaperones, if only to establish their already tenuous claim to legitimacy? Why in the past 20 years has the Middle East become the ground for three US wars, of which one has not yet ended? Are all these conflicts partly tied to unresolved conflicts like the one between the Palestinians and the Israelis? What kind of political cooperation should be pursued with regimes that have benefited from direct American support to come to power, but nonetheless adopt very narrow objectives, which are not necessarily congruent with long-term US interests? The fact that the Afghan surge was based on the Iraqi one and that General David Petraeus, who conceived of the surge for Iraq, was chosen to implement it in Afghanistan underscores the evident parallels between the two instances of insurgency, even if they are only partially comparable. This is why the idea of relegating Iraq to the dustbin does not make any sense. The path from Baghdad to Kabul is much shorter than one might assume, especially when it goes through Islamabad.

What were the lessons of the Iraq War for the United States? There are three. Some were expected, while others were less so: the destruction of a state, which will take a very long time to recover; the strength of national sentiment, which helps neither the United States nor Iran; and the emergence of an "electoral ethno-democracy," which is a reversible but undeniable development.

The Destruction of the Iraqi State

The first lesson is that the American intervention undoubtedly contributed to destroying the Iraqi state, which had deeply decayed since 1982 to an astounding extent. Between the beginning and the end of the 1990s the Iraqi gross national product (GNP) plummeted from $75 to $20 billion. This deterioration, which started with its conflict with Iran, not only bled the Iraqi society and economy, but also exacerbated all of the latent sectarian divides that have existed since its creation. The United States obviously did not set out to destroy the last shreds of the Iraqi state when it invaded the country in 2003. To the contrary, the Rumsfeld doctrine sought to overturn the Baghdad regime and replace it as quickly as possible with a new regime that would better respond to the interests of the Iraqi people and of the United States. The goal was regime change, not state building. However, this

profoundly ideological political objective of replacing a dictatorship
with a democracy simply by placing different people at the helm of
the state proved unworkable. Washington's refusal to see its intervention in Iraq as having any other aim but to topple Saddam Hussein
led it to neglect thinking about what might happen after the military
operation ended.[9] This did not stop it from implementing a massive
aid program without advance planning. Furthermore, the program was
placed under the sole control of the Defense Department, which consistently excluded other US actors with more experience in development and reconstruction. The occupation authority administering the
program, the Coalition Provisional Authority, was poorly endowed in
human capital and completely unprepared for this type of operation.
Its head, Paul Bremer, whose only relevant experience was denazifica-
tion in Germany and the American occupation in Japan, went all out
to destroy what was left of the Iraqi state on the pretext of wanting to
purify it of its Baathist elements. This terrible choice resulted in the
destruction of the last fragments of the state that were still in place,
given that most of the Baathists were Sunnis and that most Sunnis
were state officials, with many serving as officers in the army. Worse
still, he subjected the country to a vast army of American and foreign consultants on reconstruction without thinking of consulting the
Iraqis on the relevance of proposed projects.[10] These projects focused
on infrastructure programs that were lucrative for the American private
sector, but completely neglected critical areas such as agriculture, in
which investment would have made sense if only to prevent the mass
exodus of young people toward the cities and thus toward insurgency
or banditry.[11]

> The United States invaded Iraq in 2003 without meaningful plans
> for stability operations and any aspect of nation building, and then
> rapidly created a massive aid program without prior planning
> and without the mix of data and expertise needed to make that
> plan effective. It turned to contractors and ideologues to imple-
> ment these programs during the initial phases of the occupation
> in 2004. After that time, it turned to an ad-hoc interagency effort
> crippled by a lack of coordination and centralization, insufficient
> funds, time constraints, and congressional actions.[12]

In the end, Saddam Hussein's fall was the only goal of the US war. This
result was the yardstick against which Washington assessed its intervention in Iraq. Total confusion prevailed in all other areas. The American

proconsul quickly squelched the idea of a rapid political handover to the Iraqis as was initially agreed, thus preparing Iraq for a long occupation. At the same time, at the end of July 2003, the head of US armed forces was working to withdraw American troops from Iraq![13] These two entirely contradictory objectives, which had not given rise to any political arbitration, had the effect of accelerating the destruction of the state and giving birth to a widespread insurgency, which might have been eschewed if the political transition had been better managed.

Besides the policy of massive de-Baathification (in reference to the Baath, previously Iraq's only political party), the US proconsul made another decision with wide-ranging consequences: the dissolution of the Iraqi army and all security forces, that is, the last authorities able to provide a semblance of order in a country that was falling apart. This second act of destruction of the state led to the unemployment of five hundred thousand people; many had little choice but to join the camp of the Sunni insurgency.[14] Bremer had the idea that the Baath was the Nazi party, its secret services were the Gestapo, and that he was the MacArthur of Iraq.[15] The worst part of the situation is that all these decisions were taken without any form of prior deliberation with either the Iraqis, who by then had started to fear the establishment of an occupying regime. Nor did he consult with Washington, which maintained its official position to rapidly transfer sovereignty to the country's authorities:

> "When the Army was disbanded," Secretary Powell recalled, "I called Dr. Rice and said, 'What happened?' Nobody seemed to know about this and [her] answer was, 'We have to back Jerry [Bremer].' There was no meeting on it; there was no, 'Gee, is this a good idea?' You couldn't even tell who had decided it.... I saw Peter Pace, the Vice Chairman, a little later and I said, 'Peter, did you guys know about this?' He said, 'Hell, no!'"[16]

Given the gravity of the situation, the authorities in Washington decided to drastically change their strategy. The handover of full sovereignty to Iraq would now be completed within seven months: "return governing responsibilities and authorities to the people of Iraq as soon as practicable."[17] Real efforts were then made to correct the terrible mistakes of the occupation authority, but the worsening security situation significantly limited the effects of this change. The January 2005 elections for the Constituent Assembly went relatively smoothly, even if they were flawed due to a massive Sunni boycott. But they did not resolve anything. To the contrary, beginning in January 2006, they drove Iraq into a violent civil war. Bloody conflicts pitted Shiite militias against Sunni militias; Sunni militias against American forces; Shiite militias against American forces supported by the Iraqi army, which was dominated by sectarian militias (the Badr brigades) that were the avowed enemies of the Mahdi Army of imam Moqtada Sadr; Shiite militias against each other; and Sunni militias against Al Qaeda. At the beginning of 2007, Iraq was not far from being in the Hobbesian state of war of all against all. This kind of terror was a resounding testament to the fact that the problem could not be reduced to a sectarian conflict between Shiites and Sunnis, and it progressively led to three major realignments.

The first and most important one occurred in May 2007 with the political falling out between Sunni tribes in the eastern part of the country and Al Qaeda. The latter had alienated a significant section of the population by its violent nihilism.[18] This resulted in a rapprochement between the Sunni tribes and American forces. The Sunnis who had boycotted the 2005 elections were experiencing the political backlash from the fall of Saddam Hussein. They realized that their future lay in reaching a realistic political compromise with the Shiites backed by the United States. General Petraeus's genius was to understand the importance of this dynamic and to capitalize on it by agreeing to provide substantial funding to Sunni tribes before enlisting them in the battle against Al Qaeda.[19] The United States came to understand that peace could be bought more efficiently by remunerating the tribes than by launching expensive reconstruction programs whose benefits were often kept from the people they were intended to help. The second political realignment took place in August 2007, when the head of the most powerful Shiite militia, Sadr, declared a unilateral cease-fire. This decision stemmed from three factors: the effectiveness of US battering, the rejection by some Shiites of militia violence, and the completion of Baghdad's ethnic cleansing in favor of the Shiites.[20] Another factor was the deployment of additional troops (the famous surge) that nobody believed would work, including Obama who voted against it as Senator. This surge succeeded in bringing peace to Baghdad, where mixed residential zones had exacerbated sectarian violence.[21] What changed the equation with regard to the insurgency was not the surge itself, but rather its implementation in a context that made it relevant.[22] Since then, Iraq has indisputably become less violent. Nevertheless, the violence is still real and seems to have picked up again in the eastern regions of Iraq given the extremely slow progress of the authorities in

Baghdad in socially reintegrating former Sunni militias (around one hundred thousand) who are no longer directly remunerated by the United States.[23] Today Iraq's territorial integrity no longer seems to be at risk, despite the deep internal divides. The reconstruction of the state nonetheless remains the key condition to maintaining this unity. This will be an extremely long process at best. Even with $40 billion in annual oil revenue and an accumulated $50 billion in US aid, Iraq has one of the lowest standards of living in the world! The country ranks 160th, just before Gaza![24] Over half of the Iraqi population is unemployed, and the other half heavily depends on government employment to an extent that is at least equivalent to the prevailing levels under the former regime. The state's reconstruction must, however, go through a critical process: regaining legitimacy in the eyes of its citizens by responding to their fundamental needs for security and for access to basic services such as water, electricity, and waste disposal. In these areas, except perhaps for security, the everyday situation of the Iraqis remains extremely precarious. Electricity supply is particularly problematic. Iraq is the tenth largest oil producer in the world, but imports more than 10 percent of its electricity supply from Iran and Turkey due to deficiencies in its power sector.[25] This reality contrasts with the lofty promises Bremer made in August 2003 when he announced that, "About one year from now, for the first time in history, every Iraqi in every city, town, and village will have as much electricity as he or she can use; and he will have it 24 hours a day, every single day."[26] These deficiencies are emblematic of the country's disorganization and widespread corruption. The unplanned and incoherent management of US aid, as assessed in official reports, only made corruption matters worse.[27] To give an idea of the unpreparedness, total aid for Iraqi reconstruction ended up being 25 times higher than the amount initially budgeted. Moreover, more than a quarter of US-funded reconstruction projects have not yet been completed or even launched.[28] The US intervention thus ended in utter failure with regard to state reconstruction, for lack of a policy framework to guide it and the operational coherence to implement it.[29]

The Strength of National Sentiment

If the American intervention undoubtedly contributed to destroying the Iraqi state despite the huge war effort, it in no way curbed Iraqi national sentiment. In fact, it appears to have strengthened the sentiment, which in many ways does not directly benefit the United States. This reality is reflected in the terms of the agreement on the withdrawal of US troops that was signed on November 17, 2008, and that fell to the Obama administration to implement. This agreement, called SOFA in military jargon (Status of Forces Agreement), contained a number of interesting features in comparison to the hundred other agreements of this type that the United States has signed. The first is that, contrary to other agreements, it set a firm date for the final and complete withdrawal of American troops from Iraq—something the Bush administration long refused to accept.[30] Bush feared that a deadline would benefit the insurgents who would lie low until US forces left, and then go back on the offensive.[31]

The second is that the agreement stipulated that civilian contract personnel and their employers would be placed under the exclusive jurisdiction of Iraq.[32] Along these same lines, the agreement gave Baghdad the right to exercise jurisdiction over civilian and military members of the American forces for "grave pre-meditated felonies" committed while they were not on duty, or outside of their assigned areas.[33] Article 12 is important because it outlined how Iraq, as a sovereign state, determined its legal relationship with foreign forces present on its territory. It also contained a novel provision for this kind of agreement: the Article was subject to a biannual review even though the overall agreement was effective for three years.[34]

Another feature of the agreement was to define the conditions under which the US army was to maintain the security and stability of Iraq. Hence, it created a Joint Military Operations Coordination Committee. The agreement nonetheless specified that no operation could infringe on the sovereignty of Iraq and its national interests, as defined by Iraq itself.[35] Some of the provisions of the American-Iraqi agreement on the status of American forces are very telling. Indeed, the presence of foreign troops in a sovereign country is a major political challenge, including in the eyes of the public. The magnitude of the challenge is underscored by US difficulties to this day in redefining its military presence in Japan, which has been a staunch US ally for over 60 years. The Iraqi authorities obviously did their best to negotiate a final withdrawal of American troops within a relatively short time frame. When the United States transferred its occupying power back to a sovereign Iraq in 2004, it sought to negotiate an agreement on its military presence. However, the Iraqi authorities declined the request, fearing that the terms of the agreement would be less advantageous for them at a time when they were heavily dependent on the United States.[36] They ended up signing an agreement in 2008, when they deemed the balance of power to have tilted in their favor, allowing them to negotiate a final and complete withdrawal of American troops in 2011, whereas the United States had hoped to maintain an American contingent after 2011.[37] Moreover, the American-Iraqi security agreement significantly does not provide for any American security guarantee such as the one in the 1951 treaty between the United States and Japan, which states that, "Each Party recognizes that an armed attack against either Party in the territories under the administration of Japan would be dangerous to its own peace and safety and declares that it would act to meet the common danger in accordance with its constitutional provisions and processes."[38]

Why is a Shiite government that was only able to come to power because of the American military intervention, so concerned about sovereignty, and so determined to downplay the political influence of the United States in Iraq?[39] Of course, there are many explanations. Some are worth mentioning here. The first is that contrary to the Kosovars, the Iraqis (with the exception of the Kurds who have benefited from American protection since 1991) never considered the US intervention as an operation intended to liberate them from tyranny. Many saw it as a pretext for the United States to establish itself in the Middle East. From this perspective, there were no Shiites waiting for the Americans to liberate them on the one hand, and Sunnis viewing them as occupiers on the other. From the beginning, both groups viewed them as occupiers, although the Shiites also saw the intervention as an opportunity to seize power in Baghdad. This development could only worry the Sunnis, who had been in power since their country's independence. Almost all of the Shiite leaders had no other objective than to use the United States by getting it to overthrow Saddam Hussein and then to withdraw as soon as possible after the work was done. This political fact speaks volumes on the Arab political reality and the strength of national sentiment; it sheds light on what occurred. The political reality is that Arab societies are unable to freely choose their leaders and must therefore call upon outside forces to help them in this endeavor. Without US intervention, the Shiites probably never would have seized power in Baghdad. Through 2008, Nouri al-Maliki's government did not hesitate to seek assistance from Anglo-American troops, most notably in March 2008 in Bassorah, to confront Sadrist Shiite militias (named after imam Moussa Sadr, the prime minister's Shiite opponent), who controlled the city.[40] But those who rely on American support do not want to admit to this choice, especially in the Arab world where animosity toward the United States runs high. Even those who were presented, or who presented themselves, as the US picks for heading the transition (for example, Ahmed Chalabi, a neoconservative ally) only used the United States to ensconce themselves in positions of power. This same Chalabi has since become close to Tehran, after failing to gain a local foothold. Furthermore, Iraq's two main Shiite political movements (El Dawa and the Islamic Supreme Council of Iraq [ISCI]) had very few relations with Washington before the 2003 American invasion. Current Prime Minister Maliki hardly had any at all. Not that his relations with Iran are any better. After taking refuge there when the Iran-Iraq war started in 1980, he hastily left for Syria to avoid enlistment in an Iraqi Shiite militia created by Tehran to combat Iraq.[41] The Iranian question is at the heart of the conflict between the two major Shiite movements. Iyad Allawi, the Shiite but nonreligious challenger that many Sunnis have come to support since the last election, maintained closer relations with the United States, and especially the CIA.[42] However, it was a political relationship rather than one of allegiance or subordination. It is no accident that the two Iraqi political coalitions that came first in the 2010 elections were those of current Prime Minister El Maliki and of Allawi. Both have a reputation for being very independent of any foreign power. Allawi fits the mold of a moderate Arab nationalist, wary of the West and particularly hostile to Iran, even though he is a Shiite. He basically remained Baathist even though Saddam Hussein tried to have him assassinated.[43] El Maliki is clearly more sectarian, in the sense that he is particularly keen on establishing Shiite dominance in Iraq. This does not take anything away from his deep mistrust of the United States, which is completely alien to him in every respect. Vis-à-vis Iran, his position has evolved from mistrust to a more open alliance with Tehran in order to reinforce his own power against Sunnis and secularists Shiites. During his last visit to Washington, he said that he was much more concerned about Turkey than Iran. Conversely, this assessment is confirmed by the failure of the political parties that represent the Iraqi political forces close to Iran.[44] This political context has mixed implications for America. In some ways, the United States can rest assured that the arrival in power of a Shiite majority in Iraq has not, as it had feared, changed the balance of power between the Arab world and the Iranian world. In fact, the new balance of power has benefited the third regional power: Turkey. The United States has come to understand the political interest in maintaining Iraq's territorial integrity; it had hinted, when Iraq was descending into civil war, at the possibility of dividing the country or weakening its central power.[45] In the end, the United States achieved very little to nothing from the Iraq War, given the cost. On all the sensitive issues of interest to the United States, the new Iraq is not radically different from the old one, except, paradoxically, with regard to Iran, in relation to which Baghdad is forced to be prudent. The Iranian issue is all the more problematic as anti-Western and anti-American sentiment is historically more Shiite than Sunni. It is the West that for a very long time ensured the maintenance of Sunni power in Baghdad. Inversely, all the anti-Western insurgencies (1920, 1941) have largely been dominated by Shiites, whose political marginalization has only reinforced hostility toward the West.

Consequently, with the probable exception of the Kurds for whom American support has enabled the strengthening of their national sentiment and consolidation of their political autonomy since 1991, most of the Iraqi authorities as well as the Iraqi public will never show the United States the slightest appreciation.[46] To the contrary, they will constantly profess their independence from Washington, even when they need it, and probably especially when they need it. This political process, which has been under way for years, means that today US influence in Baghdad is weak relative to the huge political investment the United States made in this country. Remarkably, Washington seems to have fully internalized this reality.[47] Even the oil concessions granted in 2009 did not benefit American companies.[48]

An Electoral Ethno-Democracy

The Iraqi elites have largely reclaimed the political dynamic that was set in motion by the American intervention in 2003. This dynamic is based on three inseparable yet contradictory factors: Shiite domination over Iraqi political life, the existence of a strong Kurdish autonomy, and the improbable risk of partition given the many dividing lines that have the advantage, so to speak, of not necessarily overlapping. Indeed, if the political dynamic of 2003 was largely based on an alliance between the Kurds and Shiites to drive the Sunnis out of power, seven years later the situation is singularly more complex. Because the Sunnis' fall from power is probably permanent, their support has become necessary to the Shiite groups fighting over this power. There is no contradiction between the Shiites' shared determination not to go back to the post-2003 situation, and their division in the exercise of power.[49] Moreover, this reality is not specific to Iraq. The Sunnis face a somewhat similar problem. They know that in all likelihood they will not be able to take back power in Baghdad, and that under these circumstances they need to negotiate their buy into Shiite power with the highest bidder. It is for this very reason that many of them supported Allawi's party during the legislative elections in January 2010. Furthermore, if the Shiites and Kurds are fundamentally united against backtracking on the new political order created by the 2003 US intervention, the Shiites and Sunnis are once again united against growing Kurdish influence, especially in the contested areas of Northern Iraq (Kirkuk).[50] They also do not want revenue sharing to enable Kurdish independence from the central government. The absence of political consensus on oil-revenue sharing highlights the divide between Arabs and Kurds. The fact that the Iraqi system is basically organized along sectarian and ethnic lines, but that at the same time none of the factions can seize the political momentum, paradoxically best ensures the preservation of the new political order to the extent that no faction can govern alone unless it were to do so by force.

Iraq today is light years away from being a functional and peaceful democracy. It resembles a form of electoral ethno–democracy that is extraordinarily fragile and perhaps temporary. It took more than seven months to reach a political agreement in Baghdad to form a new government; this underscores both the tremendous difficulties that face Iraq, as well as the risk of seeing a democratically elected government refuse a changeover at the end of its term.[51] In any event, the likely entry of Sadr's supporters into the government bears testament to declining US influence in Iraq at a time of renewed political violence. For better or worse, Iraqis have partially regained control over their destiny, albeit not the destiny American neoconservatives had envisioned. Iraq demonstrated America's ability to change a political order as well as its difficulty to build a new one congruent with its objectives and interests. This reality was clearly confirmed in October 2011 when President Obama officially announced the definitive withdrawal of American troops in Iraq by December 31, 2011.[52] The United States is apparently coming to terms with Iraq by scrupulously abiding by the commitments it made in 2008. All official US statements have been perpetuating the fiction of a mission accomplished, in line with Obama's version.[53]

The reality is substantially different. The United States has done its utmost to maintain up to twenty thousand servicemen in Iraq beyond the fateful date of December 2011, because the country's situation is far from stabilized.[54] As a case in point, 16 months after the legislative elections, the government still has no minister of defense or minister of the interior. The very close outcome of the legislative elections has been accompanied by a political stalemate that the Iraqi prime minister is exploiting to consolidate his own power. The parliament has still not voted on a long-awaited oil law, thus accentuating the tension between Kurds and Arabs over resource sharing in the Kirkuk region. In addition, the political violence persists from both the Sunnis and Shiites.

Finally, and most importantly, Iran has undeniable political influence; this is America's greatest concern. Under these circumstances the United States has an understandable interest in negotiating a new agreement with the Baghdad authorities, which were in favor of extending the US presence anyway.[55] So why has this agreement that is apparently desired by both parties not materialized? The answer is relatively simple. The issue is not so much the presence of American forces, but rather their legal status. From the beginning, the two countries' positions were far apart. The United States requested immunity for its troops as a precondition for any extension. Furthermore, the immunity had to be ratified by the parliament, not just granted by the Iraqi government. The State Department set the bar very high, and perhaps even higher than what was sought by the US military, whose priority was to contain the Iranian threat in the region. Matters were not simple for Iraq either. On the one hand, part of the ruling coalition did not support a longer US presence. However, the powerful Allawi, who considers himself deprived of his election victory and accuses Prime Minister Maliki of spurning power-sharing rules following the legislative elections, has preemptively refused to endorse any agreement with the United States until he receives a satisfactory response to his political demands, which include securing the defense and interior ministries. That being said, the main difficulty stemmed from the Iraqis' extreme sensitivity on sovereignty issues and the impossibility of assuming political responsibility for an agreement that placed American forces outside of any Iraqi jurisdiction.[56] Rightly or wrongly, such provisions would have been experienced as a prolongation of the American occupation, even if many Iraqis worry about the US withdrawal.[57] In the end, with the exception of Japan, a liberated country rarely becomes an ally.[58] This key lesson applies to Baghdad and can also be expected to apply to Kabul.

CHAPTER SIX

"Good Enough for Afghanistan"

The United States definitively left Iraq in 2011, after an eight-year presence in the country. It will probably do the same in Afghanistan at the end of 2014, after dealing a symbolic blow to Al Qaeda by killing Osama Bin Laden in Pakistan in May 2011. It would seem that Barack Obama kept his end of the bargain, because he had from the outset assigned himself a limited objective in this country: "to disrupt, dismantle, and defeat al Qaeda and its safe havens in Pakistan, and to prevent their return to Pakistan or Afghanistan."[1] Furthermore, as General David Petraeus put it, the United States was not "trying to turn Afghanistan into Switzerland in a decade or less, [but] we are after what is, in a sense, good enough for Afghanistan."[2] This harks back to Lawrence of Arabia's advice: "Better to let them [the Arabs] do it imperfectly than to do it perfectly yourself, for it is their country . . . and your time is short."[3] Thus, following a well-trodden path, what initially was a fight for civilization has become a fight for the lesser of two evils. The problem is that the Afghan conflict is not quite like others in the sense that it can only be understood and solved by reference to an infinitely more important issue: the future of Pakistan. Yet US relations with this extraordinarily difficult and complicated ally reached their nadir at the end of 2011.

As a result, after a promising beginning based on a relatively accurate analysis of the situation, American policy has reached an impasse. A war of necessity may not have fared any better than a war of choice in terms of outcomes.

The Soviet Legacy

Afghanistan has historically been a coveted, but never truly dominated, territory. Until 1973, the country enjoyed exceptional stability, which was supported by all the regional and nonregional powers, including the United States and the USSR. This shows to what extent the stability of a country like Afghanistan fundamentally depends on a given regional equilibrium, which in this case was disrupted by the overthrow of the king in 1973. In that incident, a republican regime with pro-Soviet sympathies came to power in Kabul. For the Pakistani army, the advent of a pro-Soviet regime in Kabul could only benefit India, a great regional ally of the USSR. At least from the year 1973 onwards, Pakistan therefore began equipping Pashtun Islamist militias to further its foreign policy objectives in Afghanistan.[4] The violence unleashed against populations resisting forced modernization was compounded by a fierce power struggle between two communist factions, in classic Soviet style. The first communist president, Taraki, was overthrown by his rival Amin, who tapped into revolutionary radicalization to consolidate his power. The scale of ensuing abuses and political disorder disturbed the Soviets. Fearing that Islamists would take over Kabul, they decided to militarily intervene in December 1979. This triggered the beginning of two decades of war and chaos from which Afghanistan has still not recovered to this day.

Needless to say, the Kabul regime did not survive the collapse of the USSR. Afghanistan subsequently experienced a civil war whose first phase ended in 1992 with the arrival in power of a non-Pashtun regime for the first time in three hundred years.[5] The civil war escalated again when the Pakistan-backed Hekmatyar faction sought to reverse the course of events. The country then fragmented along ethnic and tribal lines as the central government virtually disappeared. This was the backdrop for the birth of the Taliban in 1994. Although they were exclusively Pashtun, the Taliban claimed, above all, to be a force for order and unity under the banner of Wahhabi Islamism, revealing a Saudi influence that had until then been largely absent from the Afghan scene. The Taliban therefore not only benefited from Pakistani sponsorship but also from Saudi and Emirati financing, as well as ideological and military support from Bin Laden, a veteran of the war against the Soviets who had returned to Afghanistan after the United States pressured Sudan to expel him in 1996. The alliance between the Taliban and Al Qaeda dates back to this time. It gradually strengthened on the basis of a relatively simple political agreement: the Taliban would control Afghanistan, while Al Qaeda would use Afghanistan as its base of operations for global jihad. Since Bin Laden was Arab and not Afghan, he could not hope to take power in Afghanistan and thereby compete with the Taliban. Rather Bin Laden's Arab legion would provide valuable services to the Taliban, helping them gain the upper hand in 2000 over their main political and military opponent— Commander Ahmad Shah Massoud's Northern Alliance army.

Pakistan played a crucial role in this new context. Feeling completely abandoned by the United States after the fall of the USSR, and subjected to substantial US sanctions over its nuclear program (Pressler Amendment), Pakistan sought to restart the jihad in Afghanistan to counter its only real enemy: India.[6] For Pakistan, controlling Afghanistan was a form of revenge for the period of Soviet control, as well as a regional compensation for America's abandonment.

The Legacy of September 11

It is now established that the Talibanization of Afghanistan was initially of little concern to Washington, despite the multiple warnings it received.

The breaking point only occurred in the aftermath of September 11, 2001. Beginning on October 7, 2001, the United States responded by launching a military operation that aimed to remove the Taliban from power in Kabul and to annihilate Al Qaeda. US strategy followed the famous Rumsfeld doctrine, which called for reducing America's political inhibitions to militarily intervene throughout the world whenever it saw its interests threatened. As a counterbalance, military commitments would remain limited in time and scope to prevent any risk of entanglement or public rejection.

The United States' undeclared strategy was to let Hamid Karzai remain bereft of arms in the capital, which would be protected by foreign forces, while relying on warlords to maintain the Pax Americana in the countryside, and on the Special Forces to oust Al Qaeda.[7] This proved to be a double-edged strategy, to say the least. In some ways it aimed to strengthen the legitimacy of the new regime across the country in the run-up to the 2004 presidential elections, but in the end it catalyzed a new insurgency ipso facto. The insurgency did not immediately gain traction since the Afghan population's support for the Karzai government remained relatively strong through 2005. Only beginning in 2006 did the situation start to deteriorate. The United States responded by increasing its engagement and encouraging its allies to do the same.

As a result, between 2006 and 2009 the contingent of foreign forces grew from thirty thousand to sixty-four thousand troops.

The Inevitable Falling-Out Between
Karzai and Washington

Placed at the head of Afghanistan in 2001 by the United States, Karzai entertained relatively trusting relations with the latter until 2006. Washington has an interest in strengthening his power, even if this entailed turning a blind eye to his methods. Meanwhile, Karzai was still too weak and isolated to stake an independent position from his protectors. With the help of the US ambassador to Kabul, an American of Afghan descent, he progressively succeeded in undermining the influence of the Northern Alliance mujahedeen, who were mostly of Tadjik and Uzbek descent and who had helped him take power, to the benefit of Pashtun reformists placed in charge of various ministries.[8]

Despite the warm personal relationship between Presidents Karzai and Bush, relations between Kabul and Washington began deteriorating in 2006 following anti-American riots in Kabul.[9] Karzai quickly understood that his political survival hinged on distancing himself from the Americans, at a time when the worsening security situation had forced the United States to bolster its military commitment. The United States had started pressuring him to lay the foundations of a modern and impartial state rooted in democracy and the rule of law, whereas Karzai did not want to pursue what appeared to him an elusive objective unless the United States allowed him to first consolidate his personal and familial power. An inevitable political misunderstanding ensued and then continued to grow and deepen after the Obama administration came into office and clearly overestimated its powers. The administration considered Karzai to be a neoconservative choice, and saw the depersonalization of American-Afghan relations as an opportunity to intensify pressure on him in the area of anti-corruption. Relatively confident in his power, however fraudulent, Karzai was keenly aware how difficult it would be for the United States to overthrow him. He understood that Washington had reached the limits of its involvement in his country and saw an opening to step up his criticism of the United States, even threatening to join the Taliban if the United States further pressed him. This resulted in a major showdown between Washington and Kabul. Remarkably, it turned out to be advantageous to the Afghan head of state, because there was no alternative. Meanwhile, the US administration was divided between the military, which wanted to accommodate Karzai, and the State Department, which wanted to excoriate him.[10]

The American-Afghan partnership is more than ever one of pure convenience. Karzai continues to have it both ways: he is strengthening his autonomous political base to make it less vulnerable to US pressure and more credible to some of the Taliban; at the same time he is using US resources, especially financial ones, to entrench his personal and familial power, while he increasingly criticizes the coalition for collateral civilian casualties caused by coalition forces. This nationalist posturing began when a number of coalition partners, in particular the British and Dutch, requested that he dismiss regional authorities whose actions were destabilizing to the country; these officials also happened to be valuable allies to the Karzai family.[11] At the national level Karzai has used the three levers of state power: the strategic appointment of regional authorities, control over security services, and foreign-aid grants. Regionally, he focused on building a powerful political base in Kandahar province through his brother Wali Karzai, who has since been assassinated by the Taliban. Wali Karzai systematically worked to prevent the emergence of political-economic rivals, including those who aimed to strengthen the central government's power.[12]

All of these issues were mentioned in General Stanley McChrystal's report, which served as the basis for the Obama administration's reevaluation of US policy in Afghanistan:

> Some local and regional power brokers were allies early in the conflict and now help control their own areas. Many are current or former members of GIRoA [Government of the Islamic Republic of Afghanistan] whose financial independence and loyal armed followers give them autonomy from GIRoA, further hindering efforts to build a coherent Afghan state. In most cases, their interests are not aligned with either the interests of the Afghan people or GIRoA, leading to conflicts that offer opportunities for insurgent groups to exploit.[13]

Yet the United States has participated, be it inadvertently, in hollowing out the state's power. It has steadily consolidated the power of the warlords, many of which did not exist before the US intervention.

This does not mean that the Afghan governance crisis should be interpreted as an ethnic one, whereby Afghanistan would be a structurally ungovernable state given its network of powerful ethnic and tribal loyalties. The most serious studies assessing the gravity of the Afghan crisis show that the collapse of confidence in Karzai's policies primarily results from his profound inability to respond to three problems that Afghans face on a daily basis: insecurity, corruption, and unemployment.[14] These three crisis factors are known to be self-reinforcing. Growing dissatisfaction is creating a wedge between the population and the government and aggravating corruption, which has become a major source of personal enrichment and political control over the people. As Afghans lose confidence in public authority, they are falling back on traditional structures (tribes, religious leaders, middlemen, and warlords) that transform conflicts into ethnic ones. Corruption is not only a problem because it is morally indefensible, but also because it most hurts the weakest and poorest while contributing to the destruction of the state. Afghanistan has become one of the most corrupt countries in the world (178th out of 180) as 25 percent of its national revenue is channeled to corrupt officials or middlemen in exchange for access to land, electricity, or justice.[15] Out of the $500 average income, corruption takes a $156 bite.[16] Moreover, the three most important ministries (interior, justice, and security) are considered to be the country's most corrupt institutions.[17]

The Weakening of the State from Foreign Aid

The weakness of state structures and public ethos accounts for much of the country's governance crisis. But it has been exacerbated by the rapid monetization of the economy that largely results from both the burgeoning drug economy, which provides the Taliban $70 to $100 million per year, and the considerable amount of foreign aid.[18] In line with how they proceed in other countries, donors have invested a lot of time and energy to create indicators and institutions on paper that are designed to strengthen the state and reduce its endemic corruption.[19] Yet the first condition for reducing corruption is that the elites internalize a public ethos, and in the process take strong ownership of the issues, priorities, and implementation of change. So long as these elites do not see any benefit to modernizing the state according to a number of principles and objectives, they will fully take advantage of its dysfunction and opacity. Rhetorical appeals from the United States and donors fighting against corruption therefore have little chance of being heard if they do not recognize this basic fact.

Unfortunately, there is no sign that foreign aid is fostering greater local ownership of change. The experience of the past few years gives reason to fear the contrary. In a state where qualified human resources and organized and competent institutions are scarce, the term "foreign aid" is literally true: it remains foreign to those it is supposed to benefit. Indeed, the aid flows through a closed loop. It is granted and disbursed by donors for donors: forty percent of all aid returns to donor countries due to tied aid and to the inflated number of consultants involved in its implementation.[20] In Afghanistan, where foreign aid represents 90 percent of public expenditure, the idea of local ownership of projects is somewhat surrealistic.[21] Two-thirds of foreign aid bypasses the central government, either because the government lacks the administrative capacity to manage the aid, or because foreign donors fear the government will divert resources to other ends than those intended—a far from groundless fear. These same obstacles hinder technical foreign assistance. Even though the intention is to provide assistance in government capacity building, the assistance is in fact reduced to a massive influx of foreign consultants who first and foremost work for their donors. The United States recently sought to address this problem by increasing the share of funds that is directly disbursed to the Afghan government. However, lingering suspicions about an administration that is profoundly corrupt and poorly endowed in human resources have resulted in the United States bypassing the very procedures that it set in place. Even when aid is officially granted to the government, it is managed by the American embassy.[22] Foreign consultants most often directly manage the aid with little real regard for the priorities defined by the Afghans themselves. Yet the consultants also enlist the services of the scarce local skilled labor. This practice has a debilitating effect on the state, which is denied these qualified human resources, given the enormous gap between the salaries offered by foreign organizations and by the state. This fundamental problem also affects the police because of the significant role played by private security forces. Foreign aid thus contributes to weakening the state that it claims to strengthen by creating parallel structures and using the locally available human resources. It also indirectly feeds corruption. Indeed, half of the aid is used to remunerate foreign consultants who in turn outsource to other foreign or local consultants, therefore creating pressure for the rapid disbursement of aid. This is conducive to the formation of networks of middlemen whose numbers grow in step with the insecurity, making it very tricky to evaluate projects. In 2009, the United States Agency for International Development (USAID) was only able to evaluate two of the nine projects it had undertaken in the agricultural sector, while it had been able to evaluate three out of four in 2006.[23] Finally, neither the donors nor the Afghans seem to have an overall view of the programs launched. American aid suffers from a considerable lack of coordination, which was already clearly identified in Iraq but has become even more flagrant in Afghanistan.[24] This can be interpreted as evidence that the United States was politically unprepared to implement nation-building programs that are so contrary to its political traditions. Given the circumstances, one might wonder whether the increase in economic aid to Afghanistan granted by the Obama administration to offset the excessively military orientation of the Bush administration will even partially succeed in overcoming these great difficulties.

Fight the War Differently?

To the Obama administration's credit, it understood from the outset that the fates of Afghanistan and Pakistan were interrelated. It accordingly tried to implement a coherent strategy based on three major goals: to overhaul the US military strategy, which had patently failed, and to more consistently prepare for the transition from foreign troops to an Afghan army; to restore the political legitimacy of the largely discredited Afghan government, even if that entailed negotiating with the Taliban; and most importantly, to involve Pakistan in conflict resolution by offering it political and strategic incentives with more long-term stability and credibility.

The Obama administration carried out a two-step reassessment of its policy on Afghanistan. The first step took place in March, when the first additional troops were deployed, and the second, in autumn 2009, when the United States unveiled a new policy after the fraudulent election of Karzai.[25] This policy is largely based on the August 30, 2009, report of General Stanley McChrystal, then commander of US forces in Afghanistan.[26] The report has often been interpreted as recommending a new military doctrine in Afghanistan based on a counterinsurgency strategy. In fact, its reach is much greater. It is an eminently political document that draws lessons from US failures in this country since 2001 while putting forward proposals to address the issues raised. Its political content strikingly highlights the influence that the military has acquired in defining American foreign policy.

Aside from its relatively dark portrayal of the politico-military situation in Afghanistan, the report conspicuously lacks an ideological vision of the Afghan conflict. This is light years away from the post-September 11, Manichean interpretation that pitted the advocates of freedom (Karzai) against the forces of obscurantism (the Taliban).

In January 2010, Defense Secretary Robert Gates conceded that the Taliban were part of Afghanistan's social fabric, thus recognizing their political legitimacy and place in any settlement.[27] Significantly, McChrystal's report does not just identify two principal actors (the government and the Taliban), but rather five: the Afghan population, the Afghan government, the insurgency, coalition forces, and finally regional actors. It implicitly suggests that the Afghan government is not one with the population. Under these circumstances the government's loss of legitimacy combined with the insurgency are the two main dangers facing Afghanistan, and they are moreover two mutually reinforcing dynamics. Contrary to conventional wisdom, McChrystal saw no clear distinction between the insurgents, criminal groups, including drug traffickers, and corrupt members of the Afghan government. Some government actors directly support insurgent groups and their attendant criminal networks, feeding the corruption that, in turn, feeds the insurrection.[28]

The report readily acknowledges that the insurgency in Afghanistan is largely Afghan, while correctly noting that the growing links between the insurgency and Al Qaeda will facilitate the latter's return to Afghanistan, even though it is only symbolically present for the time being.[29] McChrystal's report attaches great importance to Pakistan's role in resolving the problem. The new insight is his insistence that it will not be possible to engage Pakistan in conflict resolution without taking into account its strategic concerns about India's influence in Afghanistan: "While Indian activities largely benefit the Afghan people, increasing Indian influence in Afghanistan is likely to exacerbate regional tensions and encourage Pakistani countermeasures in Afghanistan or India."[30]

McChrystal weaves these various elements together to propose a new military strategy that is no longer focused on canvassing an enormous country with many underpopulated areas, where the insurgency has been highly mobile and has developed a very good information network. Rather, he proposes to develop closer ties to the local communities by responding to their economic and social needs in their households and workplaces. The objective is no longer to occupy territory, but to win over its inhabitants.[31] Hence the need to complement military action to clear areas under insurgent pressure, with civilian action to propose and implement development projects in close collaboration with the people (hold and build). The McChrystal report makes several key proposals: protect populations rather than contingents of foreign forces; minimize the use of force when civilian lives are endangered; gain the trust of local actors; and ensure the handover from foreign forces to Afghan forces. The success of these proposals was premised on the deployment of additional forces.

For several reasons, however, this strategy was not guaranteed to work. First, counterinsurgency strategy is largely based on age-old and well-known principles.[32] Winning over the hearts and minds of populations by helping them economically and socially in order to weaken the hold of insurgent forces is a classic colonial approach. The British came up with it during the Malaysian war, and France also implemented it in Algeria after its difficulties in Vietnam.[33] However, this approach has rarely been politically effective, though sometimes militarily successful, as was the case for France in Algeria. There is no doubt that the US offensive in Afghanistan has achieved sizable military results in the south and southwest of the country. The Taliban are no longer able to conduct complex operations or coordinate from these two regions. Furthermore, the Afghan army's capabilities have unquestionably grown. Despite many blunders, the huge foreign investment in this country ($440 billion from the United States alone) has enabled the achievement of a number of civilian objectives such as the increase in school enrolment from 1.2 million under the Taliban to 8.2 million today. However, it is difficult to assess these results. US military pressure in the south and southwest has caused the fighting to spill over into the east, creating a new source of tension with Pakistan. The Afghan national army is certainly more effective, but it is dominated by northern ethnic groups, limiting its role to that of a foreign army with regard to many tasks. The Afghan army will only really prove its solidity and strength the day it is able to confront and deal a blow to the Taliban in their fiefdom in Kandahar.

A public-opinion poll conducted by a nongovernmental organization in the region shortly after the US intervention reveals the limits of counterinsurgency strategy, of which perhaps too much is expected:

> Despite pronouncements and promises about hearts and minds, the offensive illustrates that the current paradigm for tackling security crises is still over-reliant on the deployment of military force. Development, aid, and counter-narcotics issues are not accorded the same level of political and financial support and effort as military endeavors, which creates a situation where those military endeavors are viewed with serious hostility by the local population whose support we seek and need.[34]

The fact that this strategy specifically sought to eradicate poppy culti-
vation even though Ambassador Richard Holbrooke, the US envoy for
Afghanistan, had stated in July 2009 that the United States would no
longer aim to do so because it was politically counterproductive, underscores the persistent internal inconsistencies of American policy.[35]

Washington's Search for an Exit Strategy

Since the inauguration of the new US head of state in January 2009,
American forces in Afghanistan have grown from twenty-three thousand to one hundred thousand, thus quadrupling in barely 18 months.[36]
Obama has strong reservations about Karzai, who is more interested in
strengthening his personal and familial power than the state. Obama
has understood that there can be no political solution in Afghanistan
without the Taliban, provided that any agreement tilts the balance
of power in the favor of non-Taliban forces. This newfound realism
may have spared America and the world more rhetoric on "the battle
between civilization and barbarism," but it does not make the search
for a political solution any easier.[37] There are still many hurdles to
overcome.

The first stems from the nature of the Afghan conflict. It is neither
a war of independence led by a single party with military forces (the
Vietnamese Vietcong and the Algerian Front de Libération Nationale
[FLN]), nor a classic civil war between two distinct camps fighting on
front lines. The insurgency actually comprises three main movements:
the actual Taliban, led by the famous Mullah Omar, with a strong base
in the southwestern part of the country, and especially in the Kandahar
region; the Gulbudin Hekmatyar faction (Hizb e islami), which formed
during the Soviet occupation, and has a notoriously cruel chief who
resides in the eastern part of the country; and finally, the equally radical
and violent Haqqani faction, based in Pakistan's North Waziristan, that
is responsible for many of the terrorist attacks in Afghanistan (notably
against the Indian embassy in Kabul) and is allegedly closely linked to
both the Pakistani intelligence services and Al Qaeda.[38] All of these
groups are militarily autonomous but politically united against the
Kabul government. They all recognize the moral authority of Mullah
Omar, who thus confers on the insurgency a non-negligible form of
Islamic legitimacy.[39] This last aspect plays an essential role in mobilizing
international support for the Taliban, especially from Saudi Arabia and
the Gulf countries, and in spreading the Taliban's Islamic-nationalist

message far beyond the Pashtu areas.[40] It is no coincidence that the mullahs have become the principal conduits for the increasing politico-military influence of the Taliban in the Uzbek and Tadjik communities, which had previously shunned them.[41]

There is obviously a fundamental political rift between these armed groups and Kabul, but that does not mean these two forces are homogenous or insulated. The overlap between the Kabul government and the insurgency is greater than one might think. It is all but official between Hekmatyar's HIG (Hizb e islami Gulbedin) and Karzai. Through its political wing, Hekmatyar and its allies have a presence in the parliament, the government, and the provinces. It is the faction that is best represented in the parliament of Kabul. Additionally, a third of provincial governors are believed to share an affiliation with Hekmatyar.[42] It is as if during the Spanish Civil War a third of nationalist-controlled provinces had in fact been under the control of people close to the republicans. The political arm of HIG claims it is independent of the military arm, but in fact, the two branches have no fundamental disagreements.[43] Hekmatyar's strategy is to both militarily pressure leaders in Kabul and infiltrate the political system.[44] Meanwhile the Kabul government is highly fragmented. Some of its factions are very close to the Taliban and quite distrustful of the Northern Alliance allies in power. Others (mostly the Tadjiks and Uzbeks) are extremely hostile to the Taliban because they fear that any political agreement with the Taliban will come at their expense. Karzai closely navigates these factions to bide time. In the face of deteriorating relations with the United States, he gives guarantees to the Taliban in a display of Afghan nationalism as the day of a post-American Afghanistan nears. At the same time, he does not want to lose the military and financial support of the United States and the international community so that he can better consolidate his power, or alternately negotiate a political agreement under the most favorable conditions for him, his family, and his clan. The complexity of the Afghan situation is not an inherently insurmountable obstacle to a political solution. But the implementation of a reconciliation process is complex.

For a long time, the United States was not interested in such a process at all, even if it heavily funded the process to help Kabul win over a number of midranked insurgents.[45] The British have been most committed to this process, which they embraced in 2006.[46] Today still they seem to be pushing for more open and official negotiations with the Taliban, even though this is not quite in line with the US position.[47] Yet in 2006, Britain's most significant initiative to advance political unification by reconciling Mullah Salaam with the leaders of Kabul ended inconclusively. The guarantees made to the mullah proved to be largely meaningless, to the point where he became a prime target for the Taliban.[48]

The official US position is to support any reconciliation process with moderate Taliban, but nobody really knows what the terms "moderate" or "salvageable" mean. US perspectives on the matter vary from one official to the next. The US intelligence chief in Kabul considers Hekmatyar and Haqqani to be politically salvageable even though the latter is certainly, and by far, the most intransigent, violent, and Al-Qaeda-affiliated leader of the insurgency.[49] He is also the primary target of US drone strikes. In 2010, 90 percent of the drone attacks launched against the Taliban were directed at North Waziristan, the bastion of Haqqani's faction.[50] Haqqani is moreover strongly backed by Pakistan. Washington would like to implement a high-visibility reconciliation process coordinated at the presidential level. If such a process yielded results, it would allow the United States to justify the beginning of a military withdrawal.[51] However, the United States only has a vague vision of reconciliation. It is less of a priority than the success of the counterinsurgency strategy or the development of an anticorruption program that might bolster the legitimacy of Karzai's government. The United States would prefer to see some kind of bottom-up reconciliation in which it would willingly take part, while leaving it to Karzai and the Pakistanis to reach an agreement with the Taliban that the United States would not have to officially sanction.[52] The second difficulty is that the United States lacks a political partner whom it can trust to negotiate a solution. This role should, in theory, naturally fall to the Afghan president. In practice, this is not the case. Karzai is today considered to be a partner by necessity who is under threat of losing US support if he does not fight against corruption, even though the United States does not have an alternative and does not want to admit that it bears considerable responsibility in this process: "If we have knowledge of things that we know are happening and the (Afghan) government doesn't respond to it, it's going to be very, very difficult for us to look American families in the eye and say, Hey, that's something worth dying for."[53] This is why the United States initially put its faith in the counterinsurgency strategy, of which one of the objectives is to enable reconciliation by creating a better balance of power on the ground.[54] The United States hopes that by militarily weakening the Taliban and by responding to the population's needs, it will set the stage for a compromise with terms that will be more acceptable to the United States.

This is the "peace of the brave" model that was reasserted by Defense Secretary Gates.[55]

American Solitude

The United States can only achieve its objective with the support of Pakistan, which the Obama administration has decided to make a strategic ally in finding a solution in Afghanistan: "We are committed to a partnership with Pakistan that is built on a foundation of mutual interest, mutual respect, and mutual trust."[56] Indeed, Washington cannot hope to exit Afghanistan until it is assured of Pakistan's ability and willingness to stabilize itself and the subregion. This is an ambitious objective given Pakistan's plight as an extraordinarily fragile state, which has functioned on the basis of three pillars since 1947: Islam as the ideology of a highly segmented society; the army as the main vehicle for national unification against India; and the United States as a provider of arms, which are necessary to anchor the military's legitimacy and its strategy against its great neighbor.[57] During the Cold War, these objectives were complementary since India was a great ally of the USSR. The culmination of the American-Pakistani alliance occurred after the USSR's invasion of Afghanistan. Pakistan was then able to leverage its position by drawing on US support, by backing the Afghan mujahedeen who depended on it and who were also supported by the United States, and ipso facto by weakening the USSR's ally, Delhi. To consolidate its position, Pakistan started backing different Islamist and jihadist movements located in the tribal zones of the Federally Administered Tribal Area (FATA), where the Pakistani military could provide support to these forces while using FATA's high level of administrative autonomy as a cover to deny any direct responsibility for these movements' actions. When the United States suddenly pulled out of the region in the 1990s, Pakistan felt abandoned and came to see Afghanistan as the strategic key to restoring balance with India. Hence the Pakistani support to the Taliban in their bid to take power in Kabul at the end of the 1990s and the tolerance of other Islamist jihadist movements, including Al Qaeda.

After September 11, the regional balance was disrupted by the United States' return to the region. The United States requested that Islamabad clearly choose its camp. Yet Pakistani strategy remained remarkably stable. Islamabad did lend US forces considerable support by allowing them to operate from its territory and by participating in military operations against Al Qaeda, in exchange for a resumption of massive US military aid. To this day most US drone strikes take place on Pakistani territory with Islamabad's consent, targeting Afghan insurgents and especially those from the Inter-Services Intelligence-supported (ISI) Haqqani faction, as well as the Pakistani Taliban.[58] Pakistani policy has in fact always differentiated between the jihadists who threaten the Pakistani state and those who fight political-military battles outside of Pakistan, and often on its behalf. Pakistan readily refers to the former group, which includes Al Qaeda, as terrorists; the latter is better tolerated. Accordingly, and because it was wary of close relations between Kabul and Delhi, Islamabad helped the Taliban reorganize after their defeat in 2001.

However, over the past years this strategic duality or political duplicity has become increasingly difficult to maintain for two main reasons. The first was the deliberate exaggeration of the Indian threat by the Pakistani army, whose strategic considerations have led it to neglect its country's economic and social development. As a result, the country has considerably weakened and become a rentier state whose revenue is linked to its external strategy. Indeed, the Pakistani state depends on the support it receives from Washington and Riyadh. The Pakistani army's inability or indifference with regard to satisfying the needs of a growing and pauperized population, which is riven by profound social and regional inequalities, has led it to defuse the pressure by using Islam as a source of unity and political coercion.[59] The army has therefore become increasingly dependent on the mosque. Meanwhile, the latter strengthened its hand by playing up the military's negligence and hostility toward the United States, which was accused, with good reason, of supporting the military. It is no accident that Pakistan is the country where public opinion is most hostile to the United States.[60] All this has led to a significant weakening of the Pakistani state at a time when it is increasingly important that the state deal with the Islamists. As the tension escalates, military confrontations have multiplied. But the Pakistani army, which was created, organized, and equipped to solely focus on a potential war with India, has never really succeeded in controlling the ever-more-powerful Islamist movement. It has therefore been forced to make compromises that increasingly benefit the latter. In exchange for their promise not to attack the Pakistani state, the Islamists were given free rein to act outside of the country, in Afghanistan, Kashmir, or India. However, the balance of power is too skewed for the Islamists to feel beholden to such an arrangement.[61] They are in a position of strength from which to pursue jihad while going after the Pakistani state. In a way, this is the complex evolution that the Lashkar e Taiba movement experienced. Initially controlled by the Pakistani special services and deployed in military operations against India in Kashmir, this movement has gradually expanded and grown independent by forming alliances with other Islamist movements such as the Pakistani Taliban, the Afghan Taliban, Al Qaeda, and even Lashkar e Jhangvi. The latter is most far removed from the Pakistani army's influence, and is probably the greatest threat to the army.[62] The Pakistani Islamists' violent opposition to the Islamabad regime reached its peak in 2009, just as the Obama administration was coming into office. At this moment the Pakistani army realized that the Islamist threat might challenge its very survival. It therefore launched an unprecedented series of military operations against the Islamists in the provinces of Swat and Bajaur beginning in February 2009. Meanwhile, the United States was developing a new strategy in the region and saw an opportunity to rebuild the American-Pakistani relationship on new foundations. The idea was no longer to request that the Pakistanis fight against Islamist movements in exchange for military aid, but rather to capitalize on the shared strategic interests of Washington and Islamabad to defeat the Islamists. This was the rationale behind the crucial *Lugar Berman Kerry Act*, which entered into force in 2009 and allocated $7.5 billion to Pakistan over five years in the form of military and economic aid.[63] The military aid came with strings attached. The act explicitly requested that elements within the Pakistani army and information services end all support for extremist and terrorist groups, and particularly for any group that had attacked the United States or coalition forces in Afghanistan.[64] The act also enjoined the State Department to provide Congress with an annual report describing "the extent to which civilian executive leaders and parliament exercise oversight and approval of military budgets, the chain of command, the process of promotion for senior military leaders, civilian involvement in strategic guidance and planning, and military involvement in civil Administration."[65] This clause offended the Pakistani military, especially since no similar conditions were placed on the economic aid. Under pressure from its military, the Pakistani government arranged for the publication of a joint American-Pakistani declaration specifying: "There is no intent to, and nothing in this act in any way suggests that there should be, any US role in micromanaging internal Pakistani affairs, including the promotion of Pakistani military officers or the internal operations of the Pakistani military."[66]

The stakes are enormous for the United States: to prevent Pakistan from collapsing and falling into the hands of Islamists, thereby transforming

Pakistan into the most powerful failed state in the world, since it is a nuclear power. In this light, Afghanistan is but a byproduct of the US strategy for Pakistan. The United States has a twofold aim: to prevent Pakistan's domestic situation from further deteriorating by strengthening its institutions, and to convince Pakistani civilian and military elites of their interest in reaching an Afghan compromise accommodating the Taliban without overturning the Kabul regime. The result would be the emergence of a new governing power in Afghanistan that is neither opposed to Islamabad nor hostile to India.

Given the scale of the challenge and the number of parameters involved, it is obviously very difficult to evaluate the results of this strategy. While the Pakistani government now recognizes the existential threat posed by the Islamist movement, there is no evidence of a change of tack. Everything points to the contrary, even after allowing for Pakistan's lack of political homogeneity. In January 2010, Pakistani authorities submitted a memorandum to Washington defining their strategy in Afghanistan; as always, the Indian factor was key. Pakistani generals continue to steadfastly believe that while the Taliban may be undisciplined and unsavory, they could be the tipping point that is keeping the existential threat from India at bay.[67] Furthermore, despite information suggesting a Pakistani policy shift in the Afghan conflict, it appears that the Pakistani secret services are in fact more than ever associated with the highest decision makers of Mullah Omar's Taliban:

> Almost all the Taliban commanders interviewed believe the ISI are represented on the Quetta Shura. One senior southern commander said: "Every group commander knows the reality—which is obvious to all of us—that the ISI is behind the Taliban, they formed and are supporting the Taliban." He also explained why it was not widely known: "Every commander knows about the involvement of the ISI in the leadership but we do not discuss it because we do not trust each other, and they are much stronger than us. They are afraid that if they say anything against the Taliban or ISI it would be reported to the higher ranks—and they may be removed or assassinated... Everyone sees the sun in the sky but cannot say it is the sun.[68]

Given that the Quetta Shura Taliban are presided over by Mullah Omar, who is the only Taliban leader Washington cannot contemplate including in a political compromise, it is apparent that the ambiguity in American-Pakistani relations persists.[69] This is not to say that the United States is completely naïf. It clearly recognizes that Pakistan's position is ambiguous and that Islamabad has a limited ability to help it weaken the Taliban and Al Qaeda.[70] The United States simply has no alternative at a time of ever-deteriorating relations with Karzai.

Islamabad is more than ever determined to prevent the emergence of a political solution in Afghanistan without it, let alone against it. This is why it has never hesitated to arrest Taliban leaders who attempted to directly negotiate with the Kabul government.[71] Pakistan continues to be both an indispensable ally and insurmountable obstacle to the United States in its Afghan strategy. This contradiction has little chance of being overcome due to three main factors.

The first lies in the fractured nature of the Pakistani state, which seems to be utterly incapable of resolving the Pakistani society's structural problems, and consequently, of producing anything resembling a coherent policy.

The second one results from the Pakistani army. It may not be homogenous, but its objectives are relatively simple: to assert its dominance over the country's public and economic life, and to weaken its Indian rival. In terms of US interests, this second objective is key. The Pakistani army is only interested in fighting the nebulous terrorist threat to the stability of Afghanistan if it leads to the weakening of India in Kashmir. This strategy is fraught with risk for the Pakistanis because of the porosity between Afghan and Pakistani terrorist forces. But Pakistan sees no contradiction in fighting the Pakistani Taliban while accommodating the Afghan Taliban. Although it is a risky strategy, Pakistan considers this risk to be smaller than that of losing precious anti-Indian allies. If the United States and Pakistan have never really succeeded in overcoming the deep distrust in their relationship, it is simply because the Pakistani military does not believe that its partnership with the United States will allow it to achieve a better balance of power with India. Indeed, the latter has vetoed any US involvement in the settlement of the Kashmir conflict, and the United States has acquiesced for lack of a better solution. Thus, Afghanistan clearly has not brought Obama the success he had hoped for, aside from the elimination of Bin Laden. The modest results confirm the growing ineffectiveness of US policy when it comes to imposing its strategy in asymmetric conflicts. In this regard, the war of necessity has not been any more satisfying than the war of choice. Consequently, after leaving Baghdad, Obama is getting ready to progressively leave Afghanistan, leaving a residual and perhaps transitional presence for a few more years. There is no question, however, that the United States has already closed the Afghan chapter to open what it sees as a more promising Asian chapter.

CHAPTER SEVEN

Breaking the Pact of Silence? Obama, the Arab Spring, and the Middle East

On January 14, 2011, Tunisian president Zine El Abidine Ben Ali fled his country following a month of public protests. This event resounded deeply throughout the Arab world. For the first time in its modern history, a leader was ousted from power by means other than a coup d'état or foreign military intervention. These revolutions posed enormous challenges for the United States because they called into question the pact of silence that Western states had implicitly signed with these regimes. The pact had simple rules: the West turned a blind eye to the nature of these regimes, which, in exchange, guaranteed at least a part of the West's security. It is still too early to know whether this pact will disintegrate given the political uncertainty that reigns in the Arab world. However, it is unlikely to endure in its current form, since it was so closely linked to the profoundly undemocratic nature of Arab regimes. Does this mean the flipside of the Arab Spring is an American Winter of sorts?[1] Nothing could be less certain.

A Brief Chronology of the Arab Spring

It turns out the Tunisian revolution had a significant domino effect on the whole Arab world, despite the country's modest influence in the region. On January 25, a day of massive protests was organized in Cairo. Three days later a new demonstration was held. But this time it was violently suppressed. The ruling party's headquarters were symbolically ransacked and burned. The Egyptian president, in power since 1981, reacted very much like his Tunisian counterpart. In his first speech, he attempted to defuse the crisis with the announcement of symbolic reforms and the formation of a new government. However, given the scale of the developing demonstrations, he made a second speech announcing, like his Tunisian counterpart, that he would not stand for another term. As in many similar situations, the concessions appeared belated and paltry. For the public, the regime was sufficiently weakened to continue the fight and too preoccupied with its survival to be able to undertake radical reforms. As a result, on February 11, 2011, then-President Hosni Mubarak announced through his newly appointed vice president that he was transferring all his power to the Supreme Council of the Armed Forces. Thus, the president of the largest Arab country relinquished power after less than two weeks of demonstrations. The speed of the Tunisian and Egyptian regimes' overthrow is of unprecedented significance in the Arab world. Tunisia was not an exception after all. The expansion of the movement challenging existing regimes spread to Egypt and the rest of the Arab world. Indeed, less than two days after the departure of President Mubarak, riots broke out in Libya. They were violently suppressed in Benghazi, where they started before quickly spreading throughout the country. On February 23, the National Transitional Council (NTC) was created in Benghazi. It established itself as the principal challenger to the Gaddafi regime, which then seemed on the brink of collapse. However, after being surprised by the scale and rapid spread of the protests, Mu'ammer Gaddafi went on the offensive again on March 6 by drawing on considerable military resources. His objective was then to take back Benghazi and crush the uprising. As if to prove his determination, he made it public in extraordinarily violent terms, which alerted the international community to the implied risks to Libya's civilian population. His plans were thwarted in extremis by a NATO military intervention that France and Great Britain strongly encouraged.

While North Africa was clearly the front line of the Arab revolutions, which quickly turned violent, it was not the only area that experienced this new political dynamic. Just four days after the departure of President Ben Ali, demonstrations were organized in Yemen. On February 26, the country saw important defections from the regime. As in the other Arab countries, protesters requested the departure of President Ali Abdullah Saleh. Not far away, in Bahrain, demonstrations were organized by the Shiite majority, which feels socially and politically marginalized by the minority Sunni power. The latter is strongly supported by Saudi Arabia and has repeatedly used the Iranian threat to perpetuate its power. However, unlike what is happening in other Arab countries, demands have focused more on reform than on bringing down the regime. Beginning with the Bahrain revolts, a fault line formed between the monarchies and the republics. In the former group, among which there are many differences (Bahrain, Morocco, Jordan), the demonstrations aim to implement constitutional political regimes. In the latter, it is simply the fall of the regime that is demanded.

On January 31, 2011, in a *Wall Street Journal* interview, the Syrian president explained that Syria was not Egypt and that its regime would not fall. He argued:

> Why is Syria stable, although we have more difficult conditions? Egypt has been supported financially by the United States, while we are under embargo by most countries of the world. (...) Despite all that, the people do not go into an uprising. So it is not only about the needs and not only about the reform. It is about the ideology, the beliefs and the cause that you have.[2]

He then gave an interesting interpretation of the Egyptian uprising: the rejection of the Camp David accords signed by Egypt and Israel in 1978 under the aegis of the United States. It does not matter that this is a questionable argument. It is worth mentioning because it shows the degree of misunderstanding by Arab leaders who are completely divorced from reality. In fact, at the end of February 2011, demonstrations in Damascus started calling for the regime's ouster.[3] Beginning in mid-March with the violent riots in Daraa, Syria fully joined the wave of Arab revolutions. Thus, in less than three months over ten Arab countries were in the throes of public protest movements seeking to either topple the existing regimes or exact substantial reforms. The fact that these protests occurred in major countries like Egypt and Syria underscores the extent of the phenomenon, even though it has spared a country as important as Saudi Arabia as well as most of the Gulf monarchies, except for Bahrain.

1848, 1989, and 2011

The Arab revolutions invite historical comparison with Central and Eastern Europe in 1989. However, the analogy is not convincing. Indeed, the 1989 revolutions stemmed from a major external political development: Mikhail Gorbachev's decision never again to intervene militarily to rescue a troubled communist regime.[4] Gorbachev put a definitive end to Leonid Brezhnev's doctrine of limited sovereignty. After that, everything became possible. The communist regimes had little legitimacy and found themselves utterly helpless. They might well have used force, but without the Union of Soviet Socialist Republic's support such a step would have only served to precipitate their downfall. The situation in the Arab world is fundamentally different. Most of the Arab regimes benefited from important external ties. However, they never expected that a Western or regional power would come to the rescue of a threatened regime. The only exception to date is Bahrain, which Saudi Arabia has always considered as an integral part of its sphere of security. In Central and Eastern Europe, popular protests spread as military nonintervention was guaranteed. Gorbachev had, in a way, implemented an Eastern European no-fly zone. The Arab revolutions were and remain much more vulnerable. Even if the Arab regimes do not have foreign protectors willing to save them, they have accumulated considerable means of repression. In fact, if the West had not militarily intervened, Gaddafi would most certainly have crushed the insurgency given the dramatically unequal balance of power on the ground. In populated and urbanized countries like Egypt or Syria the use of brute force would not have sufficed to crush the uprising. In sparsely populated countries like Libya and Bahrain, force can make a difference.

The European revolutions of 1848 seem to be a more apt comparison. As in Europe in 1848, the Arab protests aim to bring down despotic regimes with globally unprecedented life spans: Ben Ali exercised power for 23 years, Mubarak for 30 years, and Gaddafi for 42 years. In Bahrain, the real leader, the prime minister, has been in power since 1971! In Algeria, President Abdelaziz Bouteflika, who was nondemocratically elected in 1999, was his country's foreign minister the year of President John F. Kennedy's assassination! These regimes were even less likely to anticipate their downfall because they were all establishing family dynasties. This had clearly begun in Syria, where Bashar al-Assad succeeded his father in 1999, but Mubarak was also clearly preparing for his son to succeed him. It is this very possibility that gave rise to an important protest movement in 2004, as well as deep dissatisfaction within the armed forces. Gaddafi was thinking along the same lines. The only difference is that he had not yet decided which son would succeed him. The parallels between the Arab revolutions and the European revolutions in 1848 do not end here. All the European revolutions eventually had to face the forces of counterrevolution. The

Arab world may be going through a similar process.[5] This is either because some regimes are still resisting, or because in other countries like Egypt, for example, the military is increasingly seen as an impediment to democratic development; hence, the violent demonstrations of November 2011. That being said, if the parallel with 1848 were to pan out in the Arab world, then it would tend to show that the success of counterrevolutions in the short term does not preclude the victory of revolutionary ideals in the long term.[6] Therefore, it is not impossible that the Arab revolutions will follow a comparable development, even though the Arab revolutions are not liberal revolutions. They have three aspects: liberal, in the sense of anti-authoritarian; social, with regard to glaring inequalities; and identity, in opposition to the regional leaders who crush their peoples.

The United States and the Pact of Silence

The longevity of Arab regimes can be attributed to hold-over domestic social pacts with far-reaching international implications. Indeed, a lot of Arab states are oil states that are extremely dependent on international markets. The rentier-state thesis has given rise to a rich literature. Hazem Beblawi has provided a simple and enlightening definition: "A rentier economy is thus an economy where the creation of wealth is centered around a small fraction of the society; the rest of the society is only engaged in the distribution and utilization of this wealth."[7] The central idea of the rentier-state thesis is that it is based on a profoundly unequal social pact between the rent-holders and society.

The state has the wealth and redistributes it as it sees fit without requiring anything of the citizens other than their silence. This imbalance is made possible by the fact that rent sources can be sold internationally without being locally transformed. Oil states are the classic example. They extract underground resources with foreign assistance and recover the value of this extraction. They only need to meet two or three criteria: proper functioning of the rent extraction process, access to foreign markets, and security of exploitation against those who might challenge the power of the state or capture the rent. In Libya, for example, the only truly operational ministry was the oil ministry. This is far from being an isolated case. In all of the Arab oil regimes, energy and security services are the only two functional sectors. Of course, not all Arab states are oil states, and oil is not the only source of rent. In Egypt, the rents came from revenue from the Suez Canal, Egyptian immigrant workers, US aid, and tourism.[8] Rent from the latter is as precious as that from oil because it is an easy source of foreign currency. This explains the political importance of protecting touristic sites for the Egyptian, Tunisian, and Moroccan regimes.

Rents give regimes a considerable capacity to survive, as is still attested today by countries like Algeria or Saudi Arabia. To date, the only two Arab rentier regimes that have really been overthrown are those of Libya and Iraq. In both instances it took an outside intervention to unseat them, even if the Libyan and Iraqi cases are not otherwise comparable. Yet oil rents do not provide an absolute guarantee. One of the causes of the Arab Spring is the fact that the social pacts derived from the rents no longer worked correctly because they had created enormous distortions. In most Arab countries, higher general levels of education have increased demand for work that the rentier regimes are not able to satisfy precisely because their whole rentier logic aims to prevent the emergence of a middle class that is likely to use its social standing to request more political rights. This is one of the reasons why many rentier regimes use foreign labor despite massive unemployment within their populations.[9] These regimes' inability to ensure viable social pacts stems from a number of factors. In some cases, there is a deliberate intention to exclude certain parts of the population that are deemed disobedient (for example, the populations of eastern Libya and the Tunisian interior, or the Shiites in Bahrain). In other cases, the exclusion is linked to a growing predatory approach limited to an increasingly tiny sliver of people (Tunisia, Jordan). Thus, there was a clear connection between a predatory logic and familial logic in Tunisia, as well as Syria, Egypt, Bahrain, and Libya. Needless to say, these regimes owe their survival to their access to the international oil market, and accordingly to Western markets. It is interesting to note that even when Libya was subjected to an international embargo in the 1990s, oil exports were not affected. There is no doubt that rentier regimes have benefited from the benevolence of Western states.

The second international factor that played into the hands of the Arab regimes was September 11. It was a windfall for most of them because it made them indispensable to the West's security in its fight against Islamist terrorism. September 11 consolidated the pact of silence between the West and Arab regimes. In exchange for the West's silence on the repressive nature of Arab regimes, the latter committed to guaranteeing the West's security in energy, the fight against Islamist terrorism, the control of migration flows, and the renouncement of WMDs. This pact explains why steps toward political openness, which timidly began in Arab countries at the end of the 1990s and beginning of the 2000s, were brutally halted in the mid-2000s without eliciting a strong reaction from the West. Admittedly, after its fiasco in Iraq and the very negative perception of its intervention in the Arab world, the Bush administration tried to regain a modicum of political legitimacy by proposing a democratization plan for the region. However, this process was doomed to failure from the beginning since it sought a commitment to reform from authoritarian regimes on which it was also continuing to rely to maintain certain US strategic interests.

US Management of the Pact of Silence

US strategic interests in the Arab world have proven to be enduring from before Barack Obama took office to the present. They can be summarized as follows:

- maintain guaranteed access to the Middle East's energy resources
- obtain (mainly from Saudi Arabia) stable energy prices[10]
- secure the United States' strategic access to the region through the maintenance and development of military bases in order to guarantee the security of supply routes, deter Iran, and enable the projection of American forces in Asia and particularly in Afghanistan
- prevent any renewed flare-up of the Israeli-Arab conflict
- maintain Israel's strategic supremacy over its neighbors
- enlist active support from Arab regimes in the fight against terrorism
- deter Arab states from gaining access to nuclear weapons and acquiring WMDs

In exchange, the United States offered its partners forms of compensation that virtually all the Arab states, except for Syria, readily accepted:

- no challenge to the undemocratic nature of Arab regimes, despite occasional initiatives that might suggest otherwise
- substantial military aid, mainly to the Egyptian army, with the double purpose of pampering it and discouraging it from using its arms against Israel
- significant economic aid to non-oil-producing US allies (Jordan, Egypt) as well as preferential access to the US market (Jordan, Morocco)[11]

- symbolic political and economic gratification of undemocratic regimes that are strongly committed to the fight against Islamist terrorism (Algeria, Yemen)
- international political rehabilitation of countries that abandon their programs to acquire WMDs (Libya).
- security guarantee to Gulf countries against Iran.

This pact of silence worked to the benefit of both parties, thus explaining why it endured despite the Arab public's general hostility to US policy. The contradiction is understandable. The pact allowed Arab regimes to find a modus vivendi with the United States precisely because it deliberately ignored public opinion, which was acknowledged but only identified through its emotional expression ("the Arab street") rather than its thwarted citizen expression. The Bush administration was paradoxically one of the first to directly state this problem, as Condoleezza Rice did during her Cairo visit: "For 60 years, my country, the United States, pursued stability at the expense of democracy in the region. And we achieved neither."[12] However, the premises of her analysis appeared so biased to local communities that they did not come across as credible. Among the factors that most undermined the Bush administration and its democratic discourse was the assumption that the Arab-Israeli conflict resulted from the former's lack of democracy. Israel's frosty reception of the Arab revolutions a posteriori confirmed the weakness of this analysis.[13]

"Barack Obama, we love you!"

Against this background, in June 2009 Obama made one of his most important speeches, in Cairo. It carried two important messages. The first was to assert that the United States was not at war against Islam, and did not conflate Islam with terrorism.[14] In public, and in front of a Muslim audience, Obama elaborated by clearly distancing himself from any idea of a clash of civilizations. The second message was to explicitly admit that the misunderstanding between Islam and the West, and between the United States and the Muslim world, could only be truly overcome by settling the Israeli-Palestinian conflict. The Cairo speech did not get into the details of a negotiated settlement, but it expressed America's desire to be involved in one. It also established real symmetry in the obligations of the two parties (Israeli and Palestinian) with renewed emphasis on illegal settlements and the need for Israel to end them.[15] Oddly, although not by accident, democracy was only the fourth issue he addressed. After ending his discussion of this subject, though, Obama was interrupted by a listener who interjected "Barack Obama, we love you," conveying the impression that he had used the language that was expected of him. Obama recognized that the issue of democracy had been tainted by the Iraq war and that no system of government could or should be imposed on another country. At the same time, he reaffirmed the universality of fundamental rights and liberties and noted that governments that protect rights are ultimately more stable and secure, and achieve better results.[16] Finally, he pointed to the Islamists' inconsistency in supporting democracy when in the opposition and becoming intolerant once in power.[17] Obama gave unmistakable signs that he did not want his presence in Egypt to be interpreted as supporting the Egyptian regime, whose domestic policies were increasingly hardening. In fact, the speech made no reference to contemporary Egypt, let alone President Mubarak, who was pointedly ignored. Obama did not neglect the issue of democracy in the Arab world, but he understood that a messianic tone would be totally counterproductive and that the only way forward for the United States was to encourage local dynamics. This is what happened beyond all expectations. A detailed analysis of the Cairo speech shows that Obama was interrupted by public applause 37 times. The distribution of the applause is indicative of the audience's receptivity to the themes developed by the US president. Of the 37 interruptions, 14 occurred in the first part that was largely devoted to relations between the West and Islam, 6 during his discussion of the Palestinian issue, 4 when he invoked democracy, and 3 when he talked about women. By contrast, his references to the need for religious freedom were only applauded once, and mention of Iran's nuclear issue did not elicit any applause.

From Tunisia to Egypt

When Ben Ali was overthrown in January 2011, the United States cheered. It had not anticipated the importance of this first Arab revolution, which was of limited relevance to the United States, but essential to France. In his State of the Union speech on January 25, Obama paid tribute to the Tunisians.[18] However, the event was not put in perspective. The address happened to coincide with the first major demonstrations that would lead to the overthrow of Mubarak less than a month later. In fact, the day of the first large Egyptian demonstration, Hillary Clinton's initial reflex was to express support of sorts for the Egyptian regime by emphasizing its stability.[19] The parallel with Tunisia was thus implicitly rejected. This reaction revealed a certain sense of disbelief in the face of the speed of events. It also betrayed an intense fear of the consequences of a possible Egyptian revolution: Egypt was no Tunisia for the United States. While she did not necessarily disagree with the president over the right approach, Clinton was of two minds throughout the Egyptian crisis. One reflected the position of the State Department, which has traditionally valued the stability of states, and especially that of a privileged partner of over 30 years with a moderating influence in relation to Israel. She also expressed the position of two major US partners in the region: Israel and Saudi Arabia. Israel feared that the fall of Mubarak would lead to an Islamist rise to power and eventually the political neutralization of the Camp David accords.[20] Saudi Arabia also quickly understood that Mubarak's downfall was bound to have incalculable consequences for the whole Arab world. King Abdullah expressed great hostility toward the Egyptian demonstrators, whom he branded as infiltrators.[21] Even the Palestinian Authority expressed its hostility to the Arab Spring, fearing that it might reinforce Hamas position. Clinton treaded carefully. On February 5, at the Munich conference, she made it clear that the United States still wanted to give President Mubarak a last chance: "I think it's important to support the transition process announced by the Egyptian Government, actually headed by now Vice President Omar Suleiman."[22] This stance was compounded by the awkward statements, to say the least, of former US ambassador to Cairo Frank Wisner, who declared on the same day: "I believe that President Mubarak's continued leadership is critical—it's his chance to write his own legacy."[23] These comments were well out of step with President Obama's declarations. On January 28, his first remarks on the situation explicitly expressed his dismay at President Mubarak's dithering.[24] On February 1, he more firmly stated: "What is clear—and what I indicated tonight to President Mubarak—is my belief that an orderly transition must be meaningful, it must be peaceful, and it must begin now."[25] These various remarks are not substantially contradictory, but their tones were different enough that the White House felt it had to officially clarify that Wisner's views were his own.[26] As the situation on the ground deteriorated and the demonstrations grew, Obama gradually raised the tone to the point where Mubarak's departure became inevitable. Behind the scenes, what really pushed him to up the ante were the guarantees the United States obtained from the Egyptian military, with which it has maintained very close ties since the Camp David accords in 1978. The importance of the military relationship between the United States and Egypt goes a long way toward explaining the Egyptian military's behavior. Over the decades, it has professionalized and depoliticized. Even if it was part of the regime, through its very powerful economic interests, it no longer had anything to do with the very political and revolutionary army that brought Gamal Abdel Nasser to power in the 1950s. While the decision not to fire in the crowd to save Mubarak probably spurred debate among its ranks, the military's decision cannot be understood without taking account of this sociological evolution, which made it more receptive to the Pentagon's arguments about the grave implications of using force against demonstrators. To underscore the importance of Egypt and the political change it was undergoing, President Obama made a third statement on February 11 following Mubarak's decision to step down.[27]

There Is No Obama Doctrine

Having clearly paved the way for Mubarak's downfall, Obama was pressed to offer a theory for his practice. However, from the beginning of the Libyan crisis, he refused to define an Obama doctrine: "I think it's important not to take this particular situation and then try to project some sort of Obama Doctrine that we're going to apply in a cookie-cutter fashion across the board."[28] Libya was no Egypt, which itself was no Bahrain, Yemen, or Syria.

Above all Obama is pragmatic and does not want to be hemmed in by rigid positions that are ultimately likely to be held against him. He also knows that US strategic interests vary from one Arab country to another: they are strong in Bahrain, palpable in Yemen, but much more limited in Libya. The order is practically reversed for the Europeans, who have strong interests in Tunisia and Libya by dint of proximity, but much weaker ones in Bahrain and Yemen.

Bahrain, for example, is of great strategic importance to the United States because it is home to the US Fifth Fleet, which includes 30 ships and 30,000 sailors. The fleet provides security in the Arabian Sea, the Red Sea, and the western part of the Indian Ocean and Persian Gulf. It secures oil supplies from the region, fights against terrorism and piracy, and strategically deters Iran. Bahrain's important strategic value to the United States is growing, in light of expansion plans for US military facilities in 2014. In fact, Bahrain has clearly used this US shield to clamp down on any internal challenge. Manama's regime moreover benefits from Saudi Arabia's support. Notwithstanding these constraints, the Obama administration has pressured the regime to respond to the protesters' demands since the beginning of the protests. These protesters, who are mostly Shiites, have been clamoring for more equitable representation.

This country's problems have too often been portrayed in purely sectarian terms. The reality is much more complex, even though the existing regime has deliberately sought to sectarianize the crisis and lend credibility to the Iranian threat. The crux of the matter is more social than religious. As is the case in many other Arab countries, the Bahrain uprising has much to do with the development of mass unemployment, resulting from the government's inability to guarantee public employment for all graduates. Normally, the private sector should have picked up where the public left off to absorb the new graduates in the labor market. This is precisely what did not happen, since the power elite has traditionally been loath to recruit nationals, preferring less expensive foreigners who can always be expelled.[29] Bahrain is a variation of the rentier model: to keep the population at a distance is seen as way to guarantee the regime's survival. Saudi Arabia also supports this policy, in line with its longstanding priority of preventing the emergence of a Shiite challenge that might benefit Iran. Saudi Arabia's fear of Iranian Shiism is heightened by the presence of a Shiite minority in Saudi Arabia not far from Bahrain, and the concentration of oil fields in a Shiite-dominated region. The United States was careful to condemn violence and call for political dialogue. However, it is not anticipating regime change, which is not what the opposition is asking for anyway. To the contrary, Washington is backing the crown prince, who is clearly sold on the idea of a political dialogue with the opposition, against the advice of his uncle, the prime minister of Bahrain. Washington saw the emir's reshuffle in February 2011 as a sign of reform. However, this opening quickly proved illusory because it was strongly opposed within the regime by the Saudi Arabia-backed prime minister. Robert Gates returned disappointed from his trip to Manama. He considered the proposed reforms to only be "baby steps."[30] On March 13, the day when the crown prince was supposed to present the opposition with a seven-point reform plan, Saudi troops entered Bahrain.[31] This was a real blow to both the reformers and the United States. The latter nonetheless refused to condemn the Saudi military intervention, which legally conformed to the agreements linking the member states of the Gulf Cooperation Council.[32] This created a second source, after Egypt, of US tension with Saudi Arabia, which appeared as the champion of counterrevolutions, even though Riyadh had played a decisive role in the intervention in Libya just the day before. The United States also remained unconvinced by the Iranian factor that Bahrain systematically invoked to prevent any reform.[33]

Thus, even before it was formalized in May 2011,[34] US policy toward the Arab revolutions gradually and pragmatically coalesced around three principles:

- The Obama administration would support all peaceful demonstrations and condemn any violent repression.
- This position of principle would be adjusted according to the implications for US interests of political change in the different Arab countries. Since these interests vary from one country to another, the Obama administration was given wide leeway in deciding how to proceed.
- The Obama adminstration would determine the level and form of US engagement depending on availability of a credible political alternative capable of substituting the threatened regime without materially injuring US interests.

In Egypt, the identification of the armed forces as an alternative explains why the United States quickly embraced change. At the other extreme, the political confusion among the opposition in Yemen partly explains why the United States is stalling on President Saleh's refusal to step down. In May 2011, Obama called on President Saleh to comply with the Gulf Cooperation Council's resolution ordering a power transfer. However, he reiterated this position in a very succinct and almost neutral way that contrasted with his position on Egypt.[35] Since, and despite a Security Council resolution, the political deadlock continues.[36] The United States is clearly acting behind the scenes, but it refuses to unequivocally condemn President Saleh, who is doing his utmost to exploit the threat of Al Qaeda and thus retain US support in the fight against terrorism. The fact that President Obama's counterterrorism adviser John Brennan is in charge of the Yemeni case leaves no doubt as to the importance of counterterrorism in US political decisions on Yemen. This extreme caution is also apparent in Bahrain. Notwithstanding the political logjam, Obama has refrained from condemning this country's regime, but has expressed dissatisfaction with the way in which the political dialogue is unfolding.[37]

Between these two extremes the very different cases of Libya and Syria fall in the middle. The United States was much slower than France and Great Britain in recognizing the NTC in Libya because it was not sure about the NTC's orientation.[38] In Syria, it still has not recognized the opposition groups, which are admittedly not yet uni-fied. The United States has clearly chosen to outsource the settlement of the Syrian crisis to Turkey and the Arab League because it is aware of the profound distrust, even among Syrian protesters, of US policy, and also because it has no intention of committing to a military operation, be it limited to implementing a no-fly zone.

The Libyan Paradox

Libya was never a key issue for the United States. Among Arab states, it ranked far behind Egypt, Bahrain, Yemen, and Syria. Granted, in the 1980s–1990s, the United States took issue with the Libyan regime, which had become a major supporter of international terror-ism. However, in 2003 after the US intervention in Iraq, Libya clearly sought to redeem itself in the West by abandoning its chemical weap-ons program in exchange for a complete political rehabilitation on the international scene. The regime then became one of the greatest bene-ficiaries of the pact of silence, which led it, along with other Arab lead-ers, to feel invulnerable to domestic political pressures. For instance, despite its huge oil resources, Tripoli succeeded in getting Italy to agree to financially compensate Libya for controlling migratory flows from sub-Saharan Africa.[39] Gaddafi fully understood the benefits of no lon-ger being a nuisance. Meanwhile the West saw the Libyan regime as a rehabilitated one that was likely to offer vast economic opportunities. The rehabilitation process reached another milestone in 2007, with the release of Bulgarian nurses who had been detained in Libya and accused without due process of spreading acquired immune deficiency syndrome (AIDS) at the Benghazi hospital. French arms manufacturers visited Tripoli shortly before the beginning of the Libyan uprising.[40] At the same time, one of Colonel Gaddafi's sons was touring the United States. He interrupted his travels on February 17, the first day of the uprising, right before a planned visit to West Point.[41]

At first, the speed of events in the Libyan uprising seemed to indicate that the Gaddafi regime would rapidly fall. However, after Gaddafi went back on the offensive against the insurgents, the West found itself in a quandary: it could let Gaddafi proceed and risk condoning a great massacre, or it could intervene and risk delegitimizing a domes-tic uprising. Since the originality of the Arab revolutions lay in their endogenous character, there was no small danger of marring them by intervening in a region where foreign presence is an extremely sensi-tive subject.[42] Obama, who had been seeking to heal the wounds of the

Iraqi intervention since his Cairo speech, did not want to get trapped in the Arab world again.[43] This real risk explains his initial hesitation, which was then undoubtedly strengthened by domestic hostility to the intervention. Indeed, since Obama took office, the US public has entered an isolationist phase leading it to reject any idea of intervention in a little-known country, even though the Iraq experience had shown that the public could be open to military intervention, even one based on falsehoods. For its part, the US Congress did not have much sympathy for the Gaddafi regime. Except for a few committed senators such as Senator John McCain, though, it remained largely disinterested. The US Congress never actually considered the Arab Spring a major political development because of fears it might benefit Islamists and weaken Israel's regional position.

The main source of opposition to any implementation of a no-fly zone was the Pentagon, which advanced a series of highly questionable arguments.[44] First, Robert Gates argued that a no-fly zone would be very difficult to implement because of the country's vast size. But this objection was not entirely relevant. A no-fly zone was only needed over a limited coastal area from Benghazi to Tripoli where virtually all the battles were taking place. The second and more admissible argument was that the no-fly zone would not suffice given that the counteroffensive was not being carried out by air, but by ground forces, therefore implying that the no-fly zone would have to be combined with a destruction of Libyan forces. Finally, through the statements of General James Clapper, the US military underscored that the power imbalance on the ground was such that Gaddafi's troops would end up winning.[45] Such an assessment was surprising to say the least, because it either implied that Colonel Gaddafi had already prevailed, or implicitly encouraged him to finish the job. Obama rejected this hypothesis through a White House statement: "The president does not think that Qaddafi will prevail."[46] It is important to realize that behind these technical arguments lay political concerns. The Pentagon considered Libya to be outside of US strategic interests and thus of low priority at a time when the Afghani front was becoming increasingly complex. Furious to see the Europeans beginning to disengage from Afghanistan, the United States clearly did not want to appear to be automatically responding to the Europeans' military needs as they were showing reluctance to meet US demands. Gates clearly conveyed this message to his European counterparts at a NATO meeting in March 2011 during discussions about a Libyan intervention.[47] Ambassador Rice did the same, going as far as threatening France and Great Britain of voting against a resolution to establish a no–fly zone.[48] She also emphasized the military inefficiency and political uselessness of any such resolution given the high probability of a Russian and Chinese veto.[49] By contrast, within the NSC, a group led by Samantha Power called for intervention for the sake of protecting civilian populations. On the other hand, NSC head Tom Donilon expressed reservations about intervening.[50] These conflicting pressures led to a period of great uncertainty compounded by the lack of assurances about the NTC, its composition, and its objectives. Hence, the United States had no problem voting for resolution 1970, which imposed economic and financial sanctions against Libya, but it dithered on resolution 1973, which simply called for the establishment of a no–fly zone. At the United Nations, the US ambassador warned the French and British that she would not vote for the resolution, citing the Pentagon's arguments and the probable Russian and Chinese vetoes.

On March 14, 2011, at the G8 meeting in Paris, as France sought to build consensus around the idea of a military intervention, the United States refrained from taking a position. At this time, Clinton met with an NTC delegation, but made no promises. The likelihood of a military intervention then seemed very remote due to US reluctance as well as opposition from Russia and, unexpectedly, Germany. At the time, Alain Juppé expressed his extreme concern about the chances of passing draft resolution 1973, which France and Great Britain were about to introduce in the Security Council. However, over the course of a weekend the United States completely changed its position. The United States not only decided to support resolution 1973, but also amended it with the famous paragraph IV "to take all necessary measures [...] to protect civilians and civilian populated areas."[51] Three factors explain this reversal. The first was US intelligence information about an imminent attack by Gaddafi on Benghazi.[52] This would have brought the shadow of Srebrenica over Obama and sent an encouraging signal to other threatened Arab regimes: "Had we not acted along with our NATO allies and regional coalition partners, thousands would have been killed. The message would have been clear: Keep power by killing as many people as it takes."[53] Obama's political opponents, who had refrained from taking a position on Libya, would not have failed to use this misstep against him. The second factor was the Arab League's crucial vote to authorize the establishment of a no–fly zone and the protection of civilians, but to reject the idea of a foreign intervention with ground forces.[54] This was the form of legitimation that Obama had been waiting for, though the United States probably leaned heavily on the Arab League to obtain a clear commitment. Obama did not want to deploy US forces in Libya against the wishes of most Arab states. The Arab League vote was therefore decisive. It has paved the way to bring the United States into the fold of countries supporting an air intervention and furthermore prevented Russia and China from vetoing the resolution.[55]

Incidentally, the Arab League's decision was only possible because the intergovernmental organization's rules of procedure had recently changed to allow resolutions to pass by qualified majority rather than unanimity. This was a decisive change since Yemen, Syria, and Algeria voted against the resolution. The Arab League's vote can only be understood with reference to the revolutions that had just taken place in the region, and especially in the League's host country. Furthermore, Gaddafi had succeeded over his 42 years in power in uniting everyone against him. He had terrible relations with the Gulf monarchies, mainly Saudi Arabia, and with Lebanese Shiites who were angered by the mysterious disappearance of imam Moussa al-Sadr in Libya in 1978. While this Arab legitimation gave Obama license to act, he still needed to gain the US military's endorsement without humiliating it. The terms of the agreement he reached with the Pentagon were apparent in the nature and modalities of the US intervention. Obama wanted to act in a quick, efficient, and time-limited way before handing over the reins to NATO. To make a difference on the ground without taking any risk, the United States decided to primarily use Tomahawk missiles and refused to conduct air-bombing operations for fear of losing aircraft and having to intervene on the ground to pick up crews. As if to emphasize the relative importance of the US engagement in Libya, President Obama did not hesitate to proceed with his Latin American tour when the military intervention in Libya began. This was of great symbolic significance, as it is not often that a head of state takes a trip abroad while his country is involved in a military operation. However, this "leading from behind" strategy, which is how the US intervention in Libya was characterized, is not a new approach, let alone a new doctrine.[56] It is above all the formulation of a course of action that the United States wanted to pursue without making much ado. In fact, the US contribution was decisive on the ground. Without it the NATO operation would have been much more difficult, if not impossible. It was particularly important given that Gaddafi put up much stronger resistance than anticipated. The United States alone destroyed nine-tenths of the anti-aircraft missile batteries, ensured three-quarters of air-to-air refueling, scrambled communications, and provided most of the satellite information.[57] In the end, the transfer of the operation to NATO was more of a political than an operational choice. Indeed, the handover did not fundamentally change the extent of US involvement in the conflict given its key role in this institution.

The situation in Syria is especially challenging for the United States. On the one hand, it has a real strategic interest in supporting regime change in this Arab country, in contrast to the Egyptian and Libyan cases, where the benefit was not so obvious. However, Syria is the Arab country where its ability to influence local dynamics is most limited. The United States faces three major obstacles in addressing the ongoing popular uprising and the Syrian regime's resistance: Russia's blocking of Security Council action, thereby preventing total isolation of the regime; persistent divergences within the Syrian opposition, which has not succeeded in unifying and convincing its foreign partners that it is a credible alternative; finally, the fact that the Syrian regime, while severely discredited, continues to enjoy a certain level of domestic political support. Combined with the opposition's rejection of outside intervention, which would moreover be particularly difficult given the terrain, these factors have created an impossible situation. The United States knows that the fall of the Syrian regime is highly desirable, as it would also weaken the Iranian regime and the Lebanese Hezbollah. At the same time it cannot count on a viable alternative. The United States has therefore given into the natural temptation to leave the political initiative to Turkey and the Arab countries at a time when its priority in the region is Iran anyway.

Peace Settlement: A Loose Plan A without a Plan B

Even without the benefit of hindsight, Obama can be credited with handling the Arab Spring quite adroitly. He succeeded in overcoming all domestic constraints, despite the congressional Republican majority's deep hostility toward him. He was also able to get around the Pentagon's opposition to an intervention in Libya. Moreover, the Arab public seems to have welcomed the US engagement in the region (see table 7.1). In the first major public opinion poll on Arab perceptions of the revolutions, among the countries whose roles were most appreciated the United States ranked third, right behind Turkey and France.[58] Obama thus instinctively understood that the United States could not thwart the groundswell in the Arab world on the pretext that its interests in the region required maintaining existing authoritarian regimes. With regard to the evolution in the perception of US policy in the region, the

Table. 7.1 Is your attitude toward the United States positive or negative?

	2009	2010	2011
Positive	15%	10%	26%
Negative	59%	86%	84%

Source: adapted from 2011 Arab Public Opinion Poll, Doha Brookings Center, November 21, 2011, p. 24, http://www.brookings.edu/reports /2011/1121_arab_public_opinion_telhami.aspx.

opinion survey shows that the Cairo speech of June 2009 brought great hope. By 2010, however, lack of progress on the Israeli–Palestinian issue had considerably dampened enthusiasm for Obama and his policies. The year 2011 saw renewed support for the United States that can only be explained by the choices Obama made during the Arab Spring.

America's image will most likely deteriorate in 2012 given the deadlock over the settlement of the Palestinian issue. It is also probable that this factor will weigh more heavily now that the United States can no longer be held responsible for maintaining unanimously rejected Arab leaders in power.[59]

It must be acknowledged that the Obama administration has failed to make progress on this issue because it lacks an ambitious strategy and the adequate means to implement one. We will not go over the history of the Israeli–Palestinian conflict or US policy in this region. Rather, we will begin with the situation Obama faced when he came to power, and the objectives he set. Obama inherited a parlous situation in the Middle East. The Arab world considered the Bush administration too favorable to Israel. Nevertheless, the administration's quest to reach a settlement was not completely irrelevant. Through the Annapolis process launched by Washington in 2007, the Israelis and Palestinians had taken the first steps toward reaching a settlement that called for the dismantlement of part of the settlements (60,000 out of 250,000), a retreat to the 1967 borders, territory swaps, the sharing of Jerusalem, and Israel's acceptance of a small number of returning Palestinian refugees. Unfortunately, the agreement was limited by the fact that it was finalized right before Israeli elections that Ehud Olmert knew he had lost.

Obama therefore had to deal with Benjamin Netanyahu's political comeback in March 2009. Upon taking office, the new Israeli head of state outlined a settlement of the conflict that deliberately left out any prospect of creating a Palestinian state. A few days later, the head of Israeli diplomacy confirmed that his country did not feel bound by the Annapolis declaration, which had linked compliance with the road map to the negotiation of a final statute on the creation of a Palestinian state. Given the circumstances, the first meeting between Obama and Netanyahu in May 2009 was particularly difficult. For in addition to backing a two-state solution, the United States had requested a freeze on settlements. The US President confirmed this during his meeting with the Palestinian Authority in May 2009. At this time, Clinton also insisted on the centrality of the settlement freeze.[60] Washington was clearly waiting for an Israeli move, as if the United States were evaluating Israel's commitment to making real progress toward a final settlement. In June 2009, the United States thought it had achieved its objective when the Israeli government announced a temporary six-month freeze on settlements in the West Bank, with the exception of Jerusalem, which Israelis consider to be an integral part of the state of Israel. However, this hope, which Clinton too hastily called an unprecedented breakthrough, was quickly dashed. First, beginning in November 2009, a new settlement program was launched in Jerusalem. Furthermore, as forewarned, the freeze did not bring an end to new settlements. The United States lowered its expectations. Yet it did not have anything else to propose. Obama had bet that an Israeli concession on settlements would be conducive to final status negotiations. At no point did he contemplate failure. Obama thus only had a loose Plan A and no Plan B. As Martin Indyk states cogently, "When Obama speaks his rethoric is visionary. But when it comes to delivering his approach is pragmatic (...). He often fails to adjust his prophetic vision to the pragmatic outcome of his administration's diplomacy, and that produces inevitable disappointment."[61]

At a loss, Obama pulled in Dennis Ross, the principal architect of US Middle Eastern policy since the beginning of the 1980s.[62] Ross is an architect, not a strategist. While he knows the ins and outs of US policy in the region, he has no long-term strategic vision.[63] His method consists of using small steps to create a virtuous circle of mutual trust between the two parties in conflict. The approach has three advantages: it means that sensitive topics are not broached directly; it is likely to build confidence with the Israelis, who are very supportive of this process; and finally, it does not undermine America's domestic political consensus over unwavering support for the state of Israel.

Obama's Series of Retreats

It is interesting to closely examine the evolution of US policy on this subject through Obama's statements at the United Nations in 2009,

2010, and 2011. From year to year, US ambitions fell while support for Israel's positions grew. In 2009, Obama expressed a strong personal desire to be involved in the settlement of the conflict: "I will also continue to seek a just and lasting peace between Israel, Palestine, and the Arab world."[64]

He also emphasized the importance of international-community support for the bilateral negotiations between Israelis and Palestinians: "In pursuit of that goal, we will develop regional initiatives with multilateral participation, alongside bilateral negotiations."[65]

Finally, he systematically treated Israeli and Palestinian grievances equally: "The greatest price of this conflict is not paid by us. It's not paid by politicians. It's paid by the Israeli girl in Sderot who closes her eyes in fear that a rocket will take her life in the middle of the night. It's paid for by the Palestinian boy in Gaza who has no clean water and no country to call his own. These are all God's children."[66]

In 2010, when he addressed the United Nations for the second time, two significant changes were apparent. The first concerned the role of the international community, which was hardly mentioned: "Now, peace must be made by Israelis and Palestinians, but each of us has a responsibility to do our part as well."[67]

The second and more significant change concerned the consideration of both parties' perspectives. While the grievances of both camps were placed on an equal footing in 2009, the balance was disrupted in 2010. The Palestinian perspective was only briefly mentioned: "Those of us who are friends of Israel must understand that true security for the Jewish state requires an independent Palestine—one that allows the Palestinian people to live with dignity and opportunity."[68] By contrast, he expanded on the Israeli perspective:

Those who have signed on to the Arab Peace Initiative should seize this opportunity to make it real by taking tangible steps towards the normalization that it promises Israel. And those who speak on behalf of Palestinian self-government should help the Palestinian Authority politically and financially, and in doing so help the Palestinians build the institutions of their state. Those who long to see an independent Palestine must also stop trying to tear down Israel. After thousands of years, Jews and Arabs are not strangers in a strange land. After 60 years in the community of nations, Israel's existence must not be a subject for debate. Israel is a sovereign state, and the historic homeland of the Jewish people. It should be clear to all that efforts to chip away at Israel's legitimacy will only be met by the unshakeable opposition of the United

States. And efforts to threaten or kill Israelis will do nothing to
help the Palestinian people. The slaughter of innocent Israelis is
not resistance—it's injustice.[69]

The September 2011 speech reflected a new low in US ambitions
despite the May 17, 2011, statement in which Obama seemed to have
wanted to express a more ambitious position in the wake of the Arab
Spring. Obama now only insisted on one key point. The two parties
needed to reach an agreement between themselves and not expect too
much of the international community:

> I am convinced that there is no short cut to the end of a con-
> flict that has endured for decades. Peace is hard work. Peace
> will not come through statements and resolutions at the United
> Nations—if it were that easy, it would have been accomplished by
> now. Ultimately, it is the Israelis and the Palestinians who must
> live side by side. Ultimately, it is the Israelis and the Palestinians—
> not us—who must reach agreement on the issues that divide them:
> on borders and on security, on refugees and Jerusalem.[70]

Declaring on the floor of the United Nations that UN resolutions are
of little help in settling the problem was quite unprecedented, especially from a US President who claims to embrace more multilateralism. Obama justified his new position with historic examples:

> Peace depends upon compromise among people who must live
> together long after our speeches are over, long after our votes have
> been tallied. That's the lesson of Northern Ireland, where ancient
> antagonists bridged their differences. That's the lesson of Sudan,
> where a negotiated settlement led to an independent state. And
> that is and will be the path to a Palestinian state—negotiations
> between the parties.[71]

This speech revealed the self contradictory role of the United States
in pretending to be both arbitrating judge and counsel for one party.[72]
The authoritative Israeli newspaper *Haaretz* remarked in that speech
that "not one word of criticism was heard about Israel, creating unilateral physical facts on the ground. To the 2011 model Obama, only the
Palestinian approach to the UN is unilateral, objectionable and merit-
ing the death penalty. Only the very best navigators of the endless maze
of the peace process could find (...) an indirect mention of Obama

support for negotiations based on the 1967 borders and exchange of territories."[73] In dealing quasi exclusively with Jewish suffering, Obama won plaudits in Israel and among American Jewish leaders, but received lukewarm applause at the UN.[74] In Israel his standing rose significantly.[75] Of course, considering that a conflict can only be resolved if the parties have the willingness to do so seems like common sense. However, this is a highly questionable proposition. First, Obama's examples of Northern Ireland and Sudan are hardly convincing because they happen to be conflicts in which the United States was highly involved. In fact, George Mitchell, the US negotiator in Ireland, symbolically became special envoy for Middle East Peace in the first years of the Obama administration, before resigning. His work was undermined, as mentioned earlier, from the White House by Dennis Ross, who had a radically different approach to the problem.[76] In the Middle East, his plan was fought by Benjamin Netanyahu who had an intransigent position and one that was not actively endorsed by the Palestinians: "The Palestinians opposed it on the grounds, in their words, that it was worse than useless. So they refused to enter into the negotiations until nine months of the ten had elapsed. Once they entered, they then said it was indispensable. What had been worse than useless a few months before then became indispensable, and they said they would not remain in the talks unless that indispensable element were extended. We were unable to persuade the Israelis to extend it, and so the negotiations ended. Just as we were unable to persuade the Palestinians to enter into the talks and to stay in the talks."[77]

In Sudan, US involvement is such that South Sudan clearly would never have existed without its support. This is even a questionable interpretation of the Middle East. The 1978 Camp David accords between Egypt and Israel were only made possible by President Jimmy Carter's strong commitment, given how far apart their positions were despite President Anwar Sadat's trip to Jerusalem.[78] Furthermore, it is extremely surprising to hear from the president of the world's greatest power that it is no substitute for the two parties to the conflict. This would imply that the United States either has no control over them, or that it considers the status quo acceptable in relation to its global strategic interests. In 2009, the Obama administration insisted on the centrality of its role as a broker. William Burns, who was the undersecretary for the Middle East, recognized that "persistent, hard-headed, day-in-and-day-out, high-level American engagement has also been a critical ingredient for success, from Henry Kissinger's shuttle diplomacy, to Jimmy Carter at Camp David, to Jim Baker on the road to Madrid."[79] But this statement was made at the time when the administration had great expectations in the region and a lot of confidence in its capacity to pressure Israel. It was a time when the provisional freeze of Israeli settlements was considered as a decision that "falls short of the continuing Roadmap obligation for a full settlement freeze."[80] Indeed, seems unimaginable that the United States would approach a conflict between Saudi Arabia and Iran with neutrality, or express frustration about its inability to influence the parties. It is equally unthinkable that the United States would let an Asian conflict develop on the pretext that it did not have enough influence to force the parties to reach an agreement. The fact of the matter is that a great power is only powerless when it chooses to be so. The status quo undeniably hurts US strategic interests in the Middle East. However, Washington does not want a showdown with Israel, over which it wields considerable influence, but whose position in US domestic politics immunizes it against any strong pressure from the US president.

The Inevitable Abrogation of the Pact of Silence

The Arab revolutions have really only just begun. It would therefore be foolhardy to draw hasty conclusions. Yet some have already decided to interpret these revolutions as abortive political movements that will be overwhelmed by counterrevolution. In addition to being too general to explain the varying movements, this interpretation fails to explain anything at all. One would normally expect a counterrevolution to be conducted by those who oppose the revolution and hope to bring back the old order. However, there is no evidence of this. Not that the old forces are not seeking to return, as can be seen in Egypt to a certain extent. A return to the status quo nonetheless remains highly unlikely in Tunisia, Libya, and even Egypt. This is not to say that the new orders will be better than the previous ones or that Jeffersonian democracies are going to sweep over the Arab world. It simply means that a return to the past will be extremely difficult. It is quite a contradiction to speak of counterrevolution while considering the Islamists to be the likely winners of the Arab Spring. There is no doubt that Islamists did not cause the revolutions that they are now seeking to capture by democratic means. But unless revolution is equated with liberalism, the Islamists can hardly be considered counterrevolutionaries.

The Arab Spring will most likely have two major implications for US foreign policy: Arab public opinion will now have a place in Arab-American relations, and the new Arab regimes will inevitably become autonomous in relation to the West. The combination of these two elements should lead to the abrogation of the pact of silence.

The emergence of public opinion in Arab-American relations will result from the opening of Arab political systems. Now that it has more freedom to express its choices and preferences, the public will be led to opine on all economic and foreign-policy issues. Since the Arab Spring, public opinion has noticeably started to express itself much more on a number of issues. In Morocco, for example, independent experts vigorously mobilized to oppose the construction of a high-speed rail line to be built by large French companies. The desire to better control public funds and take into account the population's needs are at the heart of the Arab world's social and political demands. If the current democratic process continues, it should logically lead to a closer monitoring of economic, social, and military resources. Foreign partners will have to adapt to this new reality, as they will be dealing with much more demanding governments. Alternately, they will not be able to ignore the wishes of the population in the countries where it does not yet have a voice.

The second change is that once Arab governments are endowed with strong popular legitimacy, they will be forced to do a better job of taking into account the public's views. It is no coincidence that the new Moroccan prime minister, from the Islamist party that carried the November 2011 legislative elections, declared the following in his very first speech:

> We are aware that Morocco is a traditional ally of the EU [European Union] and the US and we have no intention to propose something different, (. . .). What we are advocating for today is to forge together and in a democratic fashion more balanced links. The balance is always to their side, with regard to certain things, [economic] interests, money and so on.[81]

Will this affect America's strategic interests in the Arab world? Caution is in order here as events continue to unfold. Moreover, several scenarios must be considered.

The first involves countries where the United States has strong strategic interests, but where political change is hindered. This applies to most of the Gulf countries, such as Saudi Arabia and Jordan. If protests were to grow in these states and the United States sided with the regimes in place, Washington's position would become increasingly awkward. For some Arab regimes, such as the Saudi regime, the United

States is viewed as a decreasingly reliable ally precisely because it has not systematically supported the status quo. Of course, this distrust is cloaked in concerns about the Israeli-Palestinian conflict, but it should not be taken at face value. The regimes criticizing the US approach to the Arab Spring are doing so because the United States did not align with their most conservative allies. That being said, even in these countries, the crisis of confidence with the United States will not have major implications. It is hard to imagine Saudi Arabia turning to Russia or China to deal with the Iranian threat. A substitute ally will be hard to find. Does this mean that the US position remains unchanged? The answer is probably no. As democratic regimes are established, their legitimacy and bargaining power will grow. A country like Egypt might not have many alternatives to US aid, but it is more than likely that this aid will now be under much greater control of a civilian government, and even more so if the army seeks to keep its privileges or block change. The United States was already starting to respond to this shift when it asked the Egyptian army to clearly commit to transferring power to a civilian authority. The most important changes in Arab policies, however, will relate to the Israeli-Palestinian conflict. Only a few months after the revolution in Egypt, the new authorities in Cairo took charge of intra-Palestinian reconciliation on a new basis by ending the blockade of Gaza requested by Israel and the United States. This does not mean that Egypt will renege on its peace agreement with Israel. Such a move would be both absolutely useless and suicidal. All it means is that Egypt, like other Arab countries, will no longer be primarily concerned with the necessity of acceding to US demands in exchange for US political accommodation. There is no indication that these new regimes are hostile to the West per se, especially since it has mostly sided with the forces of change rather than the status quo, unlike Russia, China, and other emerging powers. They simply will pursue a more autonomous path and become increasingly independent of the West. The attainment of domestic freedom will inevitably be accompanied by the attainment of foreign autonomy. While the United States can adapt to this new development, its full rehabilitation in the region will remain inextricably linked to its involvement in settling the Israeli-Palestinian conflict. Yet after showing a real willingness to engage in the settlement of this conflict, Obama backed down and also discouraged other actors such as Europe from getting involved. The Cairo speech may well have captured the sum total of Obama's policy: a lot of good will, but very few results.

CHAPTER EIGHT

Europe: The Risk-Averse Ally?

In February 2009, Barack Obama's first national security adviser, James Jones, joked that transatlantic relations had been diagnosed with terminal illness at the beginning of the 1980s.[1] It is true that in recent years the idea of a loosening of relations between Europe and the United States has increasingly taken hold, to the point of becoming a truism. The belief has only grown since Obama took office due to his low affinity for the Old World.

As always, even immediate and incomplete perceptions contain a grain of truth. The question is whether the inquiry should stop here when it is possible the issue has not been adequately framed. The United States and Europe continue to share an exceptionally wide range of interests and values at the historical, cultural, economic, and political levels. With the rise of non-Western powers such as China and India, it will not be difficult for Europeans and Americans to find common ground on many issues. At the Security Council, for example, Europeans and Americans held very similar positions on the Arab revolutions. By contrast, they were able to take stock of how their converging views on these sensitive sovereignty issues placed them at odds with the views expressed by the Russians, Chinese, and other emerging powers.[2] The only major international policy issue on which Europeans and Americans disagree concerns the settlement of the Arab-Israeli conflict. The systematic alignment of the United States with the Israeli position contrasts with the much more balanced position of most European countries, which admittedly are not unanimous. The fact that the Europeans welcomed the election of Obama with such relief, happiness, and even naïveté, underscores the scale of the old continent's expectations of the new world (see table 8.1).

Table 8.1   Obama's popularity in Europe

	2007 (Bush, in %)	2010 (Obama, in %)
Do you have a generally favorable view of the United States?		
France	39	73
Germany	30	63
Great Britain	51	65
Spain	34	61
Poland	61	74
Russia	41	57
Turkey	9	17
Egypt	21	17
China	34	58
India	59	66
Indonesia	29	59
Pakistan	15	17

Source: adapted from Pew Research Center Publications, 22-Nation Pew Global Attitudes Survey, June 17, 2001, available at : http://pewre search.org/pubs/1630/obama-more-popular-abroad-global-american -image-benefit-22-nation-global-survey.

This may be where the problem lies. There is little doubt that Europe sometimes expects a lot of the United States, which some Europeans still see as a European power; it is less certain that the United States expects as much of Europe, at least at the strategic level.[3] This imbalance is certainly not new. It has defined transatlantic relations since 1945. However, there is no question that it has increased. Europe is not a source of problems for the United States given their closely linked interests and deep interdependence. On the flip side, Europe is also not the solution to the new challenges in the world facing the United States, especially since European support on key issues can be taken for granted. As the ultimate guarantor of Europe's security, the United States has every right to ask what Europe can give in exchange for its strategic protection. What is true at the strategic level is much less so at the economic level, where the interdependence between the two partners remains very high. Indeed, the deep financial crisis Europe is undergoing is also a major US concern, which has been exacerbated by US difficulties in directly influencing its settlement. The United States is no longer the world's only economic engine. It also now needs the growth of others to jump-start its very anemic economy. This was illustrated by President Obama's unprecedented move to use the Group of Twenty (G20) summit in Cannes as an excuse to make a joint appearance with President Nicolas Sarkozy on French television. The United States and Europe have a relationship of dependency at the strategic level, and of interdependence at the economic level. The distinction between the two areas is clear-cut, although this has not always been the case.

European Downgrade?

The United States and Europe have an exceptionally strong relationship that is key to the collective well-being of their respective citizens. The vitality of this relationship is most apparent at the economic level. The value of the two-way flow of goods, services, and investment income totals $1.6 trillion, or 53 percent of the Euro-American GNP.[4] Europeans are by far the largest foreign investors in the United States, while Americans are also the largest investors in Europe.[5] Over 50 percent of US global investment is in Europe. By comparison, US investment in the BRICS (Brazil, Russia, India, China, and South Africa) accounts for no more than 7 percent of the volume of US investment in Europe.[6] In some sectors such as finance, Europe plays an even larger role. It may surprise the reader to learn that US investment in China is no larger than its investment in Spain. Perhaps even more surprisingly, US investment in the United Kingdom and the Netherlands each is larger than that in China by a factor of ten.[7] Thus the idea of US disinterest in Europe does not make much sense. By the same token, Europe's decline needs to be relativized. It would otherwise be difficult to explain the United States' interest and large presence in a supposedly ailing region of the world. This economic interdependence first clearly manifested itself during the 2008 crisis, and then during the euro crisis in 2010. The financial crisis that is shaking the euro is of vital importance to the United States because, much more so than in the past, it will affect the US recovery. Since US growth can no longer rest on the domestic market alone, it relies on foreign markets, and especially European markets, where the US position has traditionally been very strong. If Europe's deflation continues to spread, US exports and investments will suffer. Even though the exposure of US banks to sovereign risk in Southern European countries is low, their exposure to the rest of the Eurozone is much higher, making them indirectly vulnerable since European banks are most exposed to Southern European countries. This crisis has both confirmed US doubts and its weak direct influence. Its doubts stem from a failure to grasp the European model, with its national policies, intergovernmental policies, and fragments of monetary federalism. The United States was skeptical about the creation of the euro from the very beginning because it did not see how a monetary union could survive without a budgetary policy. In a way, the euro crisis proves it right, as Jacques Delors recently conceded: "When Anglo-Saxons said that a single central bank and currency without a single state would be inherently unstable, they had a point."[8] At the same time, the United States does not have a lever of decisive influence over Europe's choices. Its influence is even weaker because Europe is divided, and the most powerful of its members, Germany, has an economic culture that is the opposite of US economic culture. The Fed's proactivity is completely anathema to the German idea of a central bank's role.[9] The United States is much closer to France's approach in the sense that it would like to see the European Central Bank serve as a lender of last resort. The United States has always considered the risk of recession to be much greater and more serious than the risk of inflation. This is why it called for the implementation of a "credible firewall" in Europe that Germany is delaying by subjecting its implementation to many conditions, including a revision of European treaties.[10] This leaves the United States with only two forms of leverage: its power of persuasion and its influence in the IMF. However, the United States does not want to see greater IMF involvement until the Europeans use their own resources to deal with the crisis. This was the essence of Obama's message to the Europeans at the G20 summit in Cannes. Indeed, the resolution of the crisis is not so much a matter of means as a matter of choice.

To a certain extent the euro crisis has revealed the relative weakening of the US position in the global economy. First, the United States has become much more dependent on the growth of other regions of the world. It has also ceased to be the global economic engine. Finally, it does not have the means to directly influence the choices of European actors, particularly the most important one of all—Germany. For a long time, the United States could tell Europe, somewhat insolently, that "the dollar may be our currency, but it's your problem." Today, it is the Europeans, under duress, who are telling the United States that "the euro is our currency, but it's also your problem."

While Europeans and Americans are tied to each other when it comes to investing, they tend to diverge when it comes to trading. Transatlantic trade relations are still important, but their relative decline is just as significant. Today, 60 percent of US imports and 51 percent of its exports are with emerging and developing countries, the markets of tomorrow.[11] Europe faces the same challenge of finding new markets. However, it seems to be reacting more slowly given its history of internal trade, its social model with high standards that might be eroded by partners with lower standards, and its more marked aversion to job losses. Europe is therefore more cautious in approaching emerging countries.

This multipolar trading system has implications for the United States and Europe. Even combined, they no longer control the dynamics of global trade. They have great influence, but must increasingly deal with other actors such as China, Brazil, and India. The fact that the Doha round is currently being blocked explicitly by the United States and implicitly by China heralds a global system based on a Sino-American bipolarity encompassing multipolar relations that change depending on the issue.

While the idea of Europe's inexorable decline needs to be qualified, there is no doubt as to Europe's diminished importance relative to the emergence of new power centers. The question is why Europe's diminished influence at the economic level—the only aspect considered for the time being—affects the United States less. Indeed, by 2030 the spectacular growth of the Chinese, Indian, and Brazilian shares in global GNP will come more at the expense of Europe and Japan than of the United States. There is a simple reason for this. In the long run, the determinants of growth, wealth, and material power are demography and productivity. In both areas, Europe is at a disadvantage. Its population is less dynamic than the US population, and its productivity gains are smaller, even though one would expect the European gains to be higher since they are growing from a lower level. The United States protects its position in relation to emerging economies through strong productivity and good demographics. This explains why the erosion of its position is less marked than that of Europe.[12] In order to return to the forefront of the global competition, Europe would benefit from welcoming more immigrants and reducing market rigidities, especially in product markets that limit its productivity gains. It would also benefit from more economic and political integration to take advantage of substantial economies of scale that are key to reducing its major handicap in relation to all of its rivals: the fact that it does not constitute a uniform political entity. It is precisely on these three crucial issues that the political obstacles are the greatest because of the challenges they raise. Europeans do not want to welcome more immigrants, they are reluctant to politically integrate, and they have reservations about introducing more competition into their markets.

The Decline in Europe's Strategic Value

While Europe will continue to bring great economic prosperity to its inhabitants for years to come, this strength does not guarantee it will maintain its strategic status at the global level. The decoupling between Europe's economic and strategic values is easy to understand. As mentioned previously, Europeans and Americans share a considerable number of economic principles and values governing the market order. They both believe in the value of norms even if they disagree on their content.[13] The strategic situation is different because even in an interdependent world where everything is linked in principle, markets and security remain very distinct areas of international regulation.

Post–Cold War changes have most affected Euro-American relations in the security realm. So long as Europe was divided and the Soviet-American rift shaped the global landscape, the Euro-American relationship was based on a simple transaction. The United States guaranteed Europe's security, all the more because Europe was the frontline for its own security. In other words, the United States protected Europe, but the protection of Europe also protected the United States from the USSR. An asymmetry already existed between the protector and the protected, but what the protected offered in exchange was not negligible. Europe provided the United States with a considerable safety margin, which explains why the oft-mentioned, periodic threat of decoupling American security from European security has never actually materialized. This security margin was bolstered by a diplomatic bonus: Europeans were completely aligned with US foreign policy, except for France, which expressed its independence with even more audacity because of its conviction that the United States would ultimately guarantee its security.

Despite initial fears, the transatlantic split did not occur immediately after the Soviet Union's collapse. While the Cold War ideology instantly disappeared, it took much longer for its strategic consequences to unfold. The Balkan wars in the 1990s highlighted the importance for Europe to continue ensuring its security with US military backing (Kosovo). In the following decade the combined effects of September 11, Russia's return to the world stage, and the European Union's (EU) enlargement to Central and Eastern European countries, as well as the US neoconservative push to take on Russia, all contributed to freezing the debate. Two major crises resulted from the confluence of three factors: Moscow's bid to regain its lost status; that of former Eastern European countries to use NATO not only as a shield but also as a sword against Russia by expanding NATO's perimeter to Ukraine and potentially to any opponent of Moscow; and that of Washington to deny Moscow the legitimacy it needed to recast itself as a great power. The first was the gas crisis with Ukraine in the winter of 2005–2006, and the second, the invasion of a part of Georgia by Russian forces in the summer of 2008. In the aftermath, all the actors involved came to recognize the limits and dangers of a policy of force likely to instigate a full-blown conflict with Moscow.[14] The United States was unable to provide a security guarantee to Georgia, even though it encouraged Tbilisi to take action. Moscow faced the hostility that its conduct had raised far beyond Europe, and even in China, while major European states such as France and Germany saw the opportunity to impose a European-wide change in relations with Moscow. For Paris, as for Berlin, the prospect of a protracted confrontation with Moscow is deemed politically untenable and economically unthinkable, especially given the enormous economic opportunities offered by the Russian market, and Russia's possible participation in saving the euro. The new US policy is thus unfolding in a new context.

Should Russia Be Involved in European Security?

The new policy accords NATO a central role in the global strategy of the United States, especially because of the security guarantee that it offers Europe through this alliance. However, the United States expects more reciprocity from Europe on the ground, and not only in discourse: "We say to our friends that the alliances, treaties and international organizations we build must be credible and they must be effective. That requires a common commitment not only to listen and live by the rules, but to enforce the rules when they are, in fact, clearly violated."[15] In concrete terms, this means that the alliance should act beyond its historical geographical scope, even when the security of its members is not directly threatened:

> Because of its visibility and power, NATO may well be called upon to respond to challenges that do not directly affect its security but that still matter to its citizens and that will contribute

to the Alliance's international standing. These challenges could include the humanitarian consequences of a failed state, the devastation caused by a natural disaster, or the dangers posed by genocide or other massive violation of human rights.[16]

With the Europeans, the United States does not want to discuss Europe so much as global issues of concern that it would like for Europe to address in one way or another to unburden the United States.[17] NATO would cease to be a purely territorial alliance to become an expeditionary corps; the United States considers these two objectives to be perfectly compatible.[18]

In this context, Article 5 of the NATO treaty, stipulating that "the Parties agree that an armed attack against one or more of them in Europe or North America shall be considered an attack against them all" is understood in a larger sense. An attack might perfectly well take unconventional forms and might occur outside of member states' territories. One could argue that this already occurred in 2001 when, in the aftermath of September 11, NATO invoked the famous Article 5. The gesture had significant symbolic value, but its operational effectiveness proved to be more modest. The United States witnessed Europe's limited operational capabilities, while the Europeans experienced the Americans' reluctance to integrate them into their strategic planning. In fact, despite the triggering of Article 5, at the request of the United States the military campaign in Afghanistan did not start under the banner of NATO. It is first and foremost the Europeans who are requesting strict compliance with Article 5, whereas the United States does not want to see Article 5 become a limiting factor in NATO action: "To guard against these threats, which may or may not reach the level of an Article 5 attack, NATO must update its approach to the defense of Alliance territory while also enhancing its ability to prevail in military operations and broader security missions beyond its borders."[19] The security guarantee is important because it obviously has a direct impact on Europe's relationship with Russia, against which NATO was created. In a number of Central and Eastern European countries, where the Bush administration's hostility to Russia was perceived as an additional reassurance of security from Washington, the relativizing of the US guarantee caused genuine concern, as reflected in an open letter from political and intellectual leaders to President Obama. It is no accident that the letter criticized NATO and therefore the Americans for failing to make the Article 5 guarantee stronger and more credible: "It was a mistake not to commence with proper Article 5 defense planning for new members after NATO was enlarged."[20] Simply put, the idea was to reassert that NATO should primarily serve as a deterrent to Russia. But the United States no longer views its relations with Moscow in these exact terms. Russia is now a partner, not an opponent, even if this perspective is not universally popular in the United States, and certainly not in Congress. The most tangible sign of this strategic reappraisal was the redefined US antimissile system (the well-known "third site"), which the Bush administration sought to deploy in Poland (missile battery) and the Czech Republic (radars).[21] The official purpose of this shield was to contain a ballistic missile threat from potentially nuclear countries such as Iran, and was therefore not directly relevant to European security. However, this is not how the issue was perceived in either Eastern Europe or Russia. Central and Eastern European countries sought to capitalize on this windfall by firmly anchoring the United States to European security through an American guarantee against Russia.[22] By proposing to implement an alternative system that would deploy missiles on ships in the Mediterranean, the United States signaled its refusal to create a new source of tension with Russia. The United States recognizes that the two countries share many common objectives and interests: combating proliferation, terrorism, piracy, cybercrime, and drug trafficking from Afghanistan; joint participation in peacekeeping operations; Russia's decisive role in bringing US equipment to Afghanistan. In characterizing NATO's association with Russia, the Secretary General of NATO went as far as to declare: "NATO will never attack Russia. Never. And we do not think Russia will attack NATO. We have stopped worrying about that and Russia should stop worrying about that as well."[23] Hence the idea of moving beyond transatlantic security toward a Euro–Atlantic one bringing together the United States, Europe, and Russia: "The new Strategic Concept should reaffirm NATO's desire to help build a cooperative Euro–Atlantic security order which includes security cooperation with Russia."[24]

A formal cooperation structure between Russia and NATO (the NATO-Russia Council) has existed since 2002. However, the consensus is that it has been deficient in addressing disagreements between Americans and Russians throughout the past decade. That is why, in their open letter to President Obama, Central European authorities argued that one of the best ways to engage in dialogue with Moscow would be to revert to the practice "where NATO member countries enter into dialogue with Moscow with a coordinated position."[25] In other words, they were reaffirming the idea that Europeans and Americans should first reach an agreement among themselves before discussing anything with Moscow, precisely to prevent Russia from taking advantage of possible internal divisions that might arise. Here again, the United States has unofficially adopted a different perspective:

> The days are long since past when the United States and Europe can agree on a policy or a set of programs and then present them to the Russians and hope that the Russians will acquiesce in fait accompli. We need to have Russia at the outset of our discussions if we want them to be with us at the end.[26]

The gap between the spirit of the open letter from Eastern European leaders and the way Washington is rethinking European security has created an undeniable malaise. Not that Europe has a consistent position on this issue, especially since two levels are involved: the EU and the member states.

From the US standpoint it would be unacceptable for Europe to build up its own defense for its own purposes while continuing to benefit from the American strategic guarantee.[27] This requirement has become all the more important at a time when the United States is calling for burden sharing. The British have traditionally shared this point of view because they do not want to lose their position as intermediary between Europe and the United States, especially now that Washington no longer treats London like the special partner it would like to be. Germany is less supportive, as it envisages the formation of an autonomous European defense capability. The debate remains theoretical, though, in light of the limited progress that has been made on the issue of European defense. The lack of European consensus on this matter has allowed the United States to stay out of the debate. The United States has provisionally concluded that the EU's comparative advantage in security matters lies in civilian missions.[28] The Libyan crisis proved it right.

If the issue is considered from the perspective of member states and the role they could play in NATO's new strategic framework, Germany clearly emerges as the country that is most comfortable with the idea of including Russia in Euro-Atlantic security.[29] It is not completely by chance that a former German defense minister is calling for Russia's entry into NATO.[30] This position is admittedly a minority one in Germany, but it reflects the dual objective of German security policy: to tie the United States to European security, and to tie Russia to Europe. Hence its support for the zero option that Obama proposed in his Prague speech, as well as its approval for the implementation of a missile defense shield closely linking Russia, Europe, and the United States to deal with a potential Iranian or Korean threat.[31] While Germany is perfectly comfortable with this Euro-Atlantic security project, it has a harder time accepting the idea of NATO's transformation into an expeditionary force that would operate outside of Europe. Germany does not question the relevance of the idea, but rather fears its domestic political implications. To participate in an expeditionary force naturally involves deploying troops abroad. Here again, the Libyan case showed that Germany could go very far in balking at taking on international responsibilities. Germany not only refused to engage militarily in the conflict, but also refused to vote for the Security Council's resolution 1973, which authorized the protection of civilian populations. The German chancellor had initially suggested to the French president that Germany would vote for resolution 1973 in the Security Council. But in the end she went along with the position of the German foreign minister, who had expressed his hostility to this resolution from the outset. The German minister's choice was, however, strongly opposed by the German foreign affairs ministry. In a symbolic gesture, the German ambassador to the UN who was instructed to abstain, immediately apologized to the head of French diplomacy after the vote for resolution 1973, for which the latter had come to advocate at the UN.[32]

Germany has thus staked a middle ground, in between the countries of Central and Eastern Europe, which would like NATO to remain a territorial alliance in the classical sense, and Britain and Denmark, which have no objections to the idea of an expeditionary force under US command. Germany fully agrees with Washington that NATO should no longer be seen as an alliance that is primarily aimed at deterring Russia. Yet it is not willing to deploy German forces for operations on foreign soil, and even more unwilling to give up the caveats it imposes on the use of force—a long-standing issue for the United States.[33] The French are in line with the German position with regard to the necessity of integrating Russia into European security. France also shares Germany's reservations about turning NATO into a purely expeditionary force, not because it is reluctant to deploy troops abroad, but because it fears that such a large scope would restrict its discretion and freedom of involvement. However, France differs from Germany on the nuclear issue. It remains staunchly opposed to option zero, which would increase the strategic asymmetry between the United States and

Europe. The French argument is that equal efforts cannot be expected from powers accounting for 90 percent of the global nuclear arsenal and from those holding the remaining 10 percent. France also has greater reservations than Germany about the implementation of an antimissile defense system in Europe in the form that the United States proposed at the November 2010 NATO summit in Lisbon. France certainly formally consented to the program, but it is unlikely that France would adhere to the program if it were actually implemented because it would clearly undermine France's strategic autonomy. Former French defense minister Hervé Morin summarized the risks:

> "The anti-missile defense system, as proposed, is a program (…) with a currently unknown technological outcome. It is (…) based on American technologies and programs. At present the United States is only proposing that Europe participate in the investments linked to command and control."
>
> He added: "Of course, the Americans (…) will be the main contributors. But what is the threat? Is it only Iranian missiles? (…) What military appropriations will be affected to compensate for the new program? Obviously, if the budget remains constant, these programs will affect (…) those we need for all of today's regional crises: aircraft, helicopters, the navy, and light-armored vehicles. At a time when our hardware needs have never been so glaring, does it make sense to weaken ourselves further?"
>
> Finally, he notes: "The best way to ensure one's security and sovereignty is to be respected through military credibility. This is not an issue for the United States (…) since it has everything: deterrence and conventional armed forces. Europeans are in an altogether different situation. Defense appropriations are inexorably falling. Their armed forces are increasingly suffering from a shortfall in conventional equipment."[34]

While the French harbor reservations about the missile-defense shield, one can easily imagine that these are magnified tenfold for the Russians. The Obama administration certainly did everything to allay Russian hostility to the US project. To this end, it proposed a coupling of NATO's missile defense shield with that of Russia.[35] However, the fulfillment of this objective faces many obstacles that have stirred up the traditional mistrust between Russians and Americans. The Russians are demanding either a veto right on the missile shield's use, or a formal NATO guarantee that the shield will not affect Russian deterrence—in other words that NATO will not use it against Russia.[36] Moreover, they have requested interoperability between the Russian and American shields. These two requests are difficult for the United States to accept, especially given that the American security community still considers Russia, like China, to be a mortal threat to the United States: "The Russians still have a very formidable nuclear arsenal, which does pose potentially a mortal threat to us."[37] The strategic distrust between the United States and Russia therefore remains considerable despite Obama's determination to reduce it.

Burden Sharing: The Libyan Revelation

The key issue for the United States is strategic burden sharing among the NATO allies.

> The challenge for NATO is matching its level of ambition with its political will to resource the means to accomplish its ambitions (…). The 2010 Strategic Concept must, unlike its predecessor, address the ways and means. Absent that, once again, the disconnect between the vision—or level of ambition—and the political will to commit the resources will continue.[38]

Yet, not only has nothing changed, the problem has probably worsened, as revealed by the Libyan crisis in the spring of 2011. Indeed, at the beginning of the crisis the French and British clearly put themselves on the line. The reasons for their engagement are interesting to analyze. For France, the commitment to Libya countered its fiasco in Tunisia. In the latter country, the first to be affected by the Arab Spring, France initially gave the impression that it did not see anything coming and that it might even have been tempted to rescue Zine El Abidine Ben Ali's discredited regime. French support for Arab dictators is no accident. It results from a French realpolitik that has consisted of accepting these dictatorships as the best bulwark against Islam. This was the French version of the aforementioned pact of silence. Furthermore, there is a long-standing French tradition of always defending regimes in power and refusing to engage in dialogue with their opponents. For example, the new Tunisian president, Moncef Marzouki, did not meet with French political leaders at any point during his ten years of exile in France.[39] However, when it became apparent that the Tunisian revolution was not just a democratic accident in a sea of dictatorships but the beginning of a vast public protest movement against Arab regimes, the French position changed, even though President Sarkozy responded coolly to the news of Hosni Mubarak's fall, unlike President Obama.[40] A new reality quickly set in: France could either continue to embrace the status quo and risk losing all influence in a region it considered to be strategic, or France could be on the right side of history and accept that the legitimacy of authoritarian Arab regimes had been deeply shaken.

The Libyan crisis allowed France to regain its footing in the Arab world, even if the exact conditions under which it decided to get involved are unclear.[41] Of all the European countries France was best placed to take the lead since, independent of its own military capabilities, which allowed it to consider an operation in Libya early on, it also benefited from not having a colonial past in this country, unlike Italy and Great Britain. Along with all the other Western countries, France had renewed ties with Muammar Gaddafi, who was received in Paris with great fanfare. However, there was no historical or cultural complicity with Libya comparable to that uniting France with Maghreb countries such as Morocco, Algeria, and Tunisia. This lack of historical proximity also played well with Gaddafi's opponents. Since they did not have any historical disagreements with France, nothing stood in their way of seeking its support. America's initial reluctance to intervene militarily in Libya also spurred France. The French saw an opportunity to play a leading role.

The British motive is harder to interpret because North Africa has never been a priority area for Britain. It is nonetheless possible to find explanations for David Cameron's decision to get involved alongside France. First, the Libyan intervention was perfectly consistent with Britain's treasured tradition of liberal intervention. The Iraqi fiasco could, and presumably should, have deterred London from intervening in the Arab world again. Libya was significantly different from Iraq, however. The first difference was that the intervention in Libya undeniably enjoyed international legitimacy, which was reinforced by the Arab League's *nihil obstat*. Cameron could thus easily say that he was remaining faithful to Britain's liberal tradition without committing Tony Blair's errors. Libya was an opportunity for London to erase the memories of Iraq and to show that it could succeed where Blair had clearly failed. Another basic reason behind Britain's engagement had to do with the United States. Blair had discredited himself over Iraq by aligning with the United States. Cameron purposely did not wait to see what the Americans would do about Libya before starting to act. He understood that the United States had unilaterally ended the special relationship between them and Britain. He therefore concluded that Great Britain had to regain its autonomy and think for itself even if it does not have an alternative to its privileged relationship with the United States. Even if an alternative existed, it would certainly not be in Europe. Great Britain remains fiercely opposed to a powerful Europe. By contrast, it is extremely amenable to closely cooperating with European states individually, and especially with France. A few months before the Franco-British intervention in Libya, the two countries had signed a highly important nuclear cooperation treaty. It is quite possible that Great Britain did not want to let France intervene alone in Libya, as this could have disturbed the political and strategic parity between the two countries. British diplomacy has never sought to dominate Europe. On the flip side, it has always sought to ensure that no continental power would overtake it: Germany on the economic front, and France on the strategic front.

The End of the Suez Cycle

The Libyan crisis sheds a particularly interesting light on European dynamics at the international level, and especially in relation to the United States.

Indeed, the joint Franco-British intervention ended what could be called the Suez cycle. In 1956, the Suez intervention led by France and Great Britain to overturn Colonel Gamal Abdel Nasser following the nationalization of the Suez Canal resulted in a grand political fiasco. The French and British drew diametrically opposed lessons from this crushing failure. Great Britain concluded that its survival as a medium power required a strategic alignment with the United States. France came to the opposite conclusion. Particularly after the end of the Algerian war, it decided that its survival as a power required a distancing from the United States, with which, of course, it simultaneously did not want to jeopardize its alliance.[42] Accordingly, France withdrew from NATO's integrated military command in 1966 when the US escalation in Vietnam began. Granted, over the course of the past 50 years the French and British have seen eye-to-eye on many occasions, even on military matters: Yugoslavia, the first Gulf War, and the Kosovo war. However, the United States was very present in all of these situations. This was not the case in Libya, which can be considered the first NATO operation that the United States has not sought to lead. US operational involvement in this conflict was certainly crucial.

Politically, though, France and Great Britain were a driving force that the United States did not seek to dispute. In a paradoxical twist, tension between the English and French on the one hand and the Americans on the other flared when the former felt that the United States, which was concerned about a protracted conflict, hesitated to commit additional military resources to help hasten Gaddafi's demise. Admittedly, France was also initially reluctant to intervene in Libya. On March 6, in Cairo, Alain Juppé declared that, "France and several of its partners do not support a Western military intervention in Libya that would have very negative effects."[43] Juppé, the head of French diplomacy, was loath to intervene through NATO, which he perceived as an instrument in the hands of the United States. He first wanted to explore the possibility of a European intervention supported by the Arab League. Hence his statement to the National Assembly, where he explained: "France has taken a very clear position: NATO is not the right organization for the task."[44] This initial plan was shelved for several reasons. The first is that apart from France, all the other countries made their military intervention conditional on NATO's involvement. Even Sweden did, despite the fact that it is not a member. This instinctive preference for NATO is attributable to the habit of working through this institution. It can also be explained by the reservations that many European countries had about serving under the political and military control of France through the EU. Others were uncomfortable with EU military involvement in this conflict altogether. Finally, the United States itself made its involvement contingent on a rapid transfer of the command to NATO. In fact, NATO paradoxically gave France more leeway to act than if its actions had been placed under US command, as was the case in the first 15 days of the intervention. The Libyan intervention most likely reconciled France with NATO, even if France deplored the extremely unwieldy chain of command and the military obstacles that many European countries created through the large number of caveats placed on their forces. For example, Spanish refueling aircraft could only provide air-to-air refueling to planes that were not conducting air strikes.[45] Italian ships were anchored off the coast of Benghazi where there was no threat, but were not allowed to approach the coasts or Tripolitania, where the danger lay.[46] France did ensure from the outset that NATO would not serve as the political framework for resolving the Libyan conflict. Hence the creation of an International Contact Group on Libya that went well beyond NATO countries, including many Arab countries in the conflict resolution process.

To the same end of preventing NATO from overtaking the conflict, France did its utmost to involve the EU in Libya, especially after the great repudiation reflected in Germany's refusal to vote for resolution 1973 in the Security Council. However, France discovered a total lack of common European willingness to act in Libya on anything other than humanitarian grounds. On paper, there was a series of European agreements that could have served as a basis for European action: the 2008 Declaration on strengthening military capabilities, the 2008 Capability Development Plan, the 2010 pooling and sharing initiatives, and the 2011 Weimar agreements. When, under pressure from France, a process was launched to explore possible military options, the structures of the European External Action Service (EEAS) refused to study the options prepared by NATO.[47] Thus, as a high-level officer representing France at the NATO meetings put it, "It was as if there was a hang-up, in principle, over the idea of an instrument of power and the possible use of force."[48]

Even in the humanitarian field the results did not meet French expectations. For instance, Paris wanted to create humanitarian corridors in Libya, but faced opposition from Brussels, which saw no need for it, especially since setting up the corridors would require the deployment of armed forces. It should not be assumed, however, that political considerations prompted Brussels' refusal, or that Catherine Ashton torpedoed the French initiative, as claimed in certain French diplomatic and military circles.[49] The truth of the matter is that even the UN organization that is in charge of humanitarian issues (Office for the Coordination of Humanitarian Affairs [OCHA]) considered the implementation of these corridors to be useless.[50] Furthermore, France itself did not have internally consistent positions on the EU's role in relation to NATO. From the beginning of the Libyan operation President Sarkozy did not see NATO posing any particular problem for France, besides the unwieldy chain of command and heavy bureaucratic processes that slowed down strikes against identified targets.[51] The Quay d'Orsay's position was substantially different since the head of French diplomacy did everything to involve the EU before NATO in managing the Libyan crisis. He knew from experience that Europeans generally refuse to engage in strategic planning if NATO does so beforehand.[52] He also sought to make use of the momentum created by the Libyan crisis to revive the idea of a European military headquarters, which would have been critical in the Libyan case had the Europeans expressed a will to act collectively on the military front.

It quickly became apparent, though, that the British were, as usual, totally opposed to this idea, even if it only has symbolic value. France can claim that virtually all the European countries, apart from Great Britain, support its idea. But the concrete results of this near-unanimity are trifling. Besides France, the only other country with significant military resources is precisely Great Britain. Europe is therefore in a paradoxical situation where those who embrace a military Europe do not have the means to build it (except for France), and those who reject it have the means to take effective action (Great Britain). The Libyan crisis therefore confirmed the European paradox whereby Europe is very active through some of its members but completely inert at the community level. For some, this is a lesser evil given that the member states are, after all, members of Europe. Others see the impossibility of building a political Europe. During the NATO summit this past June, the outgoing defense secretary, Robert Gates, reiterated his concern about the survival of NATO, specifically because of the unequal burden-sharing between Americans and Europeans:

> In the past, I've worried openly about NATO turning into a two-tiered alliance: Between members who specialize in 'soft' humanitarian, development, peacekeeping, and talking tasks, and those conducting the 'hard' combat missions. Between those willing and able to pay the price and bear the burdens of alliance commitments, and those who enjoy the benefits of NATO membership—be they security guarantees or headquarters billets—but don't want to share the risks and the costs. This is no longer a hypothetical worry. We are there today. And it is unacceptable.[53]

These remarks were seconded by the bitter disappointment of the chief of staff of the French armed forces who lamented "the slow progress of Europe, which, depending on the situation, is either cacophonous or voiceless, and incapable of seeing itself as a global power on the international scene."[54]

However, the United States may not get the response that it has a right to expect. The Europeans are unlikely as ever to increase their war effort out of budgetary concerns, which the economic crisis has heightened, and political and social imperatives that underscore a strong aversion to military risk. Of all the member states of both the EU and NATO, only France, Great Britain, and Greece devote 2 percent of their GNP to defense.[55] Numerous public-opinion polls have further confirmed this aversion.

According to the 2009 Transatlantic Trends and to the German Marshall Fund of the United States, 71 percent of Americans agree that "under some conditions, war is necessary to obtain justice"; whereas only 25 percent of Europeans agree with this statement. [56] These different perceptions of war and conflict are even starker when the American and European publics are asked about a number of specific conflicts such as Iran or Afghanistan. Only 18 percent of Europeans surveyed support the possible use of military force against Iran, versus 47 percent of Americans.[57] The results are comparable for Afghanistan: 77 percent of Europeans disapprove of increasing the number of troops in Afghanistan, compared to only 19 percent who approve. This disapproval is expressed by virtually all the European states, including new member states such as Poland (80 percent) and Romania (84 percent).[58]

A report from the European Defense Agency perhaps best summarizes the European philosophy on the use of force:

> Interventions will not necessarily involve fighting battles. The presence of multinational forces (...) may well prevent hostilities from breaking out. Or they may help to stabilize a country or region after a political accord. Indeed, the scope of ESDP [European Security and Defence Policy] missions requires military contributions to be appropriately tailored, trained and readied to conduct a broad range of operations, in potentially austere areas and against diverse threats. In cases of intervention by force the main task will be to gain control of the dynamics of conflict, reduce its destructive power and break the cycle of violence. The objective of interventions is not "victory" as traditionally understood, but moderation, balance of interests and peaceful resolution of conflicts—in short, stability.[59]

This perspective goes to the heart of Europe's aversion to war.[60] To intervene militarily without making war, designating an enemy, or seeking victory is to reject Carl Schmitt's vision of politics, according to which political action is always pursued with reference to an enemy.[61] Europe envisions conducting military interventions not to make war, but to prevent it. Of the three levels of action identified in the Petersberg tasks (humanitarian and rescue tasks; peacekeeping tasks; tasks of combat forces in crisis management, including peacemaking), only the first two have served as frameworks for most European interventions. This is not surprising given that the third one involves a more significant risk of war. It is not clear in what way or how this social reality would be able to change rapidly, especially since aversion to war does not have entirely negative consequences. The disastrous results of the Iraq War as well as the ongoing political impasse in Afghanistan suggest that the benchmark for political success in increasingly asymmetric conflicts is not necessarily linked to an escalation in the use of military force. American public opinion, which was initially convinced that these forays were necessary, in retrospect now seems to be convinced that they are harmful.[62] Furthermore, while the United States is calling on Europeans to show solidarity, it is not always willing to involve them in its strategic decisions on the ground. Thus, as in the past, the major issue for Europe is not so much to determine how it should respond to US expectations, but rather to ponder its own strategic intentions, which will then enable it to better address US demands.[63] Europe is not so much a problem for the United States as it is for itself.

Conclusion: Limited Achievements

To take stock of an American president's foreign policy after a four-year term is a perilous enterprise in the absence of a clear and rigorous methodology. Take the example of the Iraq war. Barack Obama's goal was to end it and withdraw. Formally, he clearly succeeded. There have not been any US troops in Iraq since December 2011. Except that the decision to withdraw the troops was made by his predecessor at the end of his term and that the conditions under which the United States left the country are worrisome, to say the least. American political influence in Iraq is decreasing as Iran's is strengthening and as Baghdad, which is increasingly linked to Tehran, seeks to exclude the Sunnis from politics. Thus, the promise to withdraw was kept but at the price of strategic defeat. This failure is obviously not attributable to Obama, who had opposed the war. However, he was not able to either turn the situation around by extending, as he had hoped, the American presence in Iraq past 2012, or to impose a political compromise between Shiites and Sunnis. The case of Afghanistan appears to be very different since Obama clearly chose to expand the war. He did win a significant symbolic victory by eliminating Osama Bin Laden and putting the Taliban on the defensive. Yet despite the extent of American involvement in Afghanistan, it is now likely that the United States will start withdrawing after 2014 without having clearly defined the outline of a political solution in line with its interests in the region. Even more worrisome is the collapse of Obama's strategy for Pakistan. The partnership with Islamabad is in tatters, and American-Pakistani relations have fallen to pre-September 11 levels: minimal cooperation based on extreme distrust. In fact, from all the strategic challenges to US security that Obama inherited—Iran, North Korea, Iraq, Afghanistan, Pakistan, and the Israeli-Palestinian conflict—he has achieved virtually no significant political gains.

From this perspective, it can clearly be concluded that his achievements are limited. In the end, his undeniably extraordinary popularity and charisma were of little avail. Notwithstanding his skillful management of the Arab Spring, the only real strategic surprise he had to face, his credibility in the Muslim world has since steadily eroded. Rightly or wrongly, the Cairo speech's promises have not been kept. Obama's only real great breakthrough in foreign policy, and by no means an insignificant one, was to release the United States from the hold of the ideology of September 11 in which the previous administration had deliberately kept the country. Jettisoning the war-on-terror rhetoric allowed the United States to regain a strategic political legitimacy that it had partly lost, without lowering its military guard. This was no easy feat. Jimmy Carter had sought to break away from Richard Nixon and Vietnam, but US conduct was rightly or wrongly interpreted as that of a weak and indecisive state, for which he paid dearly in Iran and Afghanistan. While Obama is not Carter, he has also not been a "Nixon in China" who is able to turn the tables and propose to Iran, Pakistan, and to some extent Israel, new rules that take account of America's broader interests while incorporating those of its three partners: a declared enemy (Iran), a frenemy (Pakistan), and a key ally (Israel). This inability to change the strategic reality owes much to Obama's personality. As a careful man whose only doctrine is pragmatism, it could be said that Obama is a pragmatic doctrinaire. Due to the color of his skin, he must constantly prove that he is an American patriot, because his election has not eliminated the US color line.[1] But beyond the man is the American and global system. Obama remains a constrained president on most issues. He is constrained by the choices of his predecessors; by the severity of the economic and financial crisis that is forcing the United States to be increasingly more selective in choosing its commitments; by Congress's ideological and political influence; by the polarization of American society, which is turning its back on liberal values to endorse libertarian and antistatist values; and finally by the power structure of other international actors. When Nixon made his trip to China he only had to deal with one interlocutor, who was moreover able to maintain secrecy. Additionally, in a bipolar configuration, the gains were almost automatic: the overture to Beijing weakened the USSR.

The United States faces much more complex diplomatic and strategic relations today. Concerning Iran, Obama must confront unstable coalitions that offset each other and prevent any substantive negotiations between the two countries. The challenge in Pakistan is different, but its political fragmentation significantly hinders US policy. Finally, regarding Israel, which unlike Iran and Pakistan is a democratic state, the difficulty in shaping the policies of a country that so disrupts US strategy in the Arab world is attributable to the extreme fragility of Israel's ruling coalition. The fragility is structural and rooted in Israel's fully proportional voting system. Internal power structures constitute an undeniable constraint, as reflected in the failure of Washington's initial offer to Tehran addressing the nuclear problem. But this does not explain everything. The United States also had trouble defining the terms of a possible grand bargain. An agreement with Iran would require the consent of Israel and the Gulf countries, which do not share the same objectives or worldview. A real agreement with Islamabad would involve pressuring India, which the United States needs to counterbalance China, and which would never let itself be forced into an agreement with Islamabad by the United States. With Israel, the terms are apparently simpler: in exchange for a stronger US security guarantee, Israel would accept the existence of a Palestinian state based on the 1967 borders. An internal US constraint comes into play here: any distancing from Israel is politically unacceptable to most Americans. Israel is a domestic political topic in the United States. This is a separate issue that avoids an ultimately simple question: does America's unconditional support for Israel harm US strategic interests in the region? Obama clearly has not succeeded in escaping the domestic constraints on US foreign policy. It is for this reason that his foreign-policy record is inseparable from the US foreign policy record under his administration.

Resilient Assets

This refers to the distinctive features that underscore the continuity in America's key strengths as well as the persistence of its vulnerabilities.

An Unsurpassed Ability to Project Force around the World in Order to Punish an Opponent Threatening US Security

The United States has a vast military superiority that has considerably increased since the end of the Cold War and that Barack Obama has committed to maintaining, especially vis-à-vis China. US military expenditures account for half of global military expenditures. US surface vessels are superior to those of all the other navies in the world combined, the United States has a first-strike nuclear capability against its former Russian rival, and its military research and development program alone is equivalent to 80 percent of the Chinese military budget.[2] US military expenditures account for 4.5 percent of its GNP, versus a global average of 2.4 percent and a European average of only 1.69 percent.[3] While the financial constraints on the US economy are forcing America to adjust its military, the readjustment does not necessarily imply a decline. The Obama administration's decision to reduce the military budget will result in scaling back US conventional forces, which will no longer be able to wage wars on two fronts. However, the consequences of this reduction will remain relative. First, they will not affect the cutting edge of American military power, including its Special Forces, intelligence, and anti-cyber terrorism activities. Second, the reductions must be viewed in the context that expenditures are at an exceptionally high level, since US military expenditures in 2012 were 80 percent higher than they were in 2001.[4] Finally, and most significantly, there is an increasingly weak correlation between military means and strategic gains. Even though the United States was technically capable of waging wars on two fronts does not mean that it won them. In fact, the only real question is not whether the reduced US military expenditures affected its operational capabilities, but rather whether the reduction led to a demilitarization of US policy, that is, an attenuation of its "addiction to war" to use Steve Walt's expression.[5] It is very likely that Obama is so inclined. Even if he was driven to increase US military efforts in Afghanistan, this choice was part of a strategy à la Charles De Gaulle in Algeria, aiming to create a better military balance of power as a step toward a political solution. As for the intervention in Libya, it was carefully calibrated and ultimately very successful. As Anne Marie Slaughter put it, there will always be good and bad military interventions.[6] Obama is clearly seeking to demilitarize a US policy that had evidently failed to produce tangible results, while carefully seeking to avoid sending a signal that might be interpreted as a sign of disengagement in Beijing or Tehran. Hence the insistence on always compensating for the reduction in US forces with the determination to maintain America's military supremacy in the world.

An Ability to Assure and Reassure Allies

More than 20 years after the end of the Cold War, it is striking to see that America's ability to assure and reassure its allies has lost none of its importance or vigor. It exercises this power in the Middle East, as well as in Asia and in Europe. This is quite exceptional, although the United States must increasingly deal with independent regional actors in these three regions. Countries such as Japan, South Korea, the Philippines, Thailand, Australia, and now Vietnam seek an American security guarantee that they deem necessary either because of the North Korean threat, the Chinese threat, or both. None of these countries has the ambition or will to directly confront or create conflict with China. All are moreover increasingly important economic partners for Beijing. However, as their economies become more closely intertwined with the Chinese economy, they are almost automatically seeking an additional US guarantee, as reflected by the 2011 American-Australian agreement providing for the deployment of US troops in Australia. In some cases this rebalancing act stems from the precautionary principle. Since China is a rising power, it is appropriate to guard against its potentially baneful power. In other cases, it results from the existence of actual territorial conflicts in the South China Sea between Beijing and several Asian countries. Beijing has no interest in using force to settle these differences. It advocates peaceful bilateral solutions, but it also naturally relies on a favorable regional balance of power to advance its interests. In this respect, its priority is to prevent the United States from intervening as an arbiter between it and Asian countries. Yet this is precisely what the United States refuses to do since it does not want to be excluded in any way. It aspires to play the role of either mediating potential conflicts between China and its neighbors, or protecting the latter in the event that arbitration fails and Chinese threats emerge. Washington has succeeded in taking advantage of tension between Beijing and its neighbors by developing bilateral relations with them, but also by encouraging crosscutting and triangular cooperation: Japan-South Korea, South Korea-Australia, Japan-India and so on. These states have adjusted their China policies and broader defense strategies, and consultation between concerned countries has grown.[7]

As China pursues an Asian strategy that aims to deny the United States regional arbitration authority between China and its neighbors, the United States is seeking to frustrate China's area denial strategy by strengthening its relations with the Association of Southeast Asian Nations (ASEAN), Japan, and South Korea, and by impeding Asian economic integration around Beijing.[8] This explains the TPP (Trans-Pacific partnership) project that the United States proposed to Asian countries at the end of 2011. All are officially welcome to join in the creation of a preferential trading area between the United States and the Pacific countries. In effect, the objective is to exclude China by setting the bar too high and to decrease Asia's economic dependence on Beijing. The TPP is a political response to China's assertiveness as China asserts its territorial claims in the South China Sea, and vis-à-vis India and Japan.[9] The Obama administration is clearly disappointed with its modest strategic gains in the broader Middle East, and is therefore strategically turning its attention to Asia in order to deal with China, even if it means disengaging from the Middle East.[10] However, this political message is extremely ambiguous. It can be interpreted as a willingness to disengage from useless conflicts and wars such as Iraq, but it may also appear as a form of calculated resignation in the face of failure, or as a US refusal to bring all its weight to bear on pressing international-security problems such as the Israeli–Palestinian conflict. The political risk is to overplay a potential confrontation with China to conceal Obama's failure in the Middle East. This calculation seems all the more risky in the absence of a solution to either the Iranian crisis or the Israeli–Palestinian crisis that are likely to remind the United States of its responsibilities in the Middle East. The application of oil sanctions against Tehran will force the United States to become more involved in this crisis to remain credible, and to slide toward the inherently risky logic of regime change in Iran.[11]

While America's Asian allies are reassured by President Obama's commitment, the Europeans are much less so, precisely because the strategic threats to the old continent are much weaker and are therefore less important to the United States than they were in the past, as highlighted by the Libyan crisis. But paradoxically, this fact has had no major consequences on transatlantic relations. While the United States does not want to make up for Europe's military deficiencies, the Europeans are even less willing to bridge a possible US gap. Only a Russian or Iranian threat could change the situation. And even under this assumption, Europeans would be much more tempted to call upon the United States than to take responsibility for their own security.

Considerable Economic Potential and Attractiveness

All the evidence suggests that for the next 20 years, the United States will continue to be the leading global power by dint of its ability to include and combine the principal attributes of power: to generate material wealth on the basis of high productivity and to maintain demographic vitality, which is a prerequisite to any global ambitions. Wealth creation is rooted in improving the individual and collective well-being of citizens by controlling the complex innovation chain. This includes not only the ability to create and to invent, but also to provide an environment that fosters innovative birth and development.[12] In this area, as in many others, the United States will maintain its lead in protecting intellectual property rights, creating an environment that is conducive to innovation and encouraging creativity, but it will not be immune to an emerging power catch-up.

Demographic vitality is America's second great asset. Granted, it is not as great as that of China and especially India, but it remains incomparably stronger than that of the two other important major economic centers—Europe and Japan. The combination of these two factors explains why the redistribution of material power over the next 20 years will harm Europe and Japan more than the United States.

Between 2002 and 2006, during America's political dark years, financial inflows from abroad, especially from China, covered more than half of the US current account deficit.[13] The confidence that the US economy offers to the world in economic opportunities and legal safeguards is so great that it defies the rules of global savings flows. The economic theory is that surplus savings should flow from rich countries to poor countries, where capital is much more profitable. Yet the exact opposite is occurring as the bulk of savings flow to the United States, which can thereby easily finance its double deficit. In the aftermath of the 2008 crisis, it was common to conclude that it would be impossible for the United States to continue on this path without exacerbating global imbalances. But two years after the beginning of the worst crisis that the capitalist world has experienced since 1929, countries with high savings such as China and Japan are still financing the American deficit. Paradoxically, the crisis has intensified the awkward relation between China and the United States. China needs export growth in order to maintain job growth and preserve social stability. As China continues to run current account surpluses by exporting to the United States, it has little alternative to buying US Treasuries with the reserves it accumulates while managing its exchange rate. The United States will continue to need willing buyers for the debt issued to finance its budget deficit, especially if the household savings rate starts drifting toward precrisis levels.[14] Of course, no one knows how long this dynamic will continue. However, between the two extremes—a brutal correction whereby China would "punish" the United States by ceasing to invest its surpluses in the United States, and a gradual rebalancing whereby the Chinese would increasingly invest their savings domestically—there is a range of intermediate situations. It is not impossible that the correction will take place gradually as the Chinese economy rebalances toward increased domestic consumption. In the meantime, the reality is that, so long as China continues to accumulate reserves at a pace of around $400 billion a year, there are no alternatives to US government bond markets that are deep and liquid enough to absorb a significant portion of such massive inflows.[15]

A Very Peculiar Multipolarity

In any event, even if the erosion of American power is relative, it cannot mask the magnitude of the reallocation of global wealth to China and India. In 2025, the global power structure defined in terms of material, demographic, military, and technological wealth will continue to be led by the United States, followed by China, the EU, India, Japan, Russia, and Brazil.[16] In nominal terms, China's GNP is poised to surpass Japan's and reach America's by 2025. At this point, India's GNP is expected to equal Japan's and have surpassed that of Germany and France.[17] As always, the meaning of these figures is equivocal. The de-facto multipolarity that is developing is difficult to interpret for at least three reasons.

Multipolarity is traditionally characterized by the existence of several poles of power pursuing comparable objectives and maximizing their own power to the detriment of others' power. Like athletes in a race, these different poles compete on the basis of predetermined criteria. The model that best captures this interpretation is the European balance of power in the nineteenth and twentieth centuries, when Great Britain, France, Germany, and Russia competed to dominate the continent, even seeking arbitration from the United States. In this framework, each power tried to achieve dominance over the others by marshaling its various economic and military assets. The model was simplified by the Cold War, wherein multipolarity gave way to fairly strict bipolarity.

Multipolarity in the twenty-first century is infinitely more complex, not only because the number of actors has grown, but also because the methods of exercising power have multiplied. Interstate competition is not the global system's only dynamic.

Assuming that the international system is now organized around seven poles of power (the United States, China, the European Union, India, Japan, Russia and Brazil), one is immediately struck by the extreme variation in their structures, assets, and weaknesses. First, the poles include a particular actor in the form of the EU, which is not even a state. This significantly diminishes its ability to act collectively outside of communitarized areas. Moreover, the EU has a strategic weakness in the form of its military dependence on the United States. After the Maastricht Treaty, there may have been a sense that economic integration would necessarily lead one day to further political integration. However, Europe lacks the operational resources and flexibility of large states to act on the world stage: to trade, threat, coerce, and make conditional promises. This does not mean the idea of *governance by example* that underpins Europe should be rejected as some have hastily suggested. The United States has now adopted this idea.[18] But without the backing of real bargaining power, it becomes counterproductive by lending support to the idea that one can give in without receiving anything in return.

Japan's case is in many ways very similar to the EU. Naturally, unlike Europe, Japan is a state. Yet since 1945, as a result of well-known historical conditions, it has lost any will to play its own role on the world stage, outside of its alliance with the United States. Its strategic dependence on Washington is not only likely to continue but also to grow as China rises and extreme political instability persists in the Korean peninsula. The recent political crisis between the United States and Japan over the future of American bases has thrown into sharp focus the great weakness of a state whose security depends on an external actor.

India's establishment as a major player in the global system is, along with China's rise, the most powerful symbol of change in the international system. This rise in power would seem to be a form of historical rehabilitation of the non-Western world from the eighteenth century, since at that time China and India already produced 45 percent of global wealth. Here again, the trend of India's increasing power does not mean that the country will become America's strategic rival overnight. India has great internal imbalances, whether geographic, demographic, or social; its population suffers from tremendous poverty and low literacy, in comparison to China for example; and it is in an extremely tense regional environment where it must reckon with China's strategic assertion. All this means that for a long time India will remain a great regional power seeking more global responsibilities, but by no means being a global superpower. The same applies to Brazil, even though it is developing in an infinitely less complex and more peaceful regional context than that of India.

Russia is not an emerging power, strictly speaking, but rather a former superpower eager to regain a part of the political status it lost in the aftermath of the Cold War. To this end, Russia can draw on several

assets. One is its legacy as a great world power under the tsars and com-
munists. This is a significant asset because it makes it much easier for
Russia than for the other global players to project itself onto the global
stage, to hold a view on most key issues, to have a substantial diplomatic
corps, and to uninhibitedly voice its views on the world stage. These
assets would of course lose their relevance in the absence of material
power, but there is always a time lag between the loss of power and of
its formal attributes. Compared to the other BRICS (Brazil, Russia,
India, China, and South Africa), Russia holds an ambivalent, or even
ambiguous position. The BRICS form a coalition that allows Russia
to exist in a broader group when interacting with the West. It is no
coincidence that Moscow was most willing to politicize the BRICS at
a time when relations with Washington were deteriorating.[19] Unlike
the other BRICS, Russia is a global power without being a genuine
regional power, and it seeks to mitigate its isolation by forming coalitions with other actors. Just like the others, however, it sees this group
as a means to multilateralize its power in all the areas where its position is vulnerable. On the other hand it is careful not to play the joint
card in areas where it has particular assets. For example, Moscow is
anxious to ensure the G8 continues to function independently of the
G20 even if that no longer makes much sense. Moscow seeks to protect
its status as privileged partner of the United States, even to the detriment of other BRICS. Russia therefore has no interest in increasing
the number of permanent members in the Security Council. It could
calculate that the entry of Brazil or India might help to counterbalance the West or even China, of which Moscow remains deeply distrustful. This type of calculation is always risky, though, because it
is difficult to anticipate the behavior of states. What is certain is that
Russia sees its status as permanent member of the Security Council as
one of its principal assets next to its nuclear power. Its economic and
demographic positions are much weaker. As a rentier state, its vision of
the international economic system is warped by the very nature of its
economy, which is based on the value of hydrocarbons. Its preoccupy-
ing demographic decline further contributed to casting serious doubts
on the BRICS concept applying to Russia at all. Again, Moscow only
joins the BRICS on sovereignty-related issues, and even then, only if
the BRICS agree on what they mean by sovereignty. Moscow received
no support (or condemnation either) from the BRICS when it decided
to invade Abhkazia and Southern Ossetia in 2008, despite these two
regions being located within Georgia's internationally recognized borders. It notably did not elicit a response from China, which is extremely

stringent about respecting the territorial integrity of internationally recognized states.

As a strategic power that is intent on rivaling the United States, China is naturally an economic power with a GNP that is projected to surpass that of the United States at the nominal level in 2025. By dint of the simple fact that it has become the second greatest economic power in the world, China has seen its economic relations with the other BRICS significantly increase. China is the primary trade partner of Brazil, India, and South Africa. The interdependence among BRICS is thereby considerably deepening.[20] This development should be interpreted with caution, however. The closer economic ties among the BRICS have more to do with additional bilateral agreements than with any integration among these countries. For all the BRICS, the region remains the preferred level for economic integration processes. Moreover, China's rising economic power is a cause for concern among its partners, and especially for Brazil. The latter is worried about Chinese inroads, which it seeks to counter by strengthening economic integration within South America.[21]

This brings us to Brazil, which is unquestionably one of the central BRICS actors. Under the leadership of Luiz Lula and his Minister of Foreign Affairs Celso Amorim, Brazil played a significant role in the emergence of the BRICS. As mentioned earlier, it was a driving force in forming the Cancun front. More recently, with Turkey, it was central to a political maneuver to counter the Americans with regard to Iran by attempting to negotiate a trilateral agreement with Tehran on nuclear-waste reprocessing. Brazil sees the BRICS as an intermediary political circle in between the West—and particularly the United States, with which it enjoys close relations—and Latin America, which forms its natural economic and political sphere of influence. The complementarity of Brasilia's objectives is expressed in the fact that Lula both centrally integrated Brazil into the BRICS and crucially contributed to the creation of the Union of South American Nations (UNASUR). However, this activism has reached its limits. In a recent declaration on foreign affairs, the head of Brazilian diplomacy explicitly referred to IBSA (India, Brazil, South Africa) and did not mention the BRICS, even with reference to Syria.[22] In another statement, he emphasized that the nature of Brazilian power was different from that of China and Russia.[23] This omission is not fortuitous. Brazil now understands that China is pursuing a big-power strategy. While it might share much common ground with Chinese objectives, it certainly cannot build a strategic alliance given China's economic

expansionism and its refusal to support Brazil's accession to a permanent seat on the Security Council. More generally, beyond China, it
is apparent that Brazil's failure in the Iranian case has been instru-
mental in readjusting Brazilian diplomacy since Dilma Roussef took
office. Roussef would like to refocus on Brazil's internal problems and
regional roots. Brasilia understands that it does not have an immediate political interest in overexposing itself in areas where Brazil's main
interests are not at stake, but where its activism is likely to get it into
trouble, especially in relation to the United States. In any case, in the
Iranian matter, Brazil was not able to count on either Russia or China
when the time came to vote on the third round of sanctions against
Iran, as these two countries had already reached an agreement with
Washington beforehand.[24] As a result, Brazil found itself isolated. It
cannot be ruled out that the Russians welcomed this failure with some
relief. Indeed, if the Turks and Brazilians had reached an agreement
with Tehran, the Russians and Chinese would have found themselves
in the awkward situation of having to explain their alignment with
Western positions. Furthermore, the Russians do not want to see an
increase in the number of powers outside of the region intervening and
thus encroaching on their influence in the P5+1 (the permanent members of the UN Security Council and Germany). Also, it is not impossible that the Obama administration made Brasilia pay the price for its
independence by being tepid in its support for Brazil's possible accession to permanent membership in the Security Council. Meanwhile,
the United States has explicitly supported India's candidacy. India is
certainly not an easy partner for the United States, which refers to
India as a "sovereignty hawk."[25] However, India offers resources that
Brazil cannot when it comes to counterbalancing China. Obama thus
somewhat disappointed the Brazilians, who were probably expecting
too much from him anyway.[26]

Thus, the idea that the emergence of the BRICS might counterbalance the United States is based on two misunderstandings. First, each
of these emerging powers taken individually first and foremost aspires
to be recognized as such by the United States, which remains the greatest dispenser of strategic recognition on the world stage. Second, the
BRICS do not in fact share many interests, with the possible exception
of considering state sovereignty as an inviolable principle that can be
used against human-rights diplomacy. The combination of these two
factors means that none of the BRICS has arrived, other than verbally
in the name of multipolarity, but that all of them are eagerly seeking
a privileged relationship with the United States. This supports John

Ikenberry's argument that "the states that are emerging today do not constitute a potential united opposition bloc to the existing order."[27] This line of thought should not be taken too far, however. While the BRICS do not seek to form an anti-Western political coalition based on a counterproposal or radically different vision of the world, they are concerned with maintaining their independence of judgment and national action in a world that is increasingly economically and socially interdependent. They share a common fundamental political objective: to erode Western hegemonic claims by protecting the principle that these claims are deemed to most threaten, namely the political sovereignty of states.[28] They consider that state sovereignty trumps all, including, of course, the political nature of its underpinning regimes. Thus the BRICS—even the democratic ones—fundamentally diverge from the liberal vision of Western countries.

The Systemic Influence of the G-2

The only actor that will be able in the next 20 years to reach a level that approaches that of the United States is China. It alone has all four of the sources of power held by the United States: the ability to generate material wealth, demographic vitality, military power, and strategic instinct. The emergence in the medium term of a Sino-American duopoly therefore appears to be the strongest and most likely dynamic in the coming decades. The nature of this duopoly might easily be misinterpreted. It implies neither the return to an antagonistic bipolarity such as the one that defined the Cold War, nor automatic alignments that would force actors to choose whether to side with the United States or China. Rather, it implies that Sino-American relations have become systemic, meaning that interactions between the two countries now affect the whole international system. Sino-American relations are no longer only of concern to the Americans or the Chinese. The United States has maintained systemic relations with other actors throughout its history, but this is the first time since the beginning of the twentieth century that it has such an important systemic relation with an actor that is neither its ally nor its subordinate. Indeed, in the first half of the twentieth century, the United States had a very strong systemic relationship with Great Britain that affected all aspects of international regulation. This systemic relation culminated in the promulgation of the Atlantic Charter in 1942. The relationship was based on a very strong political, ideological, and cultural alliance.

Consequently, after the liquidation of the British Empire, London was willing to give way to the United States. In the second half of the twentieth century, Soviet-American relations took a resolutely systemic turn as competition between the two superpowers spread.[29] Yet the systemic relationship between the United States and China is stronger and more intense than the Soviet-American one for two reasons. First, it is not exclusively antagonistic. On the contrary, it is based on strong interdependence. Next, and more importantly, it affects an incomparably greater number of areas than did the Soviet-American competition. During the Cold War, trade and finance were not affected by the Soviet-American relationship. However, they were at the heart of the Euro-American relationship. The Soviet-American relationship was only truly systemic in the security realm. This was a significant area, but it did not cover everything. Since 2009, the systemic relationship between the United States and China has taken center stage precisely because it affects almost all the global systemic dynamics: economic growth, trade, currency, security, and the environment. Furthermore, the balance of power does not systematically favor the United States in all these areas. China naturally needs the US market for its exports, but the US production system is heavily dependent on a fragmented value chain organized around China to maximize profits. China also now generates a greater share of global growth than the United States, which makes it less vulnerable to possible economic sanctions in response to its currency undervaluation, for instance. Even though China does not have a trade or financial alternative to the US market, the persistence of US deficits will place the United States at a disadvantage with China in the medium term. This explains the administration's reservations about citing China as a currency manipulator, despite strong Congressional pressure. All these elements do not mean that China has overtaken the United States. Indeed, China is facing massive imbalances and multiple regional constraints. But there can no longer be any doubt that the United States must now integrate China's perspective into all of its major economic decisions. As a result, whether it is in the WTO or the G20, no global agreement is possible anymore without a prior agreement between the United States and China. The blockage and likely death of the WTO's Doha round testifies to this. The two countries do not want to open their markets any further in the current context. The Sino-American equation is, and will become, increasingly complex due to the continual intermeshing of socialization, cooperation, and competition processes.

The socialization process is very important for the United States because it will enable the United States to get to know a competitor with whom it does not have great cultural or historical affinities. This is especially true in the military area where the United States is perpetually concerned about understanding China's strategic intentions. The relationship between the US and USSR superpowers was governed by nuclear military doctrines. The strategic relationship with China is in uncharted territory. Hence the lack of strategic trust between the countries that could quickly deteriorate in the South and Eastern China Sea or the Yellow Sea. The need for socialization is even greater given that China is not a homogeneous actor. Policy toward North Korea is neither made, nor led by, the foreign ministry. It is made, managed, and protected by the liaison office of the Chinese Communist Party and by the People's Liberation Army.[30] Regarding Iran, the roles of the military and oil companies are also very important. China's multiple channels of external action largely explain the variations, nuances, and contradictory choices it might face on such issues. This is why socialization and cooperation are closely linked. As socialization grows, so does knowledge of the other. On the two major crises of North Korea and Iran, US results are ambivalent precisely because the interplay among the Chinese actors is complex. It appears that China has definitely chosen to support the North Korean regime, not due to affinity, but because the political and strategic cost of a Korean reunification is deemed extremely high.[31] The Chinese challenge is accordingly more serious but also less severe than was the Soviet one. Its security implications are less severe because of the economic interdependence between the two countries, the disappearance of any form of ideological conflict between them, and the overlap in their strategic interests, even in Asia. Their rivalry has every chance of remaining peaceful notwithstanding Washington's persistent fears about the militarization of Chinese power. China greatly needs a stable US market to develop while the United States needs Chinese resources to finance its prosperity and therefore its power.[32] At the same time the long-term challenge is more serious because, unlike the USSR, China's power rests on firm ground: material enrichment. As illustrated in the following table (9.1), China is an indispensable partner on seven important US strategic interests. It is only truly absent on two issues: human rights, which clash with the very nature of the Chinese political system, and the settlement of the Israeli-Palestinian conflict, where Americans and Israelis have agreed to keep all other actors at arm's length. China is not directly involved

Table 9.1   The systemic US-Chinese relations

Issues	Indispensable Partner	Other Partners
Growth	China	India, Brazil, Europe
Currency imbalances	China	Europe, Brazil, Japan
Trade	China	Europe, Brazil, India
Climate Change	China	India, Brazil, Europe
Nuclear disarmament and proliferation	Russia, China	Europe
Human rights	Europe	Brazil, Japan
Iran	P5, Germany, Turkey	Japan, South Korea
Afghanistan	Pakistan	China, India, Russia
North Korea	China, South Korea, Japan	Russia
Middle East	Israel	Saudi Arabia, Europe, Turkey, Russia, Palestinian Authority

in the Afghan conflict, but its close relationship with Islamabad attests to its influence in this sub-region.

American Management of Complex Multipolarity

That being said, the relationship with China is obviously not the only one with such implications. The United States also has an increasingly systemic relationship with countries such as Russia, India, Brazil, and Turkey. The scale of systemic issues covered by a bilateral relationship attests to an actor's importance on the world stage and its role as a locus of power. How does US foreign policy manage multipolarity in such a context? The Obama administration's experience points to four major objectives:

To better share the benefits of globalization in order to prevent emerging countries from securing excessive gains

To obtain greater involvement from emerging countries in addressing collective-action problems, such as climate change, nuclear proliferation, peacekeeping, and the fight against various forms of trafficking, piracy, and counterfeiting

To prevent the formation of political coalitions that are likely to prejudice US interests.

To create ad-hoc coalitions capable of settling issues that the United States cannot or does not wish to settle on its own

Better Sharing the Benefits of Globalization

It is important not to lose sight of the fact that multipolarity would not exist without the tremendous process of wealth reallocation away from the western world. In 2012, for the first time, non–OECD countries' share of global GNP equaled that of developed countries (50/50), even though just 20 years ago the proportions were 62/38 in favor of OECD members. This development has several implications for US policy. The first is that international trade now plays a much more prominent role in the US economy than it did in the past, increasing from 11 percent of US GNP at the beginning of the 1970s to 25 percent in 2009. This forced the United States to make trade policy an increasingly significant factor in its foreign policy, although Obama paradoxically ignored trade in the first two years of his term. The second change is that emerging countries have become America's primary targets for trade. In 1985, trade with the developing world accounted for 30 percent of US foreign trade. The figure is now 50 percent. This trend has become more pronounced since 2009 because of the increasing growth differential between the United States and emerging countries. The trade issue is politically important because the United States has significant trade deficits with emerging countries, and especially with China, India, and Mexico. Hence the need to secure both better access to these countries' markets and legal safeguards that are key to the growth of American investments, which have remained relatively low. Obama has a very mercantilist vision of trade relations that is rather inconsistent with trade realities, since it equates imports with job losses, and exports with job creation. Economic interest in emerging markets has, as aforementioned, dampened US enthusiasm for WTO initiatives.

It is therefore possible that Washington is ultimately seeking to stall the WTO in order to better advance two large free-trade areas: one with Europe and the other with Pacific countries, the idea being to convince major emerging countries like China, India, and Brazil to join. Thus, the creation of two great regional trade blocs is becoming a privileged instrument of US policy, although the objective is obviously not explicitly acknowledged. This is precisely why Brazil opposed the creation of a free-trade zone in the Americas in 2005, and why China realized the TPP was clearly directed against it. In fact, it is out of fear of antagonizing China that Indonesia and the Philippines have refused, for the time being, to join the TPP.

Sharing the Burden of Collective Action with Emerging Powers

As seen earlier, this second point is absolutely essential for the United States to prevent emerging countries from free riding on the resolution of collective action problems. The message is that the United States is willing to recognize them as real powers, provided they share the responsibilities of power. The scope for sharing is very broad. The issues at play range from economic ones such as trade and investment, to security and the interpenetration of societies (cybercrime, all kinds of trafficking, climate change, and so on). No objections have been raised in principle to this US requirement. Emerging countries are well aware that they cannot be better represented and heard if they do not politically and financially contribute to resolving the world's problems. However, accepting a principle need not imply agreeing to its interpretation. This is where the difficulties begin. Returning to the example of trade, multilateral negotiations are blocked because the United States wants emerging countries to make new tariff concessions, whereas the latter consider they have already done enough: "The United States in particular, strongly advocates additional liberalization for specific sectors (...) to secure more actual new market access for their manufacturers in the non-agricultural market access negotiations. While emerging markets do not completely rule out their participation in sectorals, they maintain that it should be voluntary as per the Doha declaration, which conflicts with advanced markets' demands that the mass of participants represent at least 90 percent of world trade to allay free-riding concerns. Various proposals have been floated to bridge the gap on sectorals, but without success."[33]

As the benefits of globalization are increasingly shared, the United States feels that emerging countries are not playing the reciprocity game, and has voiced its concerns: "India needs to be asking itself: Is it delivering on the global partnership?... There's no doubt this needs to be a two-way street."[34] The Indians readily share this view, except that they apply it to the United States, which they see as blocking Indian services and agricultural products from the US market. This differentiated perception of what is meant by cost-and-benefit sharing in the management of global public goods is also apparent with regard to climate change. Emerging countries insist on the historical responsibility of developed countries to request that the latter shoulder the bulk of the financial effort to reduce greenhouse-gas emissions, but the United States underscores that emerging countries are becoming the greatest emitters of greenhouse gases. From the US perspective the special treatment granted in the Kyoto Protocol is no longer warranted, while Delhi is pushing for its extension.[35] The problem is compounded when it comes to security matters, as the situation varies by case and country. For example, the Russians and Americans reacted very differently to the Korean and Iranian nuclear challenges because the former perpetually fears subjugation by the latter. As a result, the Russians are utterly opposed to an extension of US nuclear deterrence through a missile-defense shield that might destroy their deterrent capability.[36] Identifying the same threats does not mean that actors will want to respond in the same way. All the emerging powers have a strategic interest in cooperating with the United States, which still expects much from them in various areas. At the same time they are constantly seeking to ensure that these expectations do not affect their margins of maneuver or interpretation. The Indian case is once again extremely revealing here. The Bush administration signed a very important nuclear cooperation agreement with Delhi even though India was not a signatory to the nuclear nonproliferation treaty. The United States expected the agreement to align India more closely with US interests. This did not quite happen. The sale of US nuclear equipment remains blocked by the absence of adequate legal safeguards for American companies in the event of a nuclear accident. US companies deem Indian law on the matter more restrictive than the international convention on liability in the event of a nuclear accident.[37] A similar ambivalence is also apparent in the military arena. The signing of a ten-year pact between the two countries in 2005 allowed for enhanced cooperation on terrorism, maritime safety, and the fight against arms trafficking. However, it did not lead to any global form of strategic convergence, even on particularly sensitive issues for the United States, such as Pakistan. For instance, the Indians firmly refused any US mediation between India and Pakistan on the Kashmir issue, although the United States has not acknowledged this.[38] Furthermore, the Indians remain extremely vigilant in the development of their military cooperation with Washington, since they fear that Congress may some day impose political conditions on arms sales or resort to sanctions in the event of noncompliance—a risk that does not exist in dealings with either Europe or Russia.[39] India is similarly apprehensive about US political intrusiveness with regard to the transfer of sensitive technologies.[40] These examples highlight how political sovereignty remains at the core of the emerging powers' international political identity. Of course, this identity is not at odds with establishing partnerships with the United States, but it requires that partnerships not limit margins of maneuver and interpretation. As a result the United States has experienced a complex mix of satisfaction and disappointment. During the vote on resolution 1973 on Libya, the United States interpreted the abstention of emerging countries as encouraging signs of their adherence to the principle of the responsibility to protect. Since the unfolding of the Syrian crisis, however, it has realized that this is a delicate and fully reversible process. Emerging countries remain fundamentally sovereignist states that deem any outside intervention unacceptable. If it had not been for the Russian veto, the Syrian regime would likely be much weaker today. Hence, there is no doubt as to the political tension between the United States and emerging countries on the Syrian issue. Yet this tension is nothing compared to that which could arise from a possible military intervention against Iran.

Prevent the Formation of Political Coalitions That Are Likely to Prejudice US Interests

This objective is critical in a multipolar configuration because it is a major means for the dominant pole to keep its freedom of action intact. The Obama administration can clearly claim to have succeeded here, through an active but nonaggressive diplomacy that seeks to avoid creating systematically or lastingly antagonistic relations with emerging powers despite diverging views on a number of issues. The *reset* with Russia highlighted the limitations of this diplomacy, as evidenced by the ongoing crisis between the two countries over the missile-defense shield. US–Russian distrust is nonetheless much less severe now than it was under the Bush administration. The United States and Brazil have also sharply diverged, on the Iranian and Syrian issues. However, the range of bilateral issues of interest to both countries is so broad that these divergences have not undercut the relatively trusting nature of US-Brazilian relations, even if Brazil senses lukewarm US support for its bid to become a permanent member of the Security Council: "The United States sees Brazil as big, the most important country in Latin America, but not anything like a global power."[41] The same reasoning applies to Turkey. The very sharp deterioration in US-Turkish relations following the US intervention in Iraq, the crisis between Israel and Turkey, and the Turkish-Brazilian initiative on Iran has stopped. Ankara has agreed to host radar stations as part of a missile-defense shield against Iran, and to manage the Syrian issue in close coordination with Washington. Thus, while no US relationship with an emerging country is comparable to the ones it has with old allies like Japan, Korea, Australia, Canada, Mexico, and Great Britain, none of these relationships is very tense either. The United States has differences with all of them, but also shares many points of convergence. Another key factor benefits the United States: as previously noted, emerging countries do not form a homogenous bloc. None would be willing to come under the wing of another, let alone coalesce behind another to confront the United States. The logic of sovereignty that is extremely prominent in emerging countries limits America's power to compel, but by the same token makes it unlikely that an anti-American coalition will form.

Create Ad Hoc Coalitions Capable of Settling Issues That the United States Cannot Or Does Not Wish to Settle on Its Own

US results in this last area are much more ambiguous. On the highly sensitive issue of Iran, Washington succeeded in passing a resolution that was supported by China and Russia. However, the United States was not able to garner the support of Western countries and traditional allies for further steps to break all oil and financial ties with Tehran. This is why a military intervention against Iran would be as harmful to the United States as its intervention in Iraq, especially if emerging countries believed it did not first exhaust all negotiating options. This crisis is possibly the only one that could give rise to an anti-American coalition and open old, unhealed wounds from the Iraq War. Obama's handling of the Iranian crisis will therefore most likely constitute the greatest test of his foreign policy.

The Preference for Minilateralism

Consequently, and contrary to certain common ideas, the Obama administration shows no desire for multipolarity. The term is absent from Obama's discourse and was officially rejected by Hillary Clinton.[42] Of course, multipolarity cannot be decreed or rejected, but Washington's reluctance to endorse the concept is telling. To accept the reality of a multipolar world is to recognize the existence of several poles of power with equivalent resources and power seeking to manage common problems on a cooperative and egalitarian basis. This kind of multipolarity would necessitate a multilateral approach to regulating the international system. The United States is not interested in this model simply because it means the United States would have to grant other actors power and international recognition without getting anything in exchange. The United States has little interest in conferring the status of global strategic partner on India or Brazil when it only needs their support for a number of specific issues. It only makes sense for the United States to advance the position of an actor if the latter is able to provide tangible added value to problem solving or if doing so comes at no cost, such as advocating for a better allocation of voting rights within the IMF for emerging countries at the expense of Europe. The United States will therefore proceed selectively, all the more so as most of the emerging powers are seeking a status that only the United States is really able to grant them. The logical consequence of this is a bargaining of sorts whereby American recognition of an actor as a strategic partner implies that the latter is helping to resolve a problem on the basis of parameters that are congruent with US interests, or at the very least do not work against them. The policy of sanctions against Iran illustrates this very well. The United States included China and Russia in its Iranian policy because these two states could significantly hinder its strategy vis-à-vis Iran. By contrast, it does not see any pressing need to include China in the settlement of the Israeli-Palestinian conflict, or Russia in finding solutions to the issue of climate change. This is why the administration does not embrace multilateralism per se, but prefers to develop partnerships with "strong and capable"[43] actors among whom the United States intends to maintain its leadership. For each issue of importance to the United States, the goal is to involve those who can contribute because of their leverage over the protagonists (China on North Korea), their ability to use financial resources to resolve a problem (Europe in the Middle East), or their nuisance factor that might derail US plans (Russia or China on Iran).

This ad-hoc partnership strategy approximately corresponds to a minimal definition of multilateralism, but it is actually most often akin to a minilateral policy, in the sense that it involves a limited number of actors.[44] It is, however, necessary to recognize the difficulty in evaluating the multilateral aspect of a policy given the many definitions of multilateralism. A minimal definition would characterize it as a practice of coordinating national policies in groups of three or more states either through ad-hoc arrangements or institutions. In this case, Obama's foreign policy would fall within the realm of multilateralism. By contrast, if multilateralism is conceived as a belief in a universal basis of action that posits international collective action as a type of ideology, then it becomes more difficult to classify US policy as multilateral. Multilateralization through international institutions is only truly embraced in areas where the cooperation of the greatest possible number of actors is necessary.

US diplomacy has an interesting approach to the settlement of what might somewhat arbitrarily be considered the ten greatest international policy issues: Afghanistan, the Israeli-Palestinian conflict, Iran, North Korea, nuclear proliferation and disarmament, terrorism, European security, financial regulation, climate regulation, and trade regulation. There is no doubt that the United States is seeking to build partnerships in all of these areas, in a departure from the Bush administration's unilateralism. But the nature, number, and quality of these partnerships vary considerably depending on their ability, or expectations of their ability, to solve these problems. In Afghanistan, for instance, the conflict management is not actually multilateral in any way. America's chosen partner for the settlement of this conflict was Pakistan and concomitantly India, given the decisive influence of the Indian-Pakistani conflict in the Afghan equation. By contrast, the Europeans were marginalized as the war Americanized and European troops disengaged, even though the British were the first to emphasize the necessity of a political dialogue with the Taliban at the highest level, as opposed to the US preference to engage with subordinate levels. Concerning the Israeli-Palestinian conflict, the United States has just revived the peace process, but the involvement of other actors is extremely limited. This is due to US confidence in its full command of the issue and its challenges. Moreover, Israel believes that it can only trust the United States, thus preventing other actors from being involved in the settlement of the conflict. In the settlement of the Korean crisis, the United States is most interested in Chinese involvement, since China alone has the power to influence the North Korean regime. The partnerships evidently bring together a very limited number of actors when the issue at stake is US strategic security. On all the other issues the partnerships are broader, either because the United States is not the only decisive actor (climate change, trade, finance), or because the subject itself requires a multilateral solution (terrorism, nuclear proliferation). Here again, the creation of partnerships or the search for collective arrangements is based on a high selectivity of partners and priorities. The United States pursued the financial reform that it deemed best for itself, before beginning negotiations with the other blocs, and especially Europe, over its compatibility with the G20's regulatory principles. The United States has also indefinitely deferred completing the Doha round, because it has determined that it does not yet have sufficient domestic consensus to back such an agreement, and that the conclusion of this multilateral arrangement is not really urgent for the United States. Finally, with regard to climate change the United States was not preoccupied in the least about Europe's marginalization in the Copenhagen negotiations, not because the United States caused or desired it, but because it implicitly reduced international pressure on the United States. In fact, since the Copenhagen failure, the US Congress has refused to ratify the commitments that the US president made at the summit. American power is more than ever demonstrating its ability to reinvent itself while trying to remain true to its values, interests, and orientations.

APPENDICES

Methodology 1

We have compared the foreign policy discourse of George W. Bush and Barack Obama by collecting and analyzing the official speeches of the two presidents, as published on The White House website (for Bush: http://georgewbush-whitehouse.archives.gov/; for Obama: http://www.whitehouse.gov/). A complete list of the speeches is available on the website www.laidi.com under the section "publications."

The speeches were analyzed in full, except for the Q/A sessions with journalists, which have been deleted. We cover all the speeches of George W. Bush during his first and second terms (January 2005–January 2009). The text of these speeches totals 423,000 words. As for Barack Obama, we cover his foreign policy discourse from his inaugural address until his speech at West Point on May 22, 2010. The text of his speeches totals 254,000 words.

We obtained the results through the software Lexico 3, created by Université de Paris 3-Sorbonne Nouvelle.

Appendix 1

Table 10.1 Comparison of the key words in the discourses of George W. Bush and Barack Obama

Words that appear in Bush's discourse but are never or seldom used by Obama	War on Terror: 72 times–0 Free world: 33 times–1
Words that appear in Obama's discourse but are never or seldom used by Bush	Non-Proliferation Treaty NPT (x 9.36)
Words that appear at least five times more in Bush's discourse than in Obama's discourse	Democracy (x 7.21) Liberty—Freedom (x 6.8)

continued

Table 10.1—Continued

Words that appear at least five times more in Obama's discourse than in Bush's discourse	Climate change (x 5)
Words that appear 2 to 5 times more in Bush's discourse than in Obama's discourse	Weapons of mass destruction (x 3.5)
Words that appear 2 to 5 times more in Obama's discourse than in Bush's discourse	Al Qaeda (x 2.44) Nuclear power (x 2.08)
Words that appear equally in Bush's and Obama's discourse (once to twice)	United Nations (Bush x 1.97) Security (x 1.84) Peace (x 1.73) War (x 1.65) Human rights (Bush x 1.5) Terror (Bush x 1.31) NATO (Bush x 1.13)
Words that do not appear in either Bush's discourse or in Obama's	Multipolarity, multipolar, multilateralism

Appendix 2

Table 10.2 Comparison of the key words that appear in George W. Bush's and Barack Obama's discourses (in decreasing order)

George W. Bush 423,000 words	Barack Obama 254,000 words
1. Liberty (1,006)* [0.24%]**	Security (625)* [0.25%]**
2. Democracy (854)* [0.20%]**	Nuclear power (567)* [0.22%]**
3. "Terror" (843)* [0.20%]**	"Terror" (385)* [0.15%]**
4. Peace (813)* [0.19%]**	Peace (282)* [0.11%]**
5. Security (566)* [0.13%]**	War (225)* (without historical references) [0.09%]**
6. Nuclear power (454)* [0.10%]**	Leadership (147)* [0.06%]**
7. Leadership (313)* [0.07%]**	Cooperation (138)* [0.05%]**
8. United Nations (299)* [0.07%]**	NATO (136)* [0.05%]**
9. NATO (258)* [0.06%]**	Climate change (102)* [0.04%]**
10. War (230)* [0.05%]**	Liberty (90)* [0.04%]**
11. Cooperation (196)* [0.05%]**	United Nations (86)* [0.03%]**
12. Enemy (148)* [0.03%]**	Democracy (72)* [0.03%]**
13. Human rights (129)* [0.03%]**	International community (65)* [0.03%]**
14. International community (88)*	Mutual interests (57)*
15. Rule of law (76)*	Rule of law (51)*
16. Tyranny (64)*	Human rights (51)*
17. September 11 (43)*	Enemy (47)*
18. Human dignity (41)*	Mutual respect (40)*
19. Safe haven (38)*	September 11 (39)*
20. Climate change (35)*	Islam (25)*

George W. Bush *423,000 words*	Barack Obama *254,000 words*
21. European Union (29)*	International obligations (16)*
22. Multilateral (28)*	European Union (16)*
23. Ideological struggle (27)*	Multilateral (13)*
24. Islam (17)*	Norms (12)*
25. Mutual interests (12)*	International law (12)*
Unsorted: "ideology of hatred" (10)*, norm(s) (6)*, "mutual respect" (5)*, "global security" (4)*, "international obligations" (2)*	Unsorted: tyranny (9)*; "ideology of hatred" (1)*

* Number of appearances.
** Percentage of appearance in the full text of the speeches.

Appendix 3

List of the countries mentioned in official discourses (in decreasing order)

Bush	Obama
1. Iraq (561)	1. Afghanistan (328)
2. Afghanistan (393)	2. Iran (239)
3. India (360)	3. Iraq (211)
4. Iran (261)	4. Russia (170)
5. Israel (226)	5. China (166)
6. North Korea (224)	6. Pakistan (164)
7. Lebanon (223)	7. Turkey (111)
8. Russia (195)	8. Israel (103)
9. Pakistan (192)	9. North Korea (90)
10. China (151)	10. Japan (66)
11. Georgia (143)	11. India (65)
12. Syria (118)	12. South Korea (58)
13. Japan (116)	13. France (45)
14. Columbia (108)	14. Germany (42)
15. United Kingdom (75)	15. United Kingdom (26)
16. Brazil (70)	16. Brazil (24)
17. Germany (60)	17. Italy (21)
18. Kosovo (57)	18. Columbia (17)
19. Liberia (48)	19. Egypt (15)
20. Vietnam (46)	20. Spain (12)
21. South Korea (45)	21. Indonesia (11)
22. Poland (44)	22. Poland (10)
23. France (40)	23. Saudi Arabia (8)
24. Saudi Arabia (38)	24. Vietnam (7)
25. Turkey (27)	25. Palestine (7) [Palestinians (76)]

NOTES

Introduction

1. See Mitt Romney's recent critique of Obama: "Mitt Romney Contrasts His Vision with President Obama's 'Resentment of Success'": http://www.politickerny .com/2012/01/10/mitt-romney-contrasts-his-vision-with-president-obamas -resentment-of-success/.
2. In January 2012, discussions between the US government and the Taliban started in Qatar, with the apparent blessing of Pakistan and the Karzai government. But the outcome of those discussions is uncertain. On the terms of a possible political settlement in Afghanistan, see Anatol Lieven, "Afghanistan: The Best Way to Peace," *The New York Review of Books*, February 9, 2012.
3. According to Anne-Marie Slaughter, the United States does not need a grand strategy in a fluid and complex world. See Anne-Marie Slaughter,"Why the U.S Doesn't Need a Grand Strategy," *Belfer Center*, November 3, 2011: http:// belfercenter.ksg.harvard.edu/publication/21482/dr_annemarie_slaughter .html?breadcrumb=%2Fproject%2F61%2Ffuture_of_diplomacy_project. For a different point of view, see Charles Kupchan, "The Four Pillars of the Future," *Democracy Journal*, issue 23 (2012): http://www.democracyjournal.org/23/grand- strategy -the-four-pillars-of-the-future.php?page=all.

1 Legacy

1. Preelection polling data leave no doubt on this point. It is only from the end of September 2008 that Barack Obama began to pull ahead of his rival.
2. *The Times*, September 26, 2008.
3. John Gray, "A Shattering Moment in America's Fall from Power," *The Observer*, September 28, 2008.
4. Zhou Xiaochuan, "Reform the International Monetary System," *People Daily*, March 31, 2009.
5. Ibid.

6. Alan Greenspan, *The Age of Turbulence: Adventures in a New World* (New York: Penguin Press, 2007).

7. American household savings fell from 9 percent in 1980 to 6.5 percent in 1990 and 2.7 percent in 2000, before plummeting to 0.8 percent in 2005. Since the 2008 crisis, the savings rate has increased to around 3 percent, but it is unclear whether this rate is sustainable. *Financial Times*, May 4, 2010.

8. Roger C. Altman, "The Great Crash, 2008: A Geopolitical Setback for the West," *Foreign Affairs*, January–February 2009, 2–14.

9. Daniel W. Drezner, "Bad Debts, Assessing China's Financial Influence in Great Power Politics," *International Security,* 34, no. 2 (Autumn 2009): 7–45.

10. Ben S. Bernanke, "The Global Saving Glut and the U.S. Current Account Deficit," Remarks at the Sandridge Lecture, Virginia Association of Economics, Richmond, Virginia, March 10, 2005. http://www.federalreserve.gov/boarddocs/speeches/2005/20050414/default.htm.

11. The dollar's exorbitant privilege arises from the fact that since US external debt is denominated in dollars, any depreciation of the dollar automatically reduces the US current account deficit. Each percentage point of dollar depreciation yields a transfer of resources to the United States that is equivalent to a one half-percentage point of GNP. See Pierre-Olivier Gourinchas, and Hélène Rey, *From World Banker to World Venture Capitalist: US External Adjustment and The Exorbitant Privilege*, NBER Working Papers Series, August 2005. http://www.nber.org/papers/w11563.pdf; and R. Glenn Hubbard, "The US Current Account Deficit and Public Policy," *Journal of Policy Modeling*, 28 (2006): 668.

12. Michael Mastanduno, "International Relations Theory and the Consequences of Unipolarity," *World Politics,* 61, no. 1 (2009), 131 and further.

13. In the 1960s and 1970s, the United States could rightfully justify the dollar's exorbitant privileges by the nature of its military commitments to its allies. This argument does not hold anymore. Not that the United States no longer serves as military protector to a considerable number of countries, but countries like China that are at the source of America's lax monetary policy do not depend on the American security umbrella. Moreover, the United States itself has strongly encouraged their policy of investing reserves from accumulated trade surpluses in US Treasury bonds.

14. Kenneth N. Waltz, "Structural Realism after the Cold War," *International Security*, 25, no. 1 (summer 2000), 5–41.

15. John Zysman, and Laura Tyson, eds., *American Industry in International Competition: Government Policy and Corporate Strategies* (Ithaca: Cornell University Press, 1983).

16. Anthony Lake, *"Remarks: From Containment to Enlargement,"* Johns Hopkins University School of Advanced International Studies, Washington DC, September 21, 1993. http://www.mtholyoke.edu/acad/intrel/lakedoc.html.

17. It was only at the end of Clinton's first term in 2000 that this idea was revived through the joint initiative of the United States and Poland to create a community of democracies. However, the declaration's impact was lessened by

its general nature and by the quasi unanimity it commanded (France refused to support the text) throughout the world, including among antidemocratic regimes. See Ministerial Conference Final Warsaw Declaration: *Toward a Community of Democracies*, Warsaw, Poland, June 27, 2000. http://ccd21.org /articles/warsaw_declaration.htm.

18. David Lipton, D., Jeffrey Sachs, Stanley Fischer, and Janos Kornai, "Creating a Market Economy in Eastern Europe: The Case of Poland," *Brooking Papers on Economics Activity*, no. 1 (1990): 75–147.

19. I borrow this comparison from Janos Kornai, "Ten Years after 'The Road to a Free Economy': The Author's Self-Evaluation," *Paper for the World Bank Annual Bank Conference on Development Economics-ABCDE*, Washington DC, April 18–20, 2000, 25.

20. Jeffrey Sachs, cited in Philippe Rusin, "Pologne 'libérale' versus Pologne 'solidaire.' Les deux facettes de la transition vers l'économie de marché," *Études du CEFRES*, no. 9 (January 2007): 7.

21. Narcis Serra, and Jospeh E. Stiglitz, eds., *The Washington Consensus Reconsidered: Towards a New Global Governance* (Oxford: Oxford University Press, 2008).

22. Charles William Maynes, "A Workable Clinton Doctrine," *Foreign Policy*, no. 93 (Winter 1993–1994): 3–22.

23. During a vote on a resolution on Iraq (Iraqi Liberation Act) in 1998, the Congress "urged the President to take appropriate action, in accordance with the Constitution and relevant laws of the United States, to bring Iraq into compliance with its international obligations." http://www.gpo.gov/fdsys/pkg /PLAW-107publ243/html/PLAW-107publ243.htm.

24. The Powell doctrine draws on the Weinberger doctrine, named after Defense Secretary Caspar Weinberger, who held the position from 1981 to 1987, and for whom Colin Powell had worked. It includes six points: a proven threat to the vital interests of the United States or its allies; a wholehearted commitment with the intention of winning, or no commitment at all; continual reassessment of the objective's alignment with the composition of the forces; clearly defined political and military objectives with deployment of the necessary means to achieve them; congressional and public support; the commitment of troops as a last resort. See Caspar W. Weinberger, "The Uses of Military Power," Speech at the National Press Club in Washington DC, November 28, 1984, http://www .airforcemagazine.com/MagazineArchive/Documents/2004/January%20 2004/0104keeperfull.pdf.

25. In the case of Somalia, the United States had employed as translator the son of a Somali leader it was seeking to neutralize. Later, an American plane transported this very same Somali leader for negotiations.

26. Madeleine Albright, "Toward a Community of Democracies," Warsaw, Poland, June 26, 2000, http://www.fordemocracy.net/secretary-of-state-madeleine -albrights-address-to.html.

27. Henri Tajfel, *Differentiation between Social Groups: Studies in the Social Psychology of Intergroup Relations*, (London: Academic Press, 1978), 27–98, cited in Deborah

Welch Larson, and Alexei Shevchenko, "Status Seekers: Chinese and Russian Responses to U.S. Primacy" (note 14), *International Security,* 34, no. 4 (spring 2010): 63–95.

28. See William Wohlforth, "Unipolarity, Status Competition and Great Power War," *World Politics,* 61, no. 1 (January 2009): 47.

29. Deborah Welch Larson, and Alexei Shevchenko, "Status Seekers", art. cit., 70 and further.

30. Richard Haass, "Fatal Distraction: Bill Clinton's Foreign Policy," *Foreign Policy,* no. 108 (Autumn 1997): 112–123.

31. Angela E. Stent, "America and Russia: Paradoxes of Partnership," in *Russia's Engagement with the West: Transformation and Integration in the Twenty-First Century,* ed. Alexander J. Motyl, Blair A. Ruble, and Lilia Shevtsova (Armonk, NY: M. E. Sharpe, 2005), 265.

32. Robert Jervis, "Unipolarity. A Structural Perspective," *World Politics,* 61, no. 1 (January 2009): 191.

33. Cited in Fareed Zakaria, *The Post-American World and the Rise of the Rest* (London: Penguin Books, 2009).

34. Christopher Layne, "The Unipolar Illusion Revisited: The Coming End of the United States' Unipolar Moment," *International Security,* 31, no. 2 (Autumn 2006): 25.

35. Fareed Zakaria, op. cit.

36. Cited in Fareed Zakaria, ibid.

37. Ibid.

38. This thesis has been defended by Paul Kennedy in *The Rise and Fall of the Great Powers: Economic Change and Military Conflict from 1500 to 2000* (New York: Random House, 1989).

39. Robert Jervis, art. cit.

40. English distinguishes between *preemptive* and *preventive.* The former has a stronger connotation than the latter.

41. National Security Strategy, September 2002, 15, http://georgewbush-white house.archives.gov/nsc/nss/2002/.

42. Ibid.

43. Ronald R. Krebs, and Jennifer K. Lobasz, "Fixing the Meaning of 9/11: Hegemony, Coercion and the Road to War in Iraq," *Security Studies,* 16, no. 3 (July 2007): 422.

44. Ibid.

45. Statement by Celso Amorim, "Le Brésil peut aider à créer la confiance avec l'Iran," [Brazil can help build trust with Iran], *Le Monde,* May 4, 2010.

46. Albert Wohlstetter, *Moving Toward Life in a Nuclear Armed Crowd? Final Report,* 1975, 168. http://www.npec-web.org/files/19751204-AW-EtAl MovingTowards LifeNuclearArmedCrowd.pdf.

47. Ibid., 171.

48. Bob Woodward, *Plan of Attack* (New York: Simon & Schuster, 2004).

49. Cited in Robert Jervis, "Understanding the Bush Doctrine," *Political Science Quarterly,* 118, no. 3 (Autumn 2003): 372.

50. Amy Gershkoff, and Shana Kushner, "Shaping Public Opinion: The 9/11-Iraq Connection in the Bush Administration's Rhetoric," *Perspectives on Politics*, 3, no. 3 (September 2005): 525–537.

51. Paul S. Boyer, "When U.S. Foreign Policy Meets Biblical Prophecy," February 21, 2003, http://www.mail-archive.com/ctrl@listserv.aol.com/msg103467.html.

52. Jody C. Baumgartner, Peter L. Francia, and Jonathan S. Morris, "A Clash of Civilizations? The Influence of Religion on Public Opinion of U.S Foreign Policy in the Middle East," *Political Research Quarterly*, 61, no. 2 (June 2008): 171–179.

53. Ibid.

54. Ibid.

2   White House Tight Rope

1. David Mendell, *Obama: From Promise to Power* (New York: Amistad/Harper Collins Publishers, 2007), 175.

2. Ibid.

3. In 2004, 59 percent of whites and 38 percent of blacks considered themselves "very patriotic." Within the Democratic electorate, 52 percent of whites identified themselves as "very patriotic," compared to only 38 percent of blacks. See The Pew Research Center for the People and the Press, *Survey Report: The 2004 Political Landscape*, November 5, 2003, http://people-press.org /report/?pageid=752.

4. David Mendell, *Obama: From Promise to Power*, op. cit.

5. As a member of the Senate Foreign Relations Committee, Obama introduced the Cooperative Proliferation Detection, Interdiction Assistance, and Conventional Threat Reduction Act of 2006. That act, which was incorporated into the Department of State Authorities Act of 2006 and signed into law, allows for the destruction of surplus and unsecured weapons, which Obama said "make attractive targets for terrorists." See *Council on Foreign Relations*, Note on Obama: http://www.cfr.org/experts/world/barack-obama/b11603#12.

6. Text of Senate Resolution S.433 (110th) *Iraq War De-Escalation Act of 2007.* http://www.govtrack.us/congress/billtext.xpd?bill=s110–433

7. In his autobiography Barack Obama compellingly explains the distance that existed between him, the son of an African, and American blacks. This distance was reflected in the surprise of many black Americans when he mentioned his name. Neither Barack nor Obama were considered to be black names. He therefore had to integrate into the American black community and succeeded in doing so, especially by marrying a woman from this community. See Barack Obama, *Dreams from My Father: A Story of Race and Inheritance* (New York: Broadway Books, 2004).

8. This ability to unite and bridge divides is well captured in David Remnick's biography of Barack Obama, aptly entitled *The Bridge: The Life and Rise of Barack Obama* (New York: Knopf Publishers, 2010).

9. Quoted in "President Obama on American Exceptionalism," *TalkLeft*, April 5, 2009, http://www.talkleft.com/story/2009/4/5/172753/5229.

10. Barack Obama explained as follows: "I do know him because I taught at the University of Chicago. And he is Palestinian. And I do know him and I have had conversations. He is not one of my advisors; he's not one of my foreign policy people. His kids went to the Lab school where my kids go as well. He is a respected scholar, although he vehemently disagrees with a lot of Israel's policy." Quoted in "Obama's Good Friend Rashid Khalidi," *American Thinker*, May 23, 2008, http://www.americanthinker.com/blog/2008/05/obamas_good _friend_rashid_khal.html.

11. White House, Press Conference by the President, Hilton Hotel Port of Spain, Trinidad and Tobago, April 19, 2009. Available at the White House website: http://www.whitehouse.gov/the_press_office/Press-Conference-By-The -President-In-Trinidad-And-Tobago-4/19/2009.

12. "The U.S. president has been striking in his refusal—or inability—to get on with Karzai, never working to create the personal rapport the Afghan president enjoyed with his predecessor. It is Obama, not Bush, who has committed massive resources to Afghanistan while trying to improve the tattered U.S. reputation in the Muslim world. But Karzai still considers the Bush era a golden age for his presidency, a time when Karzai could pick up the phone any time and talk to the American leader." See Ahmed Rashid, "How Obama Lost Karzai: The Road of Afghanistan Runs through Two Presidents Who Just Don't Get Along," *Foreign Policy*, March/April 2011, http://www.foreignpolicy.com/articles/2011/02/22 /how_obama_lost_karzai.

13. When he came to France in June 2009, Obama declined President Sarkozy's invitation to share a family dinner at the Elysée, preferring to organize a private one with his family. This was rightly or wrongly interpreted as a refusal to personalize relations with a head of state—in this case one who had not shied away from criticizing his inexperience. See François Clemenceau, "Obama: La diplomatie au rendez-vous de l'Histoire" [Obama: his diplomacy will go down in history], *Le Journal du Dimanche*, January 23, 2010.

14. It is still unclear whether the White House's opposition to such an agreement was a substantive opposition or an irritated reaction to NIC (National Intelligence Center) director Dennis Blair's decision to take the initiative on this issue without prior consultation with the White House, which ultimately fired him over the incident. See *The New York Times*, May 21, 2010.

15. David Cameron, "A Staunch and Self-Confident Ally," *The Wall Street Journal*, July 20, 2010, http://www.freerepublic.com/focus/f-news/2555656/posts.

16. Interviews, United Nations, New York, October 2011.

17. White House, *Remarks of President Obama at Student Roundtable*, Tophane Cultural Center, Istanbul, Turkey, April 7, 2009. Available at the White House website: http://www.whitehouse.gov/the-press-office/remarks-president-barack-obama -student-roundtable-istanbul.

18. Text of the National Security Act of 1947, available at: http://www.law.cornell .edu/uscode/html/uscode50/usc_sec_50_00000401----000-notes.html.

19. I. M. Destler, "Will Obama's National Security Council Be 'Dramatically Different?'," *Foreign Affairs*, April 30, 2009, http://www.foreignaffairs.com/articles/65077/i-m-destler/jonestown.

20. Ibid.

21. Barack Obama has introduced very few structural changes to the NSC compared to his predecessor. Ibid., 9.

22. I. M. Destler, "Will Obama's National Security Council...," art. cit.

23. Ivo H. Daalder, and I. M. Destler, "In the Shadow of the Oval Office: The Next National Security Advisor," *Foreign Affairs,* January-February 2009, http://www.foreignaffairs.com/articles/63723/ivo-h-daalder-and-i-m-destler/in-the-shadow-of-the-oval-office.

24. I. M. Destler, "Donilon to the Rescue? The Road Ahead for Obama's Next National Security Adviser," *Foreign Affairs*, October 13, 2010, http://www.foreignaffairs.com/articles/66772/i-m-destler/donilon-to-the-rescue.

25. "He is so self-confident that he believes he can make decisions on the most complicated of issues after only hours of discussion." According to Leslie Gelb, cited in I. M. Destler, "Will Obama's National Security Council Be 'Dramatically Different?,'" art. cit.

26. Interviews, Princeton, October 2011.

27. "First, has Donilon ever expressed an interesting or novel foreign policy idea, or shown that he has a larger vision for what the United States' position and strategy ought to be? If so, I haven't heard about it. (...) Second, has Donilon ever taken a position that involved some level of moral courage? Has he ever done or said anything that might be regarded as controversial inside the Beltway? Given his long career as a lobbyist and political operative, that's hardly likely. What was his view on invading Iraq in 2003, for example? Did he publicly oppose that bone-headed decision? Don't think so. And given that the Obama administration's defining characteristic in foreign policy has been a tendency to spell out promising courses of action and then beat a hasty retreat from them at the first sign of serious resistance, there's little reason to expect someone with Donilon's bio to act any differently." See Steve Walt, "On Tom Donilon: A Few Questions and Reservations," *Foreign Policy*, October 12, 2010, http://walt.foreignpolicy.com/posts/2010/10/12/on_tom_donilon_%20a_few_questions_and_reservations.

28. Ryan Lizza, "The Consequentialist: How the Arab Spring Remade Obama's Foreign Policy," *The New Yorker*, May 2, 2011, http://www.newyorker.com/reporting/2011/05/02/110502fa_fact_lizza.

29. Tahman Bradley, "Kissinger Backs Clinton at State," *ABC News*, November 16, 2008, http://abcnews.go.com/blogs/politics/2008/11/kissinger-backs/.

30. "I want the Iranians to know that if I'm the president, we will attack Iran," quoted in "Pennsylvania's Six Week Primary Ends Tonight," *ABC WorldNews*, April 22, 2008, http://abcnews.go.com/WN/Vote2008/story?id=4698059&page=1.

31. Ben Smith, "Hillary Clinton Toils in the Shadows," *Politico,* June 23, 2009, http://www.politico.com/news/stories/0609/24067_Page3.html.

32. "Her voice is respected and heard and she is a strong, strong part of his overall cabinet and a leader within the foreign policy team," senior Obama adviser

Valerie Jarrett told Reuters, dismissing reports Clinton has been sidelined. See Jeff Mason, "Clinton's Influence in Team Obama: A Nuanced Role," *Reuters*, October 24, 2009, http://www.reuters.com/article/2009/10/24/us-obama -clinton-influence-analysis-idUSTRE59N0YN20091024.

33. *The Economist*, March 24, 2012.

34. Klaus Larres, ed., "Hillary Rodham Clinton as Secretary of State: A New Engagement with the World," in *The US Secretaries of State and Transatlantic Relations* (New York: Routledge/Taylor and Francis, 2010), 4–12.

35. Ryan Lizza, "The Consequentialist: How the Arab Spring Remade Obama's foreign policy," art. cit., 8.

36. For more on these conflicts, see *The New York Times*, June 22, 2010.

37. Talking about Hillary Clinton, Heather Conley, a former deputy assistant secretary said: "The challenge has been…the defining of her subject areas (. . .) She needs to identify those issues where she's the lead," quoted in Jeff Mason, "Clinton's Influence in Team Obama: A Nuanced Role," art. cit.

38. According to a poll by the Pew Research Center, 73 percent of Pakistanis are unfavorable to the United States and 69 percent perceive it as an "enemy." See "U.S. Image in Pakistan Falls No Further Following bin Laden Killing," *Pew Research Center,* June 21, 2011, 1, http://pewresearch.org/pubs/2032/pakistan -public-opinion-osama-bin-laden-india-terrorism-al-qaeda-american-image.

39. See David Weigel, "So Happy Together," *Slate Magazine,* July 17, 2009, http://www.slate.com/id/2223025/. This convergence of views was not a given; during the 2008 campaign Obama had some harsh words for Hillary, calling her "Bush-Cheney Lite." See Katharine Q. Seelye, and Michael Falcone, "Obama Says Clinton Is 'Bush-Cheney Lite,'" *The New York Times,* July 27, 2007, http://www.nytimes.com /2007/07/27/us/politics/27clinton.html.

40. *The Washington Post*, July 16, 2008.

41. "The most significant threat to our national security is our debt," CNN, August 27, 2011.

42. *The Washington Post*, October 6, 2009.

43. *Politico*, July 19, 2009.

44. Jonathan Alter, *The Promise: President Obama, Year One* (New York: Simon & Schuster, 2010).

45. Ibid. Barack Obama's firing of the commander of US forces in Afghanistan, General McChrystal, following comments that he and his staff made to *Rolling Stone* magazine, confirms the ongoing tension that exists between US political and military power. Paradoxically, the conflict is not based on substantive differences so much as it is based on the military's seemingly low regard for political power. McChrystal's dismissal had more to do with an authority problem than a disagreement over goals. See Michael Hastings, "The Runaway General," *Rolling Stones*, July 8–22, 2010.

46. Ibid.

47. *The New York Times*, August 16, 2010.
48. *International Herald Tribune,* June 24, 2010.
49. *The New York Times*, June 16, 2009.
50. Ryan Lizza, art. cit.
51. *The New York Times*, December 5, 2009.
52. *The Washington Post*, October 5, 2009.
53. Laura Rozen, "Biden on Gaza raid: 'Israel Has Right to Know' of Arms Smuggled," *Politico*, June 2, 2010, http://www.politico.com/blogs/laurarozen /0610/Biden_on_Gaza_raid_Israel_has_a_right_to_know_if_arms_being _smuggled.html?showall.
54. *The New York Times*, March 9, 2010.
55. *The Washington Post*, July 16, 2008.
56. Robert M. Gates, "A Balanced Strategy: Reprogramming the Pentagon for a New Age," *Foreign Affairs*, January-February 2009, http://www.foreignaffairs. com/articles/63717/robert-m-gates/a-balanced-strategy.
57. "The U.S. operates 11 large carriers, all nuclear powered. In terms of size and striking power, no other country has even one comparable ship. The U.S. Navy has 10 large-deck amphibious ships that can operate as sea bases for helicopters and vertical-takeoff jets. No other navy has more than three, and all of those navies belong to our allies or friends. Our Navy can carry twice as many aircraft at sea as all the rest of the world combined.

    The U.S. has 57 nuclear-powered attack and cruise missile submarines— again, more than the rest of the world combined. Seventy-nine Aegis-equipped combatants carry roughly 8,000 vertical-launch missile cells. In terms of total missile firepower, the U.S. arguably outmatches the next 20 largest navies. All told, the displacement of the U.S. battle fleet—a proxy for overall fleet capabilities—exceeds, by one recent estimate, at least the next 13 navies com-bined, of which 11 are our allies or partners. And, at 202,000 strong, the Marine Corps is the largest military force of its kind in the world and exceeds the size of most world armies." From the U.S. Department of Defense, Office of the Assistant Secretary of Defense (Public Affairs), http://www.defense.gov /speeches/speech.aspx?speechid=1460.
58. *The Washington Post,* June 16, 2008.
59. *The New York Times*, January 13, 2009.
60. "Let me be clear, the task before us is not to reduce the department's top line budget. Rather, it is to significantly reduce its excess overhead costs and apply the savings to force structure and modernization." Quoted in Gordon Adam's blog, "Cutting Defense: Is Bob Gates behind the Curve?," http://capital gainsandgames.com/blog/gordon-adams/1934/cutting-defense-bob-gates -behind-curve.
61. Susan Rice defended Obama against Hillary Clinton when she questioned his ability to deal with an international crisis. *The New York Times*, Caucus Blog, March 6, 2008.
62. *The New York Times*, September 21, 1998.

63. *PBS, Newshour*, November 17, 2006.

64. *PBS, Frontline*, October 10, 2006.

65. Idem.

66. John Brennan, "The Conundrum of Iran: Strengthening Moderates without Acquiescing to Belligerence," *The ANNALS of the American Academy of Political and Social Science*, 2008, 618, no. 1 (July 2008): 168–179.

67. *The New York Times*, August 5, 2010.

68. Barak Ravid, "Dennis Ross discovers Palestine," *Haaretz*, January 9, 2012.

69. Barak Ravid and Natasha Mozgovaya, "Obama's Mideast Adviser Steps Down Amid Stalled Peace Talks," *Haaretz*, November 10, 2011.

70. Martin S. Indyk, Kenneth G. Lieberthal and Michael O'Hanlon, *Bending History: Barack Obama's Foreign Policy* (Washington, DC: Brookings Institution Press, 2012), 133.

71. Ibid.

72. Ibid.

73. Glenn Kessler, "Understanding Obama's shift on Israel and the '1967 lines,'" *The Washington Post*, May 20, 2011.

74. "The prime minister [sic] had spoken with Secretary of State Hillary Clinton a few hours prior to the president's speech, expressing his rage over Obama's intent to support a peace accord based on the 1967 borders." Attila Somfalvi quoted in Robert Mackey, "Netanyahu to Confront Obama With 'Reality,' Israelis Say," *The New York Times*, May 20, 2011.

75. Mark Mardell, "What Does Obama's Stand on the 1967 Borders Achieve?," *BBC News*, May 19, 2011.

76. Jeffrey Goldberg, "Dear Mr. Netanyahu, Please Don't Speak to My President That Way," *The Atlantic*, May 20, 2011.

77. Robert Mackey, "Israel 'Cannot Go Back to the 1967 Lines', Netanyahu Tells Obama," *The New York Times*, May 20, 2011.

78. Helene Cooper, "Obama Presses Israel to Make 'Hard Choices,'" *The New York Times*, May 22, 2011 (emphasis added).

79. Akiva Eldar, "New U.S. envoy in Israel to clear obstacles for Obama's second term," *Haaretz*, August 5, 2011.

80. Howard L. Berman, "Turkey's New Foreign Policy Direction: Implications for U.S.-Turkish Relations," July 28, 2010 (http://international.edgeboss.net /real/international/fc07282010.smi). There has been a resurgence in the number of political grievances against Turkey. These previously overlooked grievances were now magnified: the issue of Cyprus, the treatment of non-Muslim minorities in Turkey, infringements on civil liberties, and the Armenian genocide.

81. As a result, 153 Democrats voted for a resolution in July 2010 requesting that the Obama administration set a timetable for withdrawal from Afghanistan. Only 98 Democrats voted against the resolution, which was defeated due to Republican support for the government in this matter, *The New York Times*, July 22, 2010.

82. *The Financial Times*, July 22, 2010.

83. *The New York Times*, December 7, 2011

84. Elizabeth Kolbert, "Storms Brewing," *The New Yorker,* June 13, 2011, http://www.newyorker.com/talk/comment/2011/06/13/110613taco_talk_kolbert #ixzz1cE5XkRiw.

85. *The New York Times,* March 22, 2012.

86. Al Gore, "Climate of Denial," *Rolling Stone,* June 22, 2011, http://www.rolling stone.com/politics/news/climate-of-denial-20110622#ixzz1cEockpGs.

87. The White House, "Remarks by the President in the State of the Union Address," January 24, 2012.

88. See Enrico Moretti, *The New Geography of Jobs* (Berkeley: University of California Press, 2012).

89. Global Council, *The dragon in the room: U.S. trade policy after the Doha Round,* February 23, 2012.

90. Australia, New Zealand, Brunei, Chile, Malaysia, Peru, Singapore, and Vietnam.

91. Ibid.

92. Greg Rushford, "The Rushford Report 2012: Obama's '21st Century' Trade Policies," January 30, 2012, http://www.rushfordresport.com/.

93. Foreign Policy Address at the Council on Foreign Relations, Hillary Rodham Clinton, July 15, 2009. Speech available at the State Department website: http://www.state.gov/secretary/rm/2009a/july/126071.htm.

94. "Today, we must acknowledge two inescapable facts that define our world: first, no nation can meet the world's challenges alone. The issues are too complex. Too many players are competing for influence, from rising powers to corporations to criminal cartels; from NGOs to al-Qaida; from state-controlled media to individuals using Twitter. Second, most nations worry about the same global threats, from non-proliferation to fighting disease to counterterrorism, but also face very real obstacles—for reasons of history, geography, ideology, and inertia. They face these obstacles and they stand in the way of turning commonality of interest into common action," ibid.

95. Jim Lobe, "Clinton Seeks 'Multi-Partner World', Warns Iran on Time," *IPS,* July 15, 2009, http://ipsnews.net/news.asp?idnews=47676.

96. Ibid.

97. Ibid.

98. Ibid.

99. Mancur Olson, *The Logic of Collective Action: Public Goods and the Theory of Groups* (Cambridge: Harvard University Press, 1965).

100. Ibid.

101. Foreign Policy Address at the Council on Foreign Relations, Hillary Rodham Clinton, July 15, 2009.

3   No More Monsters to Destroy?

1. Bradford Perkins, ed., "To the Monroe Doctrine," in *The Cambridge History of Foreign Relations, Vol. I, The Creation of a Republican Empire, 1776–1865* (New York: Cambridge University Press, 1995): ch. 6; Walter Russell Mead,

Special Providence, American Foreign Policy and How It Changed the World (New York: Alfred A. Knopf, 2001); Robert Litwark, *Détente and the Nixon Doctrine: American Foreign Policy and the Pursuit of Stability, 1969–1976* (New York: Cambridge University Press, 1986); James Scott, *Deciding to Intervene: The Reagan Doctrine and American Foreign Policy* (Durham, NC: Duke University Press, 1996); David Skidmore, *Reversing Course: Carter's Foreign Policy, Domestic Politics, and the Failure of Reform* (Nashville: Vanderbilt University Press, 1996); William Appleman Williams, *The Tragedy of American Diplomacy* (New York: Norton, 1988).

2. Douglas Brinkley, "Democratic enlargement: The Clinton doctrine," *Foreign Policy*, March 22, 1997, http://www.jstor.org/pss/1149177.

3. Jonathan Colman, *The Foreign Policy of Lyndon B. Johnson: The United States and the World, 1963–69* (Edinburgh: Edinburgh University Press, 2010); Meene Bose, and Rosanna Perotti, eds., *From Cold War to New World Order: The Foreign Policy of George H. W. Bush* (Westport, CT: Praeger, 2002).

4. Henry Kissinger, "The Age of Kennan," *The New York Times*, November 10, 2011, http://www.nytimes.com/2011/11/13/books/review/george-f-kennan-an -american-life-by-john-lewis-gaddis-book-review.html?pagewanted=all.

5. Walter McDougall, *Promised Land, Crusader State: The American Encounter with the World since 1776* (New York: Mariner Books, 1998).

6. Ibid.

7. Ibid.

8. Quoted in Brendon O'Connor, "American Foreign Policy Traditions: A Literature Review," *Working Paper*, October 2009, 3, http://ussc.edu.au/s /media/docs/publications/0910_oconnor_usforeignpolicy.pdf.

9. Quoted in Franck Ninkovich, *Modernity and Power: A History of the Domino Theory in the Twentieth Century* (Chicago: University of Chicago Press, 1994), 43.

10. Arthur M. Schlesinger, *The Cycles of American History* (New York: Mariner Books, 1999), 19.

11. William Widenor, *Henry Cabot Lodge and the Search for an American Foreign Policy* (Berkeley: University of California Press, 1980), 70.

12. John Ikenberry, *After Victory: Institutions, Strategic Restraints and the Rebuilding of Order after Major Wars* (Princeton, NJ: Princeton University Press, 2000).

13. Richard Grimmett, "Instances of Use of United States Armed Forces Abroad, 1798–2009," *Congressional Research Service*, January 27, 2010, 1, http://www.fas .org/sgp/crs/natsec/RL32170.pdf.

14. Ibid.

15. "War without Declaration: A Chronological List of 199 U.S. Military Hostilities Abroad without a Declaration of War. 1798–1972," *Congressional Record* 119 (July 20, 1973): S14174- S14183.

16. Ibid.

17. Richard Grimmett, "Instances of Use of United States Armed Forces Abroad, 1798–2009," art. cit.

18. In a speech on August 17, 2009, at the Veterans of Foreign Wars Convention, Obama said that the war in Afghanistan is a "war of necessity." See The White

House website: http://www.whitehouse.gov/the_press_office/Remarks-by -the-President-at-the-Veterans-of-Foreign-Wars-convention.

19. Richard Haass, *War of Necessity, War of Choice: A Memoir of Two Iraq Wars* (New York: Simon & Schuster, 2009).

20. Richard Haass, "The Restauration Doctrine," *The American Interest,* January/ February 2012, http://www.the-american-interest.com/article.cfm?piece=1164.

21. See Richard Haass, "Bleak History Lessons for Libya's Future," *The Financial Times,* March 27, 2011, http://www.ft.com/intl/cms/s/0/80b33b92–58a5 –11e0–9b8a-00144feab49a.html#axzz1iDN3AM2T; and Zaki Laïdi's response to Haass's article, "Allow the Libyan People Ownership of Their Victory," *The Financial Times,* August 30, 2011, http://www.ft.com/intl/cms/s/0/a0b42088 -cfd7–11e0-a1de 00144feabdc0.html#axzz1iDN3AM2T.

22. Richard Grimmett, op. cit.

23. Ibid.

24. Ibid.

25. Pat Towell, "Defense: FY2012 Budget Request, Authorization and App-ropriations," *Congressional Research Service,* November 25, 2011, http://www.fas .org/sgp/crs/natsec/R41861.pdf.

26. "Defense Spending," Department of Defense, May 24, 2011 http://www .defense.gov/speeches/speech.aspx?speechid=1570.

27. "An isolationist is a protectionist that builds walls around their country, they don't like the trade, they don't like to travel about the world, and they like to put sanctions on different countries. (…) So non-intervention is quite a bit different since what the founders advised was to get along with people, trade with people, and to practice diplomacy, rather than having this militancy of telling people what to do and how to run the world and building walls around our own country." Ron Paul, "Not an Isolationist but a Non-Interventionist," December 15, 2011, http://www.ronpaul.com/2011–12–15/ron-paul-not-an-isolationist-but-a -non-interventionist/.

28. Thirty-nine percent of Americans say the United States should engage with the world and help other countries deal with their problems, while a major-ity of 52 percent says the United States should be isolationist, deal with its own problems and let other countries deal with their problems as best they can. See *Pew Research Center,* "The American—Western European Values Gap," November 17, 2011, http://www.pewglobal.org/2011/11/17/the-american -western-european-values-gap/?src=prc-headline.

29. Nuno Monteiro, "Unrest Assured: Why Unipolarity Is Not Peaceful," *International Security,* 36, no. 3 (Winter 2011/12): 9–40, http://www.nunomonteiro.org /wp-content/uploads/Nuno-Monteiro-Unrest-Assured.pdf.

30. Paul Kennedy was one of the first to demonstrate the constraints on US power, even though the United States remarkably succeeded in dodging this constraint until 2009. Paul Kennedy, *The Rise and Fall of the Great Powers* (New York: Vintage, 1989).

31. According to the classification of Nuno Monteiro, "Unrest Assured: Why Unipolarity Is Not Peaceful," art. cit.

32. When John Quincy Adams served as US Secretary of State, he delivered this speech to the US House of Representatives on July 4, 1821, in celebration of American Independence Day. "John Quincy Adams on U.S. Foreign Policy," 1821, available at: http://www.fff.org/comment/AdamsPolicy.asp.

33. "Remarks by the President at the Acceptance of the Nobel Peace Prize," Oslo City Hall, *The White House*, December 10, 2009, http://www.whitehouse.gov /the-press-office/remarks-president-acceptance-nobel-peace-prize.

34. *The New York Times*, April 13, 2010.

35. For a systemic definition of realism, see Kenneth Waltz, *Theory of International Politics* (New York: McGraw-Hill, 1979). For a review of the literature, see David Baldwin, "Power and International Relations," in *Handbook of International Relations*, ed. Walter Carlsnaes, Thomas Risse, and Beth A. Simmons (Thousand Oaks, CA: Sage, 2002), 177–191.

36. Realism is not a unified collection of thought. The classics include: Hans Morgenthau, *Politics Among Nations* (New York: McGraw, 1954); Kenneth Waltz, *Theory of International Politics*, op. cit.; John Mearsheimer, *The Tragedy of Great Power Politics* (New York: Norton, 2001); Robert Keohane, *Neorealism and Its Critics* (New York: Columbia University Press, 1986); Joseph Grieco, "Modern Realist Theory and the Study of International Politics in the 21st Century," *International Studies Quarterly* 41 (1997): 295–316; Michael Nicholson, "Realism and Utopianism Revisited," *Review of International Studies*, 24, no. 5 (December 1998): 65–82; Jonathan Haslam, *No Virtue Like Necessity* (New Haven, CT: Yale University Press, 2002); Randall Schweller, *The Progressiveness of Neoclassical Realism* (Cambridge, MA: MIT Press, 2003).

37. Stephen Walt, "International Relations: One World, Many Theories," *Foreign Policy*, Spring 1998, http://www.columbia.edu/itc/sipa/S6800/courseworks /foreign_pol_walt.pdf.

38. William C. Wolforth, "Realism," in *The Oxford Handbook of International Relations*, ed. Christian Reus-Smit and Duncan Snidal (New York and Oxford: Oxford University Press, 2008), 133.

39. Kenneth Waltz, "International Politics Is Not Foreign Policy," *Security Studies*, 6, no. 1 (1996): 54–57.

40. Stephen Walt, "The Relationship between Theory and Policy in International Relations," *Annual Review of Political Science*, 8 (2005): 23–48.

41. For a detailed comparative analysis of these two sets, the reader is referred to the annex.

42. "Remarks by the President in Addresses to the New Economic School Graduation," *The White House*, July 7, 2009, http://www.whitehouse.gov/the _press_office/Remarks-By-The-President-At-The-New-Economic-School -Graduation.

43. See Zaki Laïdi, "La fin du moment démocratique" [The end of the democratic moment], *Le Débat*, March-April 2008, 52–63.

44. Juan Linz, and Alfred Stepan, *Problems of Democratic Transition and Consolidation* (Baltimore: Johns Hopkins Press, 1996), 19.

45. Georges Packer, "Iran Reveals Us," *The New Yorker,* June 16, 2009, http://www .newyorker.com/online/blogs/georgepacker/2009/06/iran-reveals-us.html.

46. William C. Potter, "India and the New Look in U.S. Non-Proliferation Policy," *Carnegie Endowment,* August 26, 2005, http://www.carnegieendowment.org /static/npp/2005conference/presentations/Potter.pdfhttp://cns.miis.edu/npr /pdfs/122potter.pdf.

47. Nuclear Suppliers Group, "Statement on Full Scope Safeguards, Meeting of Adherents to the Nuclear Suppliers Guidelines," Warsaw, March 31–April 3, 1992, INFCIRC/405/Attachment.

48. U.S. Department of Defense, "Special Briefing on the Nuclear Posture Review," *News Transcript,* January 9, 2002, http://www.defense.gov/transcripts/transcript .aspx?transcriptid=1108.

49. *Remarks by the President at the Acceptance of the Nobel Peace Prize,* Oslo City Hall, December 10, 2009. http://www.whitehouse.gov/the-press-office/remarks -president-acceptance-nobel-peace-prize.

50. John Ikenberry, *Liberal Leviathan: The Origins, Crisis, and Transformation of the American World Order* (Princeton, NJ: Princeton University Press, 2011), 308.

51. Rory Stewart, "What Could Work," *New York Review of Books,* January 14, 2010.

52. *The New York Times,* July 23, 2010.

53. Statement by Senator Richard Lugar, *The New York Times,* May 19, 2010.

54. Putin's Prepared Remarks at 43rd Munich Conference on Security Policy, *The Washington Post,* February 10, 2007, http://www.washingtonpost.com/wp-dyn /content/article/2007/02/12/AR2007021200555.html.

55. Georgia ranks eleventh among the countries George W. Bush mentioned in his speeches during his second term, right behind China!

56. *The Guardian,* December 23, 2008.

57. Hans Blix, "A Season for Disarmament," *The New York Times,* April 5, 2010.

58. Gary Schaub, and James Forsyth Jr., "An Arsenal We Can All Live With," *The New York Times,* May 24, 2010.

59. U.S. Department of Defense, *Nuclear Posture Review Report,* April 2010, www .defense.gov/npr/docs/2010 Nuclear Posture Review Report.pdf, vi.

60. Ibid., 32.

61. U.S. Department of Defense, *Nuclear Posture Review Report,* April 2010, op. cit. www.defense.gov/npr/docs/2010 Nuclear Posture Review Report.pdf, viii.

62. "The negative security assurance that we won't use nuclear weapons against non-nuclear states, in conformity with or in compliance with the Nonproliferation Treaty, is not a new thing. The new part of this is saying that we would not use nuclear weapons against a non-nuclear state that attacked us with chemical and biological weapons." Statement by Robert Gates on April 11, 2010, quoted in Daryl G. Kimball, and Greg Thielmann, "Obama's NPR: Transitional, Not Transformational," http://www.armscontrol.org/act/2010_05/Kimball -Thielmann.

63. Daryl G. Kimball and Greg Thielmann, ibid.

64. Paul Meyer, "Prague One Year Later: From Words to Deeds?," http://www .armscontrol.org/act/2010_05/LookingBack.

65. U.S. Department of Defense, *Nuclear Posture Review Report*, April 2010, art. cit. www.defense.gov/npr/docs/2010 Nuclear Posture Review Report.pdf, viii.

66. In February 2002, then-State Department spokesman Richard Boucher said it was US policy that "[i]f a weapon of mass destruction is used against the United States or its allies, we will not rule out any specific type of military response." Available at: http://www.armscontrol.org/factsheets/negsec.

67. The final declaration of the conference explicitly mentions the case of Israel, but the call for adherence to NPT provisions was made in similar terms to two other nuclear powers that are nonsignatories to the NPT—India and Pakistan. See Peter Crail, *NPT Parties Agree on Middle East Meeting*, http://www.armscontrol .org/act/2010_06/NPTMideast.

68. William Potter, Patricia Lewis, Gaukhar Mukhatzhanova, and Miles Pomper, "The 2010 NPT Review Conference: Deconstructing Consensus," *CNS Special Report*, June 17, 2010,http://cns.miis.edu/stories/pdfs/100617_npt_2010 _summary.pdf.

69. "Although many participants anticipated that the United States would be unwilling to accept the compromise language proposed by the chair, and it was unclear until mid-morning of the last day of the Conference what the final position of the United States would be, when Washington ultimately agreed to the mild reference to Israel, a deal was made that Egypt and its Arab allies could not refuse. It then was left to Iran to either make or break the conference. When Iran, at the last moment, agreed to join consensus, and the Final Document was adopted, the United States then had to put in place its damage limitation strategy directed at audiences at home and in Israel. It is noteworthy that Arab states, including Egypt, have not responded vocally to these post-RevCon reservations. As such, it appears that the post-conference statements by the United States were either part of the understanding that was reached or at least were anticipated by the Arab states," ibid., 12–13.

70. Statement by the National Security Advisor, General James L. Jones, on the Non-Proliferation Treaty Review. Conference, *The White House,* Office of the Press Secretary, May 28, 2010, http://www.whitehouse.gov/the-pressoffice /statement-national-security-advisor-general-james-l-jones-non-proliferation -treaty-.

71. *The New York Times*, March 27, 2012.

72. Charles Kupchan, *How Enemies Become Friends: The Source of Stable Peace* (Princeton, NJ: Princeton University Press, 2010).

73. Frenemy is the contraction of "friend" and "enemy." Steven Cook, "How Do You Say Frenemy in Turkish?," *Foreign Policy*, June 1, 2010, http://www.foreign policy.com/articles/2010/06/01/how_do_you_say_frenemy_in_Turkish.

74. See Matthew Kroenig, "Time to Attack Iran," *Foreign Affairs*, January–February 2012, http://www.foreignaffairs.com/articles/136917/matthew-kroenig/time- to-attack-iran; and Steve Walt, "Why Attacking Iran Is Still a Bad Idea," *Foreign*

Policy, December 27, 2010, http://walt.foreignpolicy.com/posts/2011/12/27/why_attacking_iran_is_still_a_bad_idea.

75. Mark Perry, "The Petraeus Briefing: Biden's Embarrassment Is Not the Whole Story," *Foreign Policy*, March 13, 2010, http://mideast.foreignpolicy.com/posts/2010/03/14/the_petraeus_briefing_biden_s_Embarrassment_is_not_the_whole_story.

76. Suzanne Maloney, "Progress of the Obama Administration's Policy toward Iran," Testimony before the House Subcommittee on National Security, Homeland Defense and Foreign Operations, Committee on Oversight and Government Reform, November 15, 2011, http://www.brookings.edu/testimony/2011/1115_iran_policy_maloney.aspx.

77. *The New York Times*, December 25, 2011.

78. Jeffrey Goldberg, "Robert Gates Says Israel is an Ungrateful Ally," *Bloomberg View*, September 6, 2011.

79. *The New Yorker*, August 8, 2011.

80. *The Financial Times*, February 13, 2012,

4 Repudiating the Ideology of September 11

1. John Lewis Gaddis, *Surprise, Security, and the American Experience* (Cambridge, MA: Harvard University Press, 2004), 13.

2. Cited in Edward Howland Tatum Jr., *The United States and Europe, 1815–1823, A Study in the Background of the Monroe Doctrine* (Berkeley: University of California Press, 1934), 244–245.

3. *National Security Strategy*, September 2002, 28. http://www.globalsecurity.org/military/library/policy/national/nss-020920.pdf.

4. Quoted in Robert Jervis, "Understanding the Bush Doctrine," art. cit.

5. The *Financial Times*, June 21, 2010.

6. Cited in Eric Schmitt, and Thom Shanker, "New Name for 'War on Terror' Reflects Wider U.S. Campaign," *The New York Times*, July 25, 2005.

7. "Tora Bora Revisited: How We Failed to Get Bin Laden and Why It Matters Today," *Committee on Foreign Relations United States Senate*, chaired by John F. Kerry, November 30, 2009, http://foreign.senate.gov/imo/media/doc/Tora_Bora_Report.pdf.

8. Jackson Richard, *Writing the War on Terrorism: Language, Politics and Counter-terrorism: New Approaches to Conflict Analysis* (Manchester, UK: Manchester University Press, 2005), 5.

9. Ibid., 114.

10. "Soldiers and Marines are expected to be nation builders as well as warriors," the introduction to the manual declares. "They must be prepared to help reestablish institutions and local security forces and assist in rebuilding infrastructure and basic services. They must be able to facilitate establishing local governance and the rule of law." Quoted in Nicholas Lemann, "Terrorism

Studies: Social Scientists Do Counterinsurgency," *The New Yorker*, April 26, 2010, http://www.newyorker.com/arts/critics/books/2010/04/26/100426crbo _books_lemann#ixzz0uFCmcmJ5.

11. Ibid.

12. Steve Coll, "The General's Dilemma," *The New Yorker*, September 8, 2008, http://www.newyorker.com/reporting/2008/09/08/080908fa_fact_coll.

13. *The New York Times*, June 30, 2010.

14. On this point, see the Israeli David Grossman's realist position: "Israël doit se réapproprier son destin!" [Israel should take charge of its destiny!], *Le Monde*, July 17, 2010.

15. Jane Mayer, "The C.I.A.'s Travel Agent," *The New Yorker*, October 30, 2006. Available at: http://www.newyorker.com/archive/2006/10/30/061030ta_talk _mayer#ixzz0ucNggxlA.

16. President Bush's News Conference With Prime Minister Junichiro Koizumi of Japan in Tokyo, Japan, February 18, 2002, available at: http://www .presidency.ucsb.edu/news_conferences.php?year=2002. This attempt to tie the Iraqi issue to a Palestinian settlement had already been made by the administration of George Bush Senior after the Gulf War in 1991. In a way, the United States officially held to this commitment after the war by forcing Israel to the negotiating table at the Madrid conference. The United States even threatened to suspend financing guarantees for housing programs in Israel.

17. *The White House*, "Remarks by Assistant to the President for Homeland Security and Counterterrorism John Brennan at CSIS," May 26, 2010, http:// www.whitehouse.gov/the-press-office/remarks-assistant-president-homeland -security-and-counterterrorism-john-brennan-csi.

18. The White House, "Remarks by the President at Cairo University," June 4, 2009, http://www.whitehouse.gov/the-press-office/remarks-president-cairo -university-6–04–09.

19. Doha Brookings Center, "The 2011 Arab Public Opinion Poll," November 21, 2011, http://www.brookings.edu/reports/2011/1121_arab_public_opinion _telhami.aspx.

20. Ibid.

21. Ibid.

22. Audrey Kurth Cronin, *How Terrorism Ends: Understanding the Decline and Demise of Terrorist Campaigns* (Princeton: Princeton University Press, 2009).

23. The best way to understand Al Qaeda as an organization and an idea in 2010 is to break it down into three parts: the Al Qaeda core; Al Qaeda regional affiliates and like-minded groups; and Al Qaeda-inspired radicalization and threats. See Juan C. Zarate's statement before the House Armed Services Committee, "Al Qa'ida in 2010: How Should the U.S. Respond?" *Center for Strategic and International Studies (CSIS)*, January 27, 2010, 3, http://csis.org/files/ts_100127 _Zarate.pdf.

24. Ibid., 2.

25. Ibid., 5.

26. Audrey Kurth Cronin, *How Terrorism Ends: Understanding the Decline and Demise of Terrorist Campaigns*, op. cit.

27. *National Security Strategy*, 2006, 36, http://www.comw.org/qdr/fulltext/nss 2006.pdf.

28. "Muslims Believe US Seeks to Undermine Islam," *WorldPublicOpinion.org*, April 24, 2007, http://www.worldpublicopinion.org/pipa/articles/brmiddle eastnafricara/346.php.

29. In its Ramdam ruling (2006) the Supreme Court closed military courts, while in Boumediene v. Bush (2008) it extended Habeas Corpus to Guantanamo detainees; in Congress the McCain amendment (2006) on interrogation methods further reinforced this tendency. Cited in Marc Lynch, *Rhetoric and Reality: Countering Terrorism in the Age of Obama*, Center for a New American Security, June 2010, 12, http://www.cnas.org/files/documents/publications/CNAS _Rhetoric%20and%20Reality_Lynch.pdf .

30. See Myriam Benraad, "Facing Homegrown Radicalization," *Policy Watch #1575*, Washington Institute, September 3, 2009, http://www.washington institute.org/templateC05.php?CID=3113.

31. Michael Leiter, Hearings before the Senate Committee on Homeland Security and Governmental Affairs, "Eight Years After 9/11: Confronting the Terrorist Threat to the Homeland," September 30, 2009, http://hsgac.senate.gov/public /index.cfm?FuseAction=Hearings.Hearing&Hearing_ID=5b17b0b6-afce -4488–80a0–0c3db92fe8f8.

32. This was noticeable when, in December 2009, the United States escaped a terrorist attack on a flight from Amsterdam to Detroit. Due to this incident, on January 7, 2010, Barack Obama returned to a classic discourse: "We are at war. We are at war against Al Qaeda." Remarks by the President on Strengthening Intelligence and Aviation Security. http://www.whitehouse.gov/the-press -office/remarks-president-strengthening-intelligence-and-aviation-security .

33. David Cole, "After September 11: What We Still Don't Know," *The New York Review of Books*, September 29, 2011, http://www.nybooks.com/articles /archives/2011/sep/29/after-september-11-what-we-still-dont-know.

34. This decision is contingent on obtaining funding from Congress to build a prison in Illinois.

35. *The New York Times*, May 1, 2009. The *Military Commission Act* of 2006 was, however, modified in 2009. For more on the legal differences between the two acts, see Joanne Mariner, "A First Look at the Military Commission Act of 2009," Part One, November 4, 2009, http://writ.news.findlaw.com/mariner/20091104 .html.

36. *The New York Times*, July 26, 2010.

37. David Cole, September 29, 2011, art. cit.

38. These are Michael Vickers, in charge of special operations at the Department of Defense and involved, in the 1980s, in CIA operations in Afghanistan; Steve Kappes, in charge of CIA operations; Stuart Levy, in charge of combating the financing of terrorism; Nick Rasmussen, in charge of counterterrorism at

the National Security Council; and Michael Leiter, director of the National Counterterrorism Center.

39. "There has been a lot of information that has come out from these interrogation procedures that the agency has in fact used against the real hardcore terrorists. It has saved lives," quoted in *Media matters*, January 7, 2009, http://mediamatters. org/research/200901070010.

40. *The New York Times*, November 25, 2008.

41. Jane Mayer, "The Secret History: Can Leon Panetta Move the C.I.A. Forward Without Confronting Its Past?," *The New Yorker*, June 22, 2009, http://www .newyorker.com/reporting/2009/06/22/090622fa_fact_mayer#ixzz0ubt8aj71. Leon Panetta has since become Defense Secretary and was replaced by General Petraeus.

5   Back from Baghdad

1. Richard N. Haass, "In Afghanistan, the Choice Is Ours," *The New York Times*, August 20, 2009. Richard Haass originally made the distinction between war of choice and of necessity with regard to the first and second Gulf wars. Obama expanded the comparison to Iraq and Afghanistan, but Haass disputes the idea that Afghanistan is a war of choice.

2. Barack Obama, "The World Beyond Iraq," Speech in Fayetteville, March 19, 2008. Cited in *Time*, http://thepage.time.com/full-text-of-obamas-iraq-speech/.

3. Obama speech at Camp Lejeune, NC, February 27, 2009, http://www .whitehouse.gov/the_press_office/Remarks-of-President-Barack-Obama -Responsibly-Ending-the-War-in-Iraq/.

4. R. Chuck Mason, "Status of Forces Agreement (SOFA): What Is It, and How Has It Been Utilized?," *CRS Report for Congress*, June 18, 2009, http://www.fas .org/sgp/crs/natsec/RL34531.pdf.

5. *The Washington Post*, August 3, 2010.

6. Anthony H. Cordesman, "Iraq and the United States: Creating a Strategic Partnership," *Center for International and Strategic Studies*, June 2010, 3, http://csis .org/files/publication/100622_Cordesman_IraqUSStrategicPartner_WEB.pdf.

7. Stephen Daggett, "Costs of Major U.S. War," *CRS Report for Congress*, June 29, 2010, 2, http://www.fas.org/sgp/crs/natsec/RS22926.pdf.

8. A recent excellent audit jointly prepared by the inspector generals of the Departments of State and of Defense evaluated the contract to train civil- ian police in Afghanistan. Its conclusions were very similar to those of the SIGIR audit. See Stuart W. Bowen, Jr., "Oversight: Hard Lessons Learned In Iraq and Benchmarks for Future Reconstruction Efforts," *Committee on Foreign Affairs House of Representatives One Hundred Eleventh Congress Second Session*, February 24, 2010, http://www.sigir.mil/files/USOCO/SIGIR _Testimony_10–002T.pdf.

9. For anyone interested in American foreign policy, Iraq, or the problems of foreign intervention, SIGIR's final report is highly recommended reading: SIGIR, "Hard Lessons: The Iraq Reconstruction Experience," February 2009, http://www.sigir.mil/files/HardLessons/Hard_Lessons_Report.pdf. This very rich and exceptionally rigorous report is the most damning assessment of the American intervention in Iraq.

10. Ibid., 98.

11. Ibid., 75.

12. Anthony H. Cordesman, "Iraq and the United States: Creating a Strategic Partnership," *Center for Strategic and International Studies,* June 2010, 225, http://csis.org/files/publication/100622_Cordesman_IraqUSStrategicPartner_WEB.pdf.

13. "Hard Lessons: The Iraq Reconstruction Experience," op. cit., 72.

14. Ibid., 75.

15. In his memoir Paul Bremer writes that he arrived in Baghdad with a copy of MacArthur's memoir in his luggage. It is not clear that he retained the lessons of Japan since, contrary to common perception, American success in Japan stemmed from the fact that the United States worked with the imperial institutions, see John W. Dower, *Embracing Defeat: Japan in the Wake of World War II* (New York: W.W. Norton, 1999).

16. "Hard Lessons: The Iraq Reconstruction Experience," op. cit., 76.

17. Ibid., 121.

18. International Crisis Group, "Iraq after the Surge I: The New Sunni Landscape," *Middle East Report no. 74,* April 30, 2008, http://www.crisisgroup.org/~/media/Files/Middle%20East%20North%20Africa/Iraq%20Syria%20Lebanon/Iraq/74_iraq_after_the_surge_I_the_new_sunnI_landscape.ashx.

19. According to an American analyst, "The United States has budgeted 150 million dollars to pay Sunni tribal groups this year, and the sheiks take as much as 20 percent of every payment to a former insurgent—which means that commanding 200 fighters can be worth well over a hundred thousand dollars a year for a tribal chief." Steven Simon, "The Price of the Surge. How U.S. Strategy is Hastening Iraq's Demise," *Foreign Affairs,* 87, no. 3 (May- June 2008), 65.

20. *International Crisis Group,* "Iraq's Civil War, the Sadrists and the Surge," *Middle East Report no. 72,* February 7, 2008, http://www.crisisgroup.org/~/media/Files/Middle%20East%20North%20Africa/Iraq%20Syria%20Lebanon/Iraq/72_iraq_s_civil_war_the_sadrists_and_the_surge.ashx.

21. On the history of the American surge in Iraq, which was implemented but not conceived by General Petraeus, see Steve Coll, "The General's Dilemma, David Petraeus, the Pressures of Politics, and the Road out of Iraq," *The New Yorker,* September 8, 2008, http://www.newyorker.com/reporting/2008/09/08/080908fa_fact_coll#ixzz0vlbPpByq.

22. *International Crisis Group,* "Iraq after the Surge II: The Need for a New Political Strategy," *Middle East Report no. 75,* April 30, 2008, http://www.crisisgroup.org/~/media/Files/Middle%20East%20North%20Africa/Iraq%20Syria%20

Lebanon/Iraq/75_iraq_after_the_surge_iI_the_need_for_a_new_political
_strategy.ashx.

23. "Integration of Sons of Iraq Delayed until Mid-2010," *Musings on Iraq: Iraq News, Politics, Economics, Society*, January 4, 2010, http://musingsoniraq.blog spot.com/2010/01/integration-of-sons-of-iraq-delayed.html.

24. "Iraq" in *CIA, World Factbook*, June 24, 2010, https://www.cia.gov/library /publications/the-world-factbook/geos/iz.html.

25. *The New York Times*, August 1, 2010.

26. Cited in *Hard Lessons*, op. cit., 150.

27. Ibid., 210.

28. Ibid.

29. Stuart W. Bowen, Jr., "Oversight: Hard Lessons Learned In Iraq and Benchmarks for Future Reconstruction Efforts," art. cit.

30. R. Chuck Mason, "Status of Forces Agreement (SOFA): What Is It, and How Has It Been Utilized?," art. cit.

31. Kenneth Katzman, "Iraq: Post-Saddam Governance and Security," *CRS Report for Congress*, October 28, 2009, 42, http://www.fas.org/sgp/crs/mideast /RL31339.pdf.

32. "Agreement between the United States of America and the Republic of Iraq on the Withdrawal of United States Forces from Iraq and the Organization of Their Activities during Their Temporary Presence in Iraq," Article 12, November 17, 2008, http://www.globalsecurity.org/military/library/policy/dod/iraq-sofa.htm.

33. Ibid., article 12.1.

34. Ibid., article 12.10.

35. Ibid., article 4.3.

36. R. Chuck Mason, "U.S.-Iraq Withdrawal/Status of Forces Agreement: Issues for Congressional Oversight," *CRS Report for Congress*, July 13, 2009, http:// www.fas.org/sgp/crs/natsec/R40011.pdf.

37. Robert Gates estimated that several thousand American troops would likely stay in Iraq after 2011, but he made clear this would be an Iraqi sovereign choice. "Robert Gates Talks about Residual Forces in Iraq after 2011," interview with Robert Gates in *Current Affairs*, December 17, 2008.

38. Cited in Gerard Russell, "Foreign Policy, Staying for the Longer-Term in Iraq and Afghanistan?," *Foreign Policy*, August 16, 2010, http://afpak.foreignpolicy.com /posts/2010/08/16/staying_for_the_longer_term_in_iraq_and_afghanistan.

39. It will be interesting to see if Iraq will want to negotiate a new agreement with the United States after the complete withdrawal of troops in December 2011, and if so, what provisions it would include.

40. Kenneth Katzman, "Iraq: Post-Saddam Governance and Security," art. cit..

41. Ibid., 12.

42. Ibid., 4.

43. *The Guardian*, August 5, 2010.

44. Kenneth Katzman, "Iran's Activities and Influence in Iraq," *CRS Report for Congress*, June 4, 2009, http://www.fas.org/sgp/crs/mideast/RS22323.pdf.

45. Anthony H. Cordesman, "Pandora's Box: Iraqi Federalism, Separatism, 'Hard' Partitioning, and U.S. Policy," *Center for Strategic and International Studies*, October 9, 2007, http://csis.org/files/media/csis/pubs/071009_pandorasbox.pdf.

46. Anthony H. Cordesman, "Iraq and the United States: Creating a Strategic Partnership," *Center for Strategic and International Studies,* June 2010, 6, http://csis.org/files/publication/100622_Cordesman_IraqUSStrategicPartner_WEB.pdf ; US Senator Rohrabacher stated: "I rarely hear a thank you from our Iraqis that come to visit us, and I think that we, the American people, deserve that." Quoted in "Oversight: Hard Lessons Learned in Iraq and Benchmarks for Future Reconstruction Efforts," art. cit. 6, http://www.internationalrelations.house.gov/111/55125.pdf.

47. Joost Hiltermann, "Iraq: The Impasse," *The New York Review of Books*, August 19, 2010, http://www.nybooks.com/articles/archives/2010/aug/19/iraq-impasse/.

48. Anthony H. Cordesman, "Iraq and the United States: Creating a Strategic Partnership", op. cit.

49. Kenneth Katzman, "Iraq Politics, Elections and Benchmarks," *CRS Report for Congress*, April 28, 2010, http://www.fas.org/sgp/crs/mideast/RS21968.pdf.

50. Anthony H. Cordesman, "Iraq and the United States: Creating a Strategic Partnership", op. cit., 54.

51. *The International Herald Tribune*, October 2–3, 2010.

52. "Remarks by the President on Ending the War in Iraq," *The White House,* October 21, 2011, available at: http://m.whitehouse.gov/the-press-office/2011/10/21/remarks-president-ending-war-iraq.

53. "It was well known that we were going to be out of Iraq cities in the summer of 2009, and, again, security improved; it didn't get worse. It was well known that we were going to change our mission in the summer of 2010, and the combat mission—move to an advise-and-assist mission—and get down to 50,000 troops. Again, security continued to improve; it didn't get worse. And there's something very important about the United States keeping its commitments. That sends a very strong and powerful message throughout the region—in Iraq as well as countries outside Iraq. And that's exactly what we're doing." Press Briefing by Denis McDonough, Tony Blinken, and Jay Carney, The White House, October 21, 2011, available at: http://m.whitehouse.gov/the-press-office/2011/10/21/press-briefing-denis-mcdonough-tony-blinken-and-jay-carney.

54. For more details on the negotiations and US difficulties in convincing the Iraqi authorities, see *The New York Times*, October 22, 2011.

55. No sooner had the withdrawal of US troops from Iraq been announced in December 2010, than the Pentagon indicated it was searching for ways to strengthen its strategic position in the Persian Gulf with the clear intention of signaling to Iran that withdrawal from Iraq did not imply US disinterest in the region. The new Secretary of Defense, Leon Panetta, also specified that "for Iran and anybody else who has any other ideas, let me make clear that the United States maintains 40,000 troops in that region, 23,000 in Kuwait, and

numbers of others in countries throughout that region. Let me make clear to them and to anybody else that America will maintain a presence in that part of the world." Town Hall Meeting with Secretary Panetta with U.S. Military and Japanese Defense Force Personnel at Yakota Air Base, Japan, October 24, 2011, available at the Department of Defense website at: http://www.defense.gov /transcripts/transcript.aspx?transcriptid=4911.

56. A lot of people in the political arena wanted the Americans to stay, but they could not bring themselves to translate this into a publicly held position and actually call for American immunity in Iraq, according to Ahmad Chalabi, cited in *The New York Times*, October 28, 2011.

57. "Iraq is a highly nationalistic country, and we were not able to dislodge the view that they should not have foreign troops on their soil," according to Chris Hill former US ambassador to Iraq, *The New York Times*, October 21, 2011.

58. "An invasion is never a very good basis for forming an alliance," according to Christopher Hill, *The International Herald Tribune,* October 24, 2011.

6   "Good Enough for Afghanistan"

1. *White House*, "White Paper of the Interagency Policy Group's Report on U.S. Policy toward Afghanistan and Pakistan," March 2009, 1.

2. Cited in *The New York Times*, March 16, 2011.

3. Cited in "Achieving Victory in Afghanistan Requires More Than Just 'Afghan Good Enough,'" *Small Wars Journal*, June 13, 2011. Available at: http://smallwarsjournal.com/blog/afghan-good-enough.

4. See Barnett R. Rubin, *The Fragmentation of Afghanistan* (New Haven, CT: Yale University Press, 2002).

5. Ahmed Rashid, *Descent into Chaos*, op. cit.

6. See Christine Fair, "The U.S. Strategy in Afghanistan: Impacts upon U.S. Interests in Pakistan," Testimony presented before the United States House of Representatives, Armed Services Committee, Subcommittee on Oversight and Investigations, May 24, 2011. Available at: http://www.humansecurity gateway.com/documents/USGOV_FairTestimony_StrategyInAfghanistan _ImpactUponUSInterestsInPakistan.pdf.

7. Ahmed Rashid, *Descent into Chaos*, op. cit., 133.

8. Ibid.

9. Carl Forsberg, "Politics and Power in Kandahar," *Institute for the Study of War, Afghanistan Report 5*, April 2010, http://www.understandingwar.org/files /Politics_and_Power_in_Kandahar.pdf.

10. For more details on this crisis, see Kenneth Katzman, "Afghanistan: Politics, Elections, and Government Performance," *CRS Report for Congress*, June 29, 2010, 6. http://www.fas.org/sgp/crs/row/RS21922.pdf.

11. Carl Forsberg, "Politics and Power in Kandahar," op. cit., 17–27.

12. Ibid.

13. Stanley McChrystal's "COMISAF's Initial Assessment," August 30, 2009, http://www.washingtonpost.com/wp-dyn/content/article/2009/09/21/AR2009092100110.html.

14. USAID, "Assessment of Corruption in Afghanistan," USAID, January 15–March 1, 2009, 61, http://pdf.usaid.gov/pdf_docs/PNADO248.pdf.

15. "Afghan Perceptions and Experience of Corruption: A National Survey 2010," *Integrity Watch Afghanistan*, 66.

16. Ibid.

17. Ibid.

18. Kenneth Katzman, "Afghanistan: Post-Taliban Governance, Security, and U.S. Policy," *CRS Report for Congress*, May 3, 2012

19. USAID, "Assessment of Corruption in Afghanistan," op. cit.

20. Matt Waldman, "Falling Short: Aid Effectiveness in Afghanistan," *ABCAR Advocacy Series*, March 2008, 1, http://www.ciaonet.org/pbei/oxfam/0003419/f_0003419_2530.pdf.

21. Ibid., 1.

22. United States Government Accountability Office, "Afghanistan Development USAID Continues to Face Challenges in Managing and Overseeing U.S. Development Assistance Programs," Testimony Before the Subcommittee on State, Foreign Operations, and Related Programs, Committee on Appropriations, July 15, 2010, 8, http://www.gao.gov/products/GAO-10-932T.

23. Ibid., 5.

24. "Despite numerous reports highlighting this problem in Iraq and Afghanistan over the last eight years, one of our first audits found that the United States still does not have a system that would allow agencies to share information about reconstruction programs." Statement of Arnold Fields, Special Inspector General for Afghanistan Reconstruction before the House Armed Services Committee Hearing, "Oversight Issues in Afghanistan," May 20, 2010, 2, http://www.sigar.mil/pdf/testimony/05_20_10SIGARTestimonyHouseIOSubcommittee.pdf.

25. See Katzman, "Afghanistan: Post-Taliban Governance, Security, and U.S. Policy," op. cit.

26. Stanley Mc Chrystal, "COMISAF's Initial Assessment," op. cit., August 30, 2009.

27. *The New York Times*, January 22, 2010.

28. Stanley McChrystal, "COMISAF's Initial Assessment," op. cit.

29. James Jones, Obama's security adviser, estimated there are one hundred Al Qaeda members in Afghanistan. See "State of the Union," *CNN*, October 4, 2009, http://transcripts.cnn.com/TRANSCRIPTS/0910/04/sotu.05.html.

30. Stanley McChrystal, "COMISAF's Initial Assessment," op. cit.

31. Ibid.

32. "Best practice COIN integrates and synchronizes political, security, economic, and informational components that reinforce governmental legitimacy and effectiveness while reducing insurgent influence over the population. COIN

strategies should be designed to simultaneously protect the population from insurgent violence; strengthen the legitimacy and capacity of government institutions to govern responsibly and marginalize insurgents politically, socially, and economically." "Counterinsurgency Guide: United States Government Interagency Counterinsurgency Initiative," *US Department of State, Bureau of Political-Military Affairs*, Washington (January 2009), 12, http://www.state.gov /documents/organization/119629.pdf.

33. Sir Robert G. K. Thompson, *Defeating Communist Insurgency: The Lessons of Malaya and Vietnam* (New York: Praeger, 1966): 112–113.

34. *ICOS,* "Operation Moshtarak: Lessons Learned," May 2010. http://smallwars journal.com/documents/moshtarak1.pdf.

35. Kenneth Katzman, "Afghanistan: Post-Taliban Governance, Security, and U.S. Policy," op. cit., 20.

36. NATO, "International Security Assistance Force," http://www.nato.int/isaf /docu/epub/pdf/placemat_archive/isaf_placemat_090112.pdf.

37. This is empty rhetoric. If the future of civilization were at stake in Afghanistan, it would be difficult to understand why almost all the countries involved in the conflict are searching for good reasons to withdraw their troops, and why a growing number of foreign players are calling for negotiations with the Taliban. As long as the West's military losses were limited, the cause of civilization was strongly supported as a justification for war. However, as soon as the losses started to grow, it was coyly set aside. In France, Nicolas Sarkozy has perfectly illustrated this trajectory. In fairness to him, though, almost all of his European counterparts have reacted in the same way.

38. Thomas Ruttig, "The Other Side: Dimensions of the Afghan Insurgency: Causes, Actors and Approaches to 'Talks,'" *Afghan Network Analysis, AAN Thematic Report 01,* July 2009, http://www.aan-afghanistan.org/uploads/200907%20 AAN%20Report%20Ruttig%20-%20The%20Other%20Side.PDF.

39. Ibid., 16.

40. Ibid., 21.

41. See Antonio Giustozzi, and Christoph Reuter, "The Northern Front. The Afghan insurgency Spreading beyond the Pashtuns," *Afghan Network Analysis, AAN Thematic Report 03,* June 2010, http://aan-afghanistan.com/uploads /20100623NORTH.pdf.

42. Talatbek Masadykov, Antonio Giustozzi, and James Michael Page, "Negotiating with the Taliban: Toward a Solution for the Afghan Conflict," *Crisis States Working Papers Series no. 2, Working Paper no. 66,* January 2010, 11, http://www .crisisstates.com/download/wp/wpSeries2/WP66.2.pdf.

43. Ibid.

44. Thomas Ruttig, "The Other Side: Dimensions of the Afghan Insurgency: Causes, Actors and Approaches to 'Talks,'" op. cit., 11.

45. Matt Waldman, "Golden Surrender? The Risks, Challenges, and Implications of Reintegration in Afghanistan," *Afghan Network Analysis, AAN Thematic*

Report 3, April 2010, 3,http://aan-afghanistan.org/uploads/2010_AAN_Golden _Surrender.pdf.

46. Kenneth Katzman, "Afghanistan: Post-War Governance, Security and US Policy," op. cit.

47. Ibid., 28.

48. Michael Semple, *Reconciliation in Afghanistan* (Washington, DC: United States Institute for Peace, 2009).

49. "Flynn, the intelligence chief, went so far as to suggest that the insurgent leaders Jalaluddin Haqqani and Gulbuddin Hekmatyar are both 'absolutely salvageable.' The HIG already have members in Karzai's government, and it could evolve into a political party, even though Hekmatyar may be providing al Qaeda leaders refuge in Kunar. Hekmatyar has reconcilable ambitions. As for the Haqqani network, I can tell you they are tired of fighting, but are not about to give up. They have lucrative business interests to protect: the road traffic from the Afghanistan-Pakistan border to Central Asia." Robert Kaplan, "Man versus Afghanistan," *The Atlantic,* April 2010, http://www.theatlantic.com/magazine /archive/2010/03/man-versus-afghanistan/7983/1/.

50. Bill Roggio, and Alexander Mayer, "Charting the Data for US airstrikes in Pakistan, 2004–2010," *The Long War Journal,* August 24, 2010, http://www .longwarjournal.org/pakistan-strikes.php.

51. Talatbek Masadykov, Antonio Giustozzi, and James Michael Page, op. cit., 12.

52. Holbrooke is cited in "US Backs Kabul's Direct Talks with Islamabad," *Dawn. com,* July 26, 2010, http://www.dawn.com/wps/wcm/connect/dawn-content -library/dawn/news/world/16-karzai-pakistani+holbrooke-hs-01.

53. Senator Kerry, "Karzai Must Fight Graft or Lose Support," *Dawn.com,* August 18, 2010, http://www.guardian.co.uk/world/feedarticle/9224264.

54. To offer amnesty or a seemingly generous compromise can also cause divisions among the insurgency and provide opportunities to break or weaken it. *US Military Joint Publication 324, Counterinsurgency Operations,* October 2009, vi, 20–21. Richard Holbrooke declaration: "Discussions on a Political Level Are Going to Reflect Battlefield Realities," *Reuters,* February 25, 2010, http:// uk.reuters.com/article/idUKN25186088.

55. Al Pessin, "Gates: Low Level Reconciliation Growing in Afghanistan", *VOA News,* March 24, 2010.

56. Address by President Obama, United States Military Academy at West Point, December 1, 2009, http://www.whitehouse.gov/the-press-office/remarks -president-address-nation-way-forward-afghanistan-and-pakistan.

57. Statement of Husain Haqqani, Director, Center for International Relations, Boston University in U.S. Policy Toward Pakistan, *Hearing Before the Subcommittee on the Middle East and South Asia Committee on Foreign Affairs House of Representatives One Hundred Tenth Congress First Session,* March 21, 2007, 9–10, http://foreignaffairs.house.gov/110/34239.pdf.

58. For more details on the drone program (number, targets, victims, and so on), see Bill Rogio, and Alexander Mayer, "Charting the Data for US Airstrikes in Pakistan, 2004–2010," op. cit.

59. Statement of Husain Haqqani, op. cit., 15.

60. In 2010, 17 percent of Pakistanis favorably viewed the United States. This is by far the lowest figure among countries that were polled. This figure has not been affected by Obama's arrival in the White House since it totaled 19 percent in 2008. See "Obama More Popular Abroad Than at Home, Global Image of U.S. Continues to Benefit," *Pew Global Project Attitudes*, June 17, 2010, http://pewglobal.org/files/pdf/Pew-Global-Attitudes-Spring-2010-Report.pdf.

61. Statement of Lisa Curtis, Senior Research Fellow, Asia Studies Center, *Heritage* Foundation in U.S. Policy Toward Pakistan, op. cit., 27.

62. Marvin Weinbaum, "Bad Company: Lashkar E–Tayyiba and the Growing Ambition of Islamist Militancy in Pakistan," *Hearing before the Subcommittee on the Middle East and South Asia of the Committee on Foreign Affairs House of Representatives One Hundred Eleventh Congress Second Session*, March 11, 2010, 13, http://www.internationalrelations.house.gov/111/55399.pdf.

63. Enhanced Partnership with Pakistan Act 2009, Title II, Section 203(c)(2)(A), http://www.cfr.org/publication/20422/joint_Explanatory_statement_Enhanced_partnership_with_pakistan_act_of_2009.html.

64. Ibid.

65. Cited in Anwar Iqbal, "US Note Dilutes Some Conditions in Kerry-Lugar Bill," *Dawn.com*, October 14, 2009, http://archives.dawn.com/archives/99491.

66. Ibid.

67. *The New Yorker*, March 1, 2010.

68. Matt Waldman, "The Sun in the Sky: The Relationship between Pakistan's ISI and Afghan Insurgents," *Crisis States Discussion Paper 18*, June 2010, 6, http://www.longwarjournal.org/threat-matrix/multimedia/20106138531279734lse-isi-taliban.pdf.

69. "Mullah Omar and the Taliban's hard core that have aligned themselves with al Qaeda are not reconcilable and we cannot make a deal that includes them." Cited in "White Paper of the Interagency Policy Group's Report on U.S. Policy toward Afghanistan and Pakistan," op. cit., 4.

70. Steve Coll "American Officials Believe That ISI Has Considerably More Leverage with the Afghan Taliban Than It Is Willing to Admit," *The New Yorker*, May 24, 2010.

71. "The ISI control the Quetta Shura. When Mullah Baradar and Mullah Omar talked directly to the Afghan government—peace talks—the ISI arrested Baradar...because they want peace talks to fail." Account of a Taliban commander cited in Matt Waldman, "The Sun in the Sky: The Relationship between Pakistan's ISI and Afghan Insurgents", op. cit., 20. This account is largely confirmed by other sources. See *The New York Times*, August 23, 2010.

7 Breaking the Pact of Silence? Obama, the Arab Spring, and the Middle East

1. See Aaron David Miller, "For America, An Arab Winter," *Wilson Quarterly*, Summer 2011, http://www.wilsonquarterly.com/article.cfm?aid=1967.
2. *The Wall Street Journal*, January 31, 2011, http://online.wsj.com/article/SB10001 424052748703833204576114712441122894.html.
3. *International Crisis Group*, "Syria: Quickly Going beyond the Point of No Return," May 3, 2011, http://www.crisisgroup.org/en/publication-type/media -releases/2011/syria-quickly-going-beyond-the-point-of-no-return.aspx.
4. Tony Judt, *Postwar: A History of Europe since 1945* (New York: Vintage, 2010).
5. Hussein Agha, and Robert Malley, "The Arab Counterrevolution," *The New York Review of Books*, September 29, 2011, http://www.nybooks.com/articles /archives/2011/sep/29/arab-counterrevolution/?pagination=false.
6. Sylvie Aprile, *La révolution de 1848 en France et en Europe* [The revolution of 1848 in France and Europe] (Paris: Editions Sociales, 1998).
7. Hazem Beblawi, "The Rentier State in the Arab World," in *The Rentier State*, ed. Hazem Beblawi and Giacomo Luciani (New York: Instituto Affari Internazionale, 1987), 51.
8. Ibid. 57.
9. According to the CIA Factbook, Egypt is ranked 101st in the world for its unemployment rate, Morocco is ranked 103rd, Algeria is ranked 109th, and Tunisia is ranked 136th.
10. Saudi Arabia is the United States' third-largest oil supplier after Canada and Mexico, which also control prices. It has constantly worked to prevent oil-price increases that might be harmful to consumer countries, in contrast to other oil-producing countries, which are primarily concerned with maximizing their revenue.
11. USAID to Jordan, for example, amounts to more than $800 million per year, placing the country right behind Israel as the second largest recipient of US aid per inhabitant.
12. Condoleezza Rice, quoted in *The American Cause*, January 27, 2005, http:// www.theamericancause.org/a-pjb-050627-rice.htm.
13. Benjamin Netanyahu considers the Arab revolutions to be an "anti-Western, anti-liberal, anti-Israeli and anti-democratic wave," *The Telegraph*, November 26, 2011.
14. The White House, "Remarks by the President at Cairo University," June 4, 2009, http://www.whitehouse.gov/the_press_office/Remarks-by-the-President-at -Cairo-University-6-04-09.
15. "The United States does not accept the legitimacy of continued Israeli settle-ments. This construction violates previous agreements and undermines efforts to achieve peace. It is time for these settlements to stop." Ibid.
16. "Governments that protect these rights are ultimately more stable, successful and secure." Ibid.

17. "And we will welcome all elected, peaceful governments—provided they govern with respect for all their people. This last point is important because there are some who advocate for democracy only when they're out of power; once in power, they are ruthless in suppressing the rights of others." Ibid.

18. The White House, "Remarks by the President in State of the Union Address," January 25, 2011, http://www.whitehouse.gov/the-press-office/2011/01/25/remarks-president-state-union-address.

19. "Our assessment is that the Egyptian government is stable and is looking for ways to respond to the legitimate needs and interests of the Egyptian people," Hillary Clinton, quoted in *Reuters*, January 25, 2011, http://af.reuters.com/article/topNews/idAFJOE70O0KF20110125.

20. It is important to note, however, that the Palestinian Authority also expressed support for President Mubarak. "President Mahmoud Abbas called Mubarak and affirmed his solidarity with Egypt and his commitment to its security and stability," quoted on *CNN*, January 29, 2011, http://articles.cnn.com/2011–01–29/world/egypt.middle.east.reaction_1_Egyptian-people-egyptian-president-hosni-mubarak-populous-arab-nation?_s=PM:WORLD.

21. "Saudi Arabia slammed protesters in Egypt as 'Infiltrators,'" *CNN*, January 29, 2011, http://articles.cnn.com/2011–01–29/world/egypt.middle.east.reaction_1_Egyptian-people-egyptian-president-hosni-mubarak-populous-arab-nation?_s=PM:WORLD.

22. Quoted in *Reuters*, February 6, 2011, http://af.reuters.com/article/topNews/idAFJOE71502520110206.

23. Quoted on *BBC*, February 5, 2011, http://www.bbc.co.uk/news/mobile/world-us-canada-12374753.

24. *The White House*, "Remarks by the President on the Situation in Egypt," January 28, 2011, http://www.whitehouse.gov/the-press-office/2011/01/28/remarks-president-situation-egypt.

25. *The White House*, "Remarks by the President on the Situation in Egypt," February 1, 2011, http://www.whitehouse.gov/the-press-office/2011/02/01/remarks-president-situation-egypt.

26. "The views he expressed today are his own. He did not co-ordinate his comments with the US government." Quoted in *BBC*, February 5, 2011, http://www.bbc.co.uk/news/mobile/world-us-canada-12374753.

27. *The White House*, "Remarks by the President on Egypt," February 11, 2011, http://www.whitehouse.gov/the-press-office/2011/02/11/remarks-president-egypt.

28. "'I've got no doctrine,' Obama says," *Politico*, March 29, 2011, http://www.politico.com/politico44/perm/0311/case_by_case_d3c7f152–61fa–4d63–b2a4–9f20ccd22369.html.

29. Laurence Louër, "Bahrein, la fin des compromis" [Bahrain and the end of compromise], *CERI Papers*, September 2011, http://www.ceri-sciencespo.com/archive/2011/septembre/dossier/art_ll.pdf.

30. *The New York Times*, March 12, 2011.

31. Hillary Clinton has indeed indicated that Bahrain's government is "on the wrong track." Quoted in *The Washington Post*, March 16, 2011, http://www

.washingtonpost.com/politics/clinton-bahrain-government-on-the-wrong
-track/2011/03/16/ABfhoSg_video.html.

32. Hillary Clinton called the intervention in Bahrain "alarming." Quoted on *CNN*, March 16, 2011,http://articles.cnn.com/2011–03–16/us/us.bahrain_1_bahraini -state-hillary-clinton-jay-carney?_s=PM:US.

33. "Bob Gates expressed the view that we had no evidence that suggested that Iran started any of these popular revolutions or demonstrations across the region," *The New York Times*, March 12, 2011.

34. *The White House*, "Remarks by the President on the Middle East and North Africa," May 19, 2011, http://www.whitehouse.gov/the-press-office /2011/05/19/remarks-president-middle-east-and-north-africa.

35. "President Saleh needs to follow through on his commitment to transfer power." Quoted in Ibid.

36. See UN Security Council Resolution 2014 on Yemen, October 21, 2011. Article 4 of the Resolution *"calls on* all parties in Yemen to commit themselves to implementation of a political settlement based upon this initiative, *notes* the commitment by the President of Yemen to immediately sign the Gulf Cooperation Council initiative and encourages him (…) to do so, and to implement a political settlement based upon it, and *calls* for this commitment to be translated into action, in order to achieve a peaceful political transition of power." Text available at: http://articles.cnn.com/2011–03–16/us/us.bahrain_1_bahraini-state -hillary-clinton-jay-carney?_s=PM:US.

37. "The only way forward is for the government and opposition to engage in a dialogue, and you can't have a real dialogue when parts of the peaceful opposition are in jail. The government must create the conditions for dialogue, and the opposition must participate to forge a just future for all Bahrainis." Ibid.

38. "There is a great deal of caution that is being exercised with respect to any actions that we might take other than in support of humanitarian missions. (…) We don't know these players," declaration by Hillary Clinton at the Senate, March 2, 2011, http://webb.senate.gov/newsroom/pressreleases/03–02–2011–02.cfm?render forprint=1.

39. "Italy-Libya Sign Agreement to Fight Illegal Immigration by Sea," December 9, 2010, http://www.timesofmalta.com/articles/view/20101209/local/immigration .340123.

40. Interview with a French official, Paris, July 2011.

41. Daniel Wagner, "Muammar Gaddafi's Son, Khamis Gaddafi, Toured U.S. In Weeks before Libya Conflict," *The Huffington Post*, March 25, 2011.

42. See "2011 Arab Public Opinion Poll: Results of Arab Opinion Survey Conducted October 2011," *Brookings Doha Center*, November 21, 2011, available at: http:// www.brookings.edu/reports/2011/1121_arab_public_opinion_telhami.aspx.

43. "The president has been clear that what's sweeping across the Middle East is organic to the region, and as soon as we become a military player, we're at risk of falling into the old trap that Americans are stage-managing events for their own benefit." An American official quoted in *The New York Times*, March 2, 2011.

44. "A no-fly zone begins with an attack on Libya to destroy the air defences. That's the way you do a no-fly zone. Then you can fly planes around the country and not worry about our guys being shot down. That is the way it starts. It also requires more airplanes than you would find on a single aircraft carrier," he said. "It is a big operation by a big country." Quoted in "US Defense Secretary Robert Gates Slams 'Loose Talk' about No-Fly Zones," *The Burning Platform,* March 3, 2011, http://www.theburningplatform.com/?p=12273.

45. "I think over the longer term that the (Gaddafi) regime will prevail," quoted in "Top U.S. Intelligence Official Tells Congress Gaddafi 'Will Prevail' In Libya," *The Huffington Post,* March 10, 2011, http://www.huffingtonpost .com/2011/03/10/top-us-intelligence-official-gaddafi-prevail_n_834334 .html. The statement was subtly denied the following day by Tom Donilon, Obama's security adviser: "My view is—as the person who looks at this quite closely every day and advises the President—is that things in the Middle East right now and things in Libya in particular right now need to be looked at not through a static but a dynamic, and not through a unidimensional but a multi-dimensional lens. And if you look at it in that way, beyond a narrow view, on just the kind of numbers of weapons and things like that, you get a very different picture. The lost legitimacy matters. The isolation of the region matters. Denying the regime resources matters. And this can affect the sustainability of their efforts over time. Motivation matters. Incentives matter. The people of Libya are determined to effect their future." In *The White House,* "Briefing by National Security Advisor Tom Donilon and Deputy National Security Advisor Ben Rhodes on Libya and the Middle East," March 10, 2011.

46. *The New York Times,* March 10, 2011.

47. According to Robert Gates "Frankly, there is too much talk about leaving and not enough talk about getting the job done right," he said. "Too much discussion of exit and not enough discussion about continuing the fight. Too much concern about when and how many troops might redeploy and not enough about what needs to be done before they leave." *The New York Times,* March 12, 2011.

48. Interviews, United Nations, New York, October 2011.

49. Ibid.

50. Massimo Calabresi, "Why the U.S. Went to War: Inside the White House Debate on Libya," *Time Magazine,* March 20, 2011, http://swampland.time .com/2011/03/20/why-the-u-s-went-to-war-inside-the-white-house-debate -on-libya/#ixzz1eMzBOggf.

51. Article 4 of UN Resolution 1973 "*Authorizes* Member States that have notified the Secretary-General, acting nationally or through regional organizations or arrangements, and acting in cooperation with the Secretary-General, to take all necessary measures, notwithstanding paragraph 9 of resolution 1970 (2011), to protect civilians and civilian populated areas under threat of attack in the Libyan Arab Jamahiriya, including Benghazi, while excluding a foreign occupation force of any form on any part of Libyan territory, and *requests* the Member States

concerned to inform the Secretary-General immediately of the measures they take pursuant to the authorization conferred by this paragraph which shall be immediately reported to the Security Council." Text of the resolution available at: http://www.un.org/News/Press/docs/2011/sc10200.doc.htm#Resolution.

52. For the details, see Ryan Lizza, "The Consequentialist," *The New Yorker*, May 2, 2011, http://www.newyorker.com/reporting/2011/05/02/110502fa_fact_lizza.

53. Barack Obama, "Remarks by the President on the Middle East and North Africa," *The White House*, May 19, 2011, available at: http://www.whitehouse .gov/the-press-office/2011/05/19/remarks-president-middle-east-and-north -africa.

54. Article 1 of the declaration of the Arab League on March 12, 2011 asks "the UN Security Council (...) to impose immediately a no-fly zone over Libya, and to establish secure zones in the areas under attack as a preventive measure that would allow for the protection of Libyan people (...) while respecting neighboring countries' sovereignty and regional peace."

55. Since its accession to the United Nations, China has actually only used its veto twice: in Burma and Zimbabwe. In both cases it invoked the fact that voting for sanctions against these two states was not backed by their respective regional organizations. Even if this interpretation might be considered an excuse, it cannot be completely dismissed. The moment of truth over Syria will come if the United Nations considers Arab League-backed sanctions.

56. The expression is from Ryan Lizza, "The Consequentialist," art. cit.

57. Interview with a French official, Paris, July 2011.

58. To the question: "Looking at the international reaction to the events in the Arab world in the past few months, which countries do you believe played the most constructive role?," 50 percent of the Arabs polled answered Turkey, while 30 percent chose France, and 24 percent chose the United States. See "2011 Arab Public Opinion Poll," op. cit.

59. Significantly, this same study shows that US support for existing regimes is ranked last in the list of objections to US policy. Indeed, to the question: "What two steps by the United States would improve your views of the United States the most?," only 8 percent of the Arabs polled answered "stopping aid to Arab governments," See "2011 Arab Public Opinion Poll," op. cit.

60. Interview, Al Jazeera.

61. Martin Indyk, Kenneth Lieberthal, and Michael E. O'Hanlon, *Bending History*, op. cit., 139.

62. William Quandt, "Obama's Middle East Straddle—Time to Get off the Fence," *Foreign Policy*, April 21, 2010, available at: http://mideast.foreignpolicy.com /posts/2010/04/21/obamas_middle_East_straddle_time_to_get_off_the_fence.

63. Interview, United Nations, October 2011.

64. "Remarks by the President to the United Nations General Assembly," *The White House*, September 23, 2009 http://www.whitehouse.gov/the-press -office/remarks-president-united-nations-general-assembly.

65. Ibid.

66. Ibid.
67. "Remarks by the President to the United Nations General Assembly," *The White House*, September 23, 2010, http://www.whitehouse.gov/the-press-office/2010/09/23/remarks-president-united-nations-general-assembly.
68. Ibid.
69. Ibid.
70. "Remarks by the President in Address to the United Nations General Assembly," *The White House*, September 21, 2011, http://www.whitehouse.gov/the-press-office/2011/09/21/remarks-president-obama-address-united-nations-general-assembly.
71. Ibid.
72. Geoffrey Wheatcroft, "Can They Ever Make a Deal?," *New York Review of Books*, April 5, 2012.
73. *Haaretz*, September 9, 2011.
74. Martin Indyk, Kenneth Lieberthal. and Michael E. O'Hanlon, *Bending History*, op. cit., 135.
75. The 2011 Public Opinion Poll of Jewish and Arab Citizens of Israel, http://www.brookings.edu/reports/2011/1201_israel_poll_telhami.aspx.
76. According to Aaron Miller, a US insider, Ross and Mitchell "have different conceptions of how they see the process and how they see one another's needs." Qtd. in *Haaretz*, May 25, 2011.
77. "The Middle East in the 21st Century: A Conversation with David Miliband and George Mitchell," October 17, 2011, http://www.chathamhouse.org/sites/default/files/public/Meetings/Meeting%20Transcripts/171011miliband_mitchell.pdf.
78. William Quandt, "Obama's Middle East Straddle—Time to Get off the Fence," art. cit.
79. *Haaretz*, November 13, 2009
80. Ibid.
81. *The Financial Times*, November 27, 2011.

8   Europe: The Risk-Averse Ally?

1. "I know it has become fashionable in some quarters to suggest that the United States has somehow neglected the transatlantic partnership. To some extent, this assertion is not surprising. One report noted that 'the relationship...is in the early stages of what could be a terminal illness.' That report was from nearly 30 years ago—in the early 1980s." Speech at the 46th Munich Security Conference, February 6, 2010, available at: http://regards-citoyens.over-blog.com/article-speech-of-james-l-jones-at-the-46th-munich-security-conference-44560815.html.
2. Zaki Laïdi, "The BRICS Against the West ?," *CERI Strategy Papers*, no 11, Hors-Série, November 2011, http://www.ceri-sciencespo.com/ressource/n11_112011.pdf.

3. "An Open Letter to the Obama Administration from Central and Eastern Europe," *Radio Free Europe/Radio Free Liberty*, July 16, 2009, available at: http://www.rferl.org/content/An_Open_Letter_To_The_Obama_Administration _From_Central_And_Eastern_Europe/1778449.html.

4. Derek E. Mix, "The United States and Europe: Current Issues," *CRS Report for Congress*, August 5, 2009, 10, http://www.fas.org/sgp/crs/row/RS22163.pdf.

5. James K. Jackson, "U.S. Direct Investment Abroad: Trends and Current Issues," *CRS Report for Congress*, July 28, 2010, 3, http://www.fas.org/sgp/crs/misc /RS21118.pdf.

6. Robert D. Hormats, "On Strengthening the Transatlantic Economy: Moving beyond the Crisis," December 9, 2009, 1, *The Senate Foreign Relations Committee Subcommittee on European Affairs,* http://foreign.senate.gov/imo/media/doc /HormatsTestimony091209p(2).pdf.

7. James K. Jackson, "U.S. Direct Investment Abroad: Trends and Current Issues", op. cit.

8. Interview with *The Telegraph*, December 4, 2011, http://www.telegraph .co.uk/finance/financialcrisis/8932647/Euro-doomed-from-start-says -Jacques-Delors.html.

9. Raymond J. Ahearn, and Paul Belkin, "The German Economy and U.S.-German Economic Relations," *CRS Report for Congress*, November 30, 2009, http://www.fas.org/sgp/crs/row/R40961.pdf.

10. Barack Obama, "A Firewall to Stop Europe's Crisis Spreading," *The Financial Times*, October 28, 2011, http://www.ft.com/intl/cms/s/0/8bea546a-ffc5 −11e0−8441−00144feabdc0.html#axzz1juKcMIAu.

11. James K. Jackson, "U.S. Direct Investment Abroad: Trends and Current Issues," op. cit.

12. See *OECD*, "Going for Growth 2010" (Paris: OECD, 2010).

13. Zaki Laïdi, "Normative Empire. The Unintended Consequences of European Power," *Garnet Policy Brief*, no. 6, February 2008, http://www.garnet-eu.org /fileadmin/documents/policy_briefs/Garnet_Policy_Brief_No_6.pdf.; and more generally, Zaki Laïdi, *La norme sans la force* (Paris: Presses de Sciences-Po, 2008). [Zaki Laïdi, *Norms Over Force: The Enigma of European Power* (New York: Palgrave Macmillan, 2008).]

14. Thomas Graham, in "Transatlantic Security in the 21st Century: Do New Threats Require New Approaches?," *Hearing Before the Committee on Foreign Affairs House of Representatives*, March 17, 2010, http://www.international relations.house.gov/111/55514.pdf.

15. "Remarks by Vice President Biden at 45th Munich Conference in Security Policy," *The White House*, February 7, 2009, http://www.whitehouse.gov/the _press_office/RemarksbyVicePresidentBidenat45thMunichConferenceonSecurity Policy.

16. Madeleine K. Albright, and Jeroen van der Veer, "NATO 2020: Assured Security, Dynamic Engagement: Analysis and Recommendations of the Group of Experts on a New Strategic Concept for NATO," Brussels, NATO, May 17, 2010, 15, http://www.nato.int/nato_static/assets/pdf/pdf_2010_05/2010_05_D8B67

F56A5CD4F44805365DB21B29108_Expertsreport_fr.pdfhttp://carnegieen dowment.org/pdf/20100517_100517_Expertsreport.pdf.

17. Damon Wilson, "NATO Post-60: Institutional Challenges Moving Forward," May 6, 2009, Hearing before the Committee on Foreign Relations United States Senate, http://foreign.senate.gov/imo/media/doc /WilsonTestimony090506p1.pdf.

18. "There is no inherent contradiction between force projection and collective defense since just about any conflict will probably require deployable forces," *U.S. Department of Defense,* "Remarks as Delivered by Secretary of Defense Robert M. Gates," February 23, 2011, http://www.defense.gov/speeches/speech.aspx? speechid=1423.

19. Madeleine K. Albright, and Jeroen van der Veer, "NATO 2020: Assured Security, Dynamic Engagement," art. cit., 9.

20. "An Open Letter to the Obama Administration from Central and Eastern Europe," art. cit.

21. Americans refer to it as the third site in reference to the first two, which are located in California and Alaska.

22. "An Open Letter to the Obama Administration from Central and Eastern Europe," art. cit.

23. "NATO Secretary General Completes Visit to Russia," NATO, December 17, 2009, http://www.nato.int/cps/en/natolive/news_60224.htm.

24. Madeleine K. Albright, and Jeroen van der Veer, "NATO 2020: Assured Security, Dynamic Engagement," art. cit., 10.

25. "An Open Letter to the Obama Administration from Central and Eastern Europe," art. cit.

26. Thomas Graham, in "Transatlantic Security in the 21st Century: Do New Threats Require New Approaches?," March 17, 2010, Hearing before the Committee on Foreign Affairs House of Representatives, 10, http://www .internationalrelations.house.gov/111/55514.pdf..

27. Albright's report implicitly makes this point by stating that the complementarity between NATO and the EU is only possible "if non-EU NATO members and non-NATO EU members are accorded the same degree of transparency and involvement when joint activities are conducted." Madeleine K. Albright, and Jeroen van der Veer, "NATO 2020: Assured Security, Dynamic Engagement," art. cit., 26.

28. Ibid.

29. "A common effort of the United States, Europe and Russia is therefore strongly needed to finally realize a sustainable Euro-Atlantic security architecture," Testimony of Ambassador Wolfgang Ischinger, director of the Munich Security Conference and co-director of the Euro-Atlantic security initiative, http:// www.securityconference.de/Monthly-Mind-Detail-View.67+M5fdbdf2167c .0.html?&L=1.

30. "Open Letter. It's Time to Invite Russia to Join NATO," *Der Spiegel,* March 8, 2010, http://www.spiegel.de/international/world/0,1518,682287,00.html.

31. Sam Nunn, Igor Ivanov, and Wolfgang Ischinger, "All Together Now: Missile Defense," *The International Herald Tribune*, July 21, 2010, http://carnegieen dowment.org/2010/07/21/all-together-now-missile-defense/5go.

32. Interviews at the Quai d'Orsay in Paris in July 2011, and at the United Nations in October 2011 with a witness.

33. "Allies should minimize the national caveats that they attach when contributing troops to Alliance operations; any caveats that are imposed should be clearly and explicitly stated and their impact carefully evaluated during force generation and operational planning," Madeleine K. Albright, and Jeroen van der Veer, "NATO 2020: Assured Security, Dynamic Engagement," art. cit., 32.

34. Hervé Morin, *Arrêtez de mépriser les Français: Pour une société de la reconnaissance.* [Stop despising the French: For a society of recognition] (Paris: Flammarion, 2011), 58–59.

35. "An absence of trust: Why Russia Is No Closer to Working with NATO on Missile Defence," *The Economist*, November 19, 2011.

36. "We insist on only one thing: that we're an equal part of it," Ivanov said of the antimissile system. "In practical terms, that means our office will sit, for example, in Brussels and agrees on a red-button push to start an antimissile, regardless of whether it starts from Poland, Russia or the U.K.," Russian Deputy Prime Minister Sergei Ivanov, quoted in "Russia Demands 'Red-Button' Role in NATO Missile Shield," *Global Security Newswire*, March 22, 2011.

37. Luis Martinez, "Russia, China Major Threats? Intel Director Clapper's Comments Perplex Senators," *ABC News*, March 10, 2012, http://abcnews .go.com/Politics/russia-china-major-threats-national-intelligence-director -james/story?id=13104936.

38. John Craddock, "Oral Statement for the Senate Foreign Relations Committee," Hearing on the NATO Strategic Concept, October 22, 2009, http://foreign .senate.gov/imo/media/doc/CraddockTestimony091022a.pdf.

39. One year after the Tunisian revolution started, Franco-Tunisian relations remain very strained, as evidenced by President Marzouki's indictments against it. See *Le Journal du Dimanche*, December 18, 2011.

40. The turning point in French diplomacy occurred on March 1, when the French Minister of Foreign Affairs, Alain Juppé, was visiting Cairo and declared: "Look at what is happening throughout the Arab world and even beyond. The people are no longer supporting the dictators." See http://www.diplomatie .gouv.fr/fr/le-ministere/le-ministre-d-etat-et-les/alain-juppe/presse-et -media-20656/#sommaire_10.

41. French essayist Bernard Henri Lévy takes credit for having been the first to alert the French head of state to the gravity of the Libyan situation follow- ing the first contacts he established with the National Transitional Council. However, it seems that French military headquarters already started consider- ing the aerial option at the end of February. This would explain how French strikes were able to immediately begin after resolution 1973 passed. See *Le Monde*, November 10, 2011.

42. Zaki Laïdi, "Gaddafi's Threats Had to Be Taken at Face Value," *The Financial Times*, March 30, 2011, http://www.ft.com/intl/cms/s/0/55a3db64–5a5d -11e0–8367–00144feab49a.html#a.

43. *Le Point*, March 6, 2011.

44. "Libya—Alain Juppé's Answer to a Question on Current Affairs at the National Assembly," Assemblée Nationale, Paris, March 8, 2011, http://www.diplomatie .gouv.fr/fr/le-ministere/le-ministre-d-etat-et-les/alain-juppe/interventions -a-l-assemblee-20662/article/libye-reponse-d-alain-juppe-a-une.

45. Interviews with a high-level French military officer who was directly involved in the Libyan crisis. Paris, July 2011.

46. Ibid.

47. Ibid.

48. Ibid.

49. Interview with a high-level French diplomat. Paris, July 2011.

50. Interview at the United Nations with a high-level UN diplomat, New York, October 2011.

51. Interview with a French officer general, Paris, July 2011.

52. Interview with a French officer general, Paris, July 2011.

53. Robert Gates, "The Security and Defense Agenda (Future of NATO)," Speech in Brussels, Belgium, June 10, 2011, http://www.defense.gov/speeches/speech. aspx?speechid=1581.

54. Remarks by Admiral Edouard Guillaud, chief of staff of the French armed forces, at the Institute for Higher National Defense Studies, May 20, 2011.

55. Robert Gates, "The Security and Defense Agenda (Future of NATO)," op. cit.

56. German Marshall Fund of the United States (GMF); *Transatlantic Trends (2009 Topline Data,* http://trends.gmfus.org/doc/2010_English_Top.pdf).

57. Ibid.

58. Ibid.

59. "An Initial Long-Term Vision for European Defense Capability and Capacity Needs," *European Defense Agency* (EDA), October 3, 2006, http://europa .eu/legislation_summaries/foreign_and_security_policy/cfsp_and_esdp _implementation/l33238_en.htm.

60. Zaki Laïdi, "Europe as a Risk-Averse Power: A Hypothesis," *Garnet Policy Brief*, no. 11, February 2010, http://www.garnet.eu.org/fileadmin/documents /policy_briefs/Garnet_Policy_Brief_No_11.pdf.

61. According to Carl Schmitt, who defined politics as the means to distinguish between friends and enemies.

62. See CNN/Opinion Research Corporation Poll, September 1–2, 2010, http:// www.pollingreport.com/iraq.htm.

63. Cf. Nick Witney, and Jeremy Shapiro, "Towards a Post-American Europe: A Power Audit of EU-US Relations," *ECFR*, November 2, 2009, http://ecfr.3cdn .net/05b80f1a80154dfc64_x1m6bgxc2.pdf.

9 Conclusion: Limited Achievements

1. Randall Kennedy, *The Persistence of the Color Line: Racial Politics and the Obama Presidency* (New York: Pantheon, 2011).
2. Nuno Monteiro, "Unrest Assured: Why Unipolarity Is Not Peaceful," *International Security*, 36, no. 3 (2011): 9.
3. Sipri, *Recent Trends in Military Expenditures*, Stockholm, January 2010.
4. See SIPRI, *SIPRI Yearbook 2010*, 196–198, 202, http://www.sipri.org/year book/2011/files/SIPRIYB1104–04A-04B.pdf.
5. Steve Walt, "Is American Addicted to War?" *Foreign Policy*, April 4, 2011, http://www.foreignpolicy.com/articles/2011/04/04/is_america_addicted_to_war?hidecomments=yes.
6. Anne-Marie Slaughter, "Wilsonianism in the Twenty-first century," in *The Crisis of American Foreign Policy: Wilsonianism in the Twenty-First Century*, ed. Anne-Marie Slaughter, John Ikenberry, Thomak Knock, and Tony Smith (Princeton, NJ: Princeton University Press, 2009), 89–119.
7. "China's Foreign Policy: Challenges and Players," *Hearing before the US-China Economic and Security Review Commission*, April 13, 2011, 82, http://www.uscc.gov/hearings/2011hearings/transcripts/11_04_13_trans/11_04_13_final_transcript.pdf.
8. "China locked into an area denial strategy in order to gain the space in the Western Pacific that it feels it needs to defend its vital interests and even its sovereignty. The U.S. locked into a strategy in the Western Pacific of making sure that area denial fails, not by conquering anything, but by having the capabilities to overcome an area denial strategy." *Carnegie Endowment*, May 2011.
9. Jagdish Bhagwati, "America's Threat to Trans-Pacific Trade," *Project Syndicate*, 2011, http://www.project-syndicate.org/commentary/bhagwati20/English.
10. "to rebuild its reputation, extricate itself from the Middle East and Afghanistan, and turn its attention toward Asia and China's unchecked influence in the region. America was 'overweighted' in the former and 'underweighted' in the latter." Ryan Lizza, "The Consequentialist: How The Arab Spring Remade Obama's Foreign Policy," *The New Yorker*, May 2, 2011, http://drezner.foreignpolicy.com/posts/2011/04/25/is_there_such_a_thing_as_a_consequentialist_grand_srategy.
11. Suzanne Maloney, "Obama's Counterproductive New Iran Sanctions: How Washington Is Sliding toward Regime Change," *Foreign Affairs*, January 5, 2012, http://www.foreignaffairs.com/articles/137011/suzanne-maloney/obamas-counterproductive-new-iran-sanctions?page=2.
12. National Intelligence Council, *Global Trends 2025: A Transformed World*, November 2008, http://www.dni.gov/nic/PDF_2025/2025_Global_Trends_Final_Report.pdf.
13. Eswar Prasad, "The U.S.-China Economic Relationship: Shifts and Twists in the Balance of Power," Hearing on "U.S. Debt to China: Implications and Repercussions," *U.S-China Economic and Security Review*

Commission, March 10, 2010, http://prasad.dyson.cornell.edu/doc/policy/USCESRCTestimony.Rev01Mar10.pdf.

14. Ibid., 5.
15. Ibid., 8.
16. National Intelligence Council, op. cit., 29.
17. Goldman Sachs, "Dreaming with BRICs: The Path to 2025," *Global Economics Paper*, no. 99, October 2003, http://www2.goldmansachs.com/our-thinking/brics/brics-reports-pdfs/brics-dream.pdf.
18. See Richard Haass, "The Age of Nonpolarity: What Will Follow U.S. Dominance," Foreign Affairs, May/June 2008, http://www.foreignaffairs.com/articles/63397/richard-n-haass/the-age-of-nonpolarity.
19. Zaki Laïdi, "The BRICS against the West?," art. cit.
20. In 2001, Chinese exports to India, Russia, and Brazil did not exceed $3 billion each. In 2009, Chinese exports to these three countries respectively reached $30, $17, and $14 billion. In less than ten years, Chinese exports to India have thus increased tenfold. Source: the World Bank.
21. According to Dilma Roussef, "regional integration is the best way to strengthen Brazil's position with regard to the Asian products that are inundating the region," cited in *La Folha*, July 29, 2011.
22. Interview in *l'Estado de Sao Paulo*, July 17, 2011.
23. The New chief of Brazilian diplomacy, Antonio Patriota, provides insights into the new directions of Brazilian diplomacy under the new presidency, in a subtle speech in *Woodrow Wilson Center for Scholars*, May 31, 2011, http://www.wilsoncenter.org/sites/default/files/1310524380-Palestra%2520Min%2520Patriota%2520Wilson%2520Center,%2520FINAL.pdf.
24. With regard the Teheran agreement of May 17, 2010, the former chief of Brazilian diplomacy writes: "The insistence on sanctions against Iran—effectively ignoring the Declaration of Tehran, and without even giving Iran time to respond to the comments of the 'Vienna Group' (the U.S., France and Russia)—confirmed the opinions of many analysts who claimed that the traditional centers of power will not share gladly their privileged status." This interpretation is not false in and of itself. However, the chief of Brazilian diplomacy is careful not to explain why China and Russia ended up voting for sanctions against Iran. See Celso Amorim, "Let's Hear from the New Kids on the Block," *The New York Times*, June 14, 2010.
25. Interview with Strobe Talbott, "U.S. Interest in Sino-Indian Cooperation," *Journal of International Affairs*, Spring 2011, http://findarticles.com/p/articles/mi_hb6705/is_201104/ai_n57429606/.
26. Interviews in *Itamaraty*, May 2011, Brasilia.
27. John Ikenberry, Liberal Leviathan: The Origins, Triumph, Crisis, and Transformation of the American World Order (Princeton, NJ: Princeton University Press, 2011), 341.
28. This point is cogently noticed by John Ikenberry in the conclusion of his most recent book *Liberal Leviathan: The Origins, Triumph, Crisis, and Transformation of the American World Order* (Princeton, NJ: Princeton University Press, 2011).

29. See Aaron L. Friedberg, *A Contest For Supremacy. China, America and the Struggle for Mastery in Asia* (New York: Norton, 2011).

30. "Prepared Statement for Dr. Victor Cha," in "China's Foreign Policy: Challenges and Players," art. cit., 104.

31. "Despite China's Frustration with Its Poor and Pathetic Neighbor, It Will Never Abandon It," ibid., 105.

32. See Daniel Drezner, "Bad Debts: Assessing China's Financial Influence in Great Power Politics," *International Security*, no. 34, Autumn 2009, http://belfercenter. ksg.harvard.edu/files/IS3402_pp007–045_Drezner.pdf.

33. International Monetary Fund, *The WTO Doha Trade Round: Unlocking the Negotiations and Beyond*, paper prepared by the Strategy, Policy, and Review Department and approved by Tamim Bayoumi, September 20, 2011.

34. Congressional Research Service, *India: Domestic Issues, Strategic Dynamics, and U.S. Relations*, by K. Alan Kronstadt et al., Report No. RL33529, September 1, 2011, 76.

35. "BASIC pushes for Kyoto Protocol's extension," *The Economic Times*, December 6, 2011.

36. According to Russian Deputy Foreign Minister Sergei Ryabkov "they [the US] want to nullify the potential of the strategic nuclear forces of the Russian Federation." Quoted in "NATO Missile Shield Aimed at Neutralizing Russian Strategic Deterrent: Official," *Global Security Newswire*, January 27, 2012, http://www.nti.org/gsn/article/nato-missile-shield-aimed-neutralizing -russian-deterrent-official-claims/.

37. "India Risks Nuclear Isolation with Break From Chernobyl Accord," *Bloomberg*, August 26, 2010; "India Liability Bill Seen Shaking Up Nuclear Trade, Liability Regime," *Nucleonics Week*, September 2, 2010.

38. *The Telegraph*, November 18, 2009.

39. Josy Joseph, "Army Chief Warns against Govt-to-Govt Deals with US," *Times of India* (Delhi), May 25, 2010.

40. Sandeep Dikshit, "India Averse to Inking Military Pacts With U.S.," *Hindu* (Chennai), June 23, 2011.

41. Simon Romero and Jackie Calmes, "Brazil and U.S. Accentuate the Positive," *The New York Times*, April 9, 2012.

42. Hillary Clinton is partial to "tilting the balance away from a multi-polar world and toward a multi-partner world," *The Washington Post*, July 16, 2009.

43. National Security Strategy, op. cit., 26.

44. For more on these debates, see Robert O. Keohane, "Multilateralism: An Agenda for Research," *International Journal*, 45, no. 4(1990): 731–764; Miles Kahler, "Multilateralism with Small and Large Numbers," *International Organization*, 46, no. 3 (1992): 681–708; James Caporaso, "International Relations Theory and Multilateralism: The Search for Foundations," *International Organization*, 46, no. 3 (1992): 599–632; John Gerard Ruggie, "Multilateralism: Anatomy of an Institution," in *Multilateralism Matters: The Theory and Praxis of an Institutional Form*, ed. John Gerard Ruggie (New York: Columbia University Press, 1993): 3–47.

BIBLIOGRAPHY

Note: This bibliography is limited to articles, books, and testimonies quoted in the book.

Books

Alter, Jonathan. *The Promise: President Obama, Year One.* New York: Simon & Schuster, 2010.

Bader, Jeffrey. *Obama and China's Rise: An Insider's Account of America's Asia Strategy.* Washington DC: Brookings Institution Press, 2012.

Baldwin, David. "Power and International Relations." In *Handbook of International Relations*, edited by Walter Carlsnaes, Thomas Risse, and Beth A. Simmons, 177–191. New York: Sage, 2002.

Berry, Mary, Josh Gotheimer and Theodore Sorensen. *Power in Words: The Stories Behind Barack Obama's Speeches, from the State House to the White House.* Boston: Beacon Press, 2011.

Betts, Richard. *American Force: Dangers, Delusions, and Dilemmas in National Security.* New York: Columbia University Press, 2011.

Bostdorff, Denise. *Proclaiming the Truman Doctrine: The Cold War Call to Arms.* College Station, TX: Tamu Press, 2008.

Carothers, Thomas. *Democracy Policy under Obama: Revitalization or Retreat?* Washington DC: Carnegie Endowment for International Peace, 2011, 58.

Colman, Jonathan. *The Foreign Policy of Lyndon B. Johnson: The United States and the World, 1963–69.* Edinburgh: Edinburgh University Press, 2010.

Cox, Michael. *U.S. Foreign Policy after the Cold War: Superpower without a Mission?* Stamford, CT: Thomson Learning, 1995.

Cox, Michael, and Doug Stokes, eds. *U.S. Foreign Policy.* Oxford: Oxford University Press, 2012.

Cronin, Audrey. *How Terrorism Ends: Understanding the Decline and Demise of Terrorist Campaigns.* Princeton, NJ: Princeton University Press, 2009.

Dower, John. *Embracing Defeat: Japan in the Wake of World War II.* New York: W.W. Norton, 1999.

Foot, Rosemary and Andrew Walter. *China, the United States and Global Order.* New York: Cambridge University Press, 2011.

Friedberg, Aaron. *A Contest for Supremacy: China, America, and the Struggle for Supremacy in Asia.* New York: Norton, 2001.

Friedman, Thomas, and Michael Mandelbaum. *That Used to Be Us: How America Fell Behind in the World That It Invented and How We Can Come Back.* New York: Farrar, Straus & Giroux, 2011.

Gaddis, John Lewis. *Surprise, Security, and the American Experience.* Cambridge: Harvard University Press, 2004.

Gerges, Fawaz. *Obama and the Middle East: The End of America's Moment.* New York: Palgrave, 2012.

Greenspan, Alan. *The Age of Turbulence: Adventures in a New World*. New York: Penguin Press, 2007.

Haass, Richard. *War of Necessity, War of Choice: A Memoir of Two Iraq Wars*. New York: Simon & Schuster, 2009.

Haslam, Jonathan. *No Virtue Like Necessity*. New Haven, CT: Yale University Press, 2002.

Ikenberry, John. *After Victory: Institutions, Strategic Restraints and the Rebuilding of Order after Major Wars*. Princeton, NJ: Princeton University Press, 2000.

————. *Liberal Leviathan: The Origins, Crisis, and Transformation of the American World Order*. New York: Cloth, 2011.

Ikenberry, John, Michael Mastanduno, and William Wohlforth. *International Relations Theory and the Consequences of Unipolarity*. New York: Cambridge University Press, 2011.

Ikenberry, John, Anne-Marie Slaughter, Tony Smith, and Thomas Knock. *The Crisis of American Foreign Policy: Wilsonianism in the Twenty-First Century*. Princeton: Princeton University Press, 2009.

Indyk, Martin, Kenneth Lieberthal, and Michael O'Hanlon. *Bending History? Barack Obama's Foreign Policy*. Washington, DC: Brookings Institution Press, 2012.

Judt, Tony. *Postwar: A History of Europe since 1945*. New York: Vintage, 2010.

Kantor, Jodi, and Robin Miles. *The Obamas*. Paris: Hachette, 2012.

Kennedy, Paul. *The Rise and Fall of the Great Powers*. New York: Vintage, 1989.

Kennedy, Randall. *The Persistence of the Color Line: Racial Politics and the Obama Presidency*. New York: Pantheon, 2011.

Keohane, Robert. *Neorealism and Its Critics*. New York: Columbia University Press, 1986.

Kupchan, Charles. *The End of the American Era: U.S. Foreign Policy and the Geopolitics of the Twenty-First Century*. New York: Vintage, 2003.

————. *How Enemies Become Friends: The Source of Stable Peace*. Princeton: Princeton University Press, 2010.

————. *No One's World: The West, the Rising Rest, and the Coming Global Turn*. New York: Oxford University Press, 2012.

Larres, Klaus. *The US Secretaries of State and Transatlantic Relations*. London: Routledge/Taylor and Francis, 2010.

Linz, Juan, and Alfred Stepan. *Problems of Democratic Transition and Consolidation*. Baltimore: Johns Hopkins Press, 1996.

Litwark, Robert. *Détente and the Nixon Doctrine: American Foreign Policy and the Pursuit of Stability, 1969–1976*. New York: Cambridge University Press, 1986.

McDougall, Walter. *Promised Land, Crusader State: The American Encounter with the World since 1776*. New York: Mariner Books, 1998.

Mead, Walter Russell. *Special Providence, American Foreign Policy and How It Changed the World*. New York: Alfred A. Knopf, 2001.

Mearsheimer, John. *The Tragedy of Great Power Politics*. New York: Norton, 2001.

Mearsheimer, John, and Stephen Walt. *The Israel Lobby and U.S. Foreign Policy*. New York: Farrar, Straus & Giroux, 2007.

Meena, Bose, and Rosanna Perotti. *From Cold War to New World Order: The Foreign Policy of George H. W. Bush*. Westport, CT: Praeger, 2002.

Mendell, David. *Obama: From Promise to Power*. New York: Amistad/Harper Collins Publishers, 2007.

Morgenthau, Hans. *Politics among Nations*. New York: McGraw, 1954.

Motyl, Alexander, Blair A. Ruble, and Lilia Shevtsova. *Russia's Engagement with the West: Transformation and Integration in the Twenty-First Century*. New York: Sharpe, 2005.

Nawaz, Shuja. *Crossed Swords*. New York: Oxford University Press, 2008.

Ninkovich, Franck. *Modernity and Power: A History of the Domino Theory in the Twentieth Century*. Chicago: University of Chicago Press, 1994.

Nye, Joseph. *The Future of Power*. New York: PublicAffairs, 2011.

―――. *The Powers to Lead*. New York: Oxford University Press, 2010.

Obama, Barack. *Dreams from My Father: A Story of Race and Inheritance*. New York: Broadway Books, 2004.

Olson, Mancur. *The Logic of Collective Action: Public Goods and the Theory of Groups*. Boston: Harvard University Press, 1965.

Pape, Robert. *Dying to Suicide: The Strategic Logic of Suicide Terrorism*. New York: Random House Trade Paperbacks, 2006.

Parsi, Trita. *A Single Roll of the Dice: Obama's Diplomacy with Iran*. New Haven: Yale University Press, 2012.

Perkins, Bradford. "To the Monroe Doctrine." In *The Cambridge History of Foreign Relations*. Vol. 1, *The Creation of a Republican Empire, 1776–1865*. New York: Cambridge University Press, 1995.

Pratt, Julius. *A History of US Foreign Policy*. Englewood Cliffs, NJ: Prentice-Hall, 1980.

Remnick, David. *The Bridge: The Life and Rise of Barack Obama*. New York: Knopf, 2010.

Reus-Smit, Christian, and Duncan Snidal. *The Oxford Handbook of International Relations*. Oxford: Oxford University Press, 2008.

Richard, Jackson. *Writing the War on Terrorism: Language, Politics and Counter-Terrorism. New Approaches to Conflict Analysis*. Manchester: Manchester University Press, 2005.

Rubin, Barnett. *The Fragmentation of Afghanistan*. New Haven, CT: Yale University Press, 2002.

Ruggie, John Gerrard. *Multilateralism Matters: The Theory and Praxis of an Institutional Form*. New York: Columbia University Press, 1993.

Schlesinger, Arthur. *The Cycles of American History*. New York: Mariner Books, 1999.

Schmidt, John. *The Unraveling: Pakistan in the Ages of Jihad*. New York: Farrar, Straus & Giroux, 2011.

Schweller, Randall. *The Progressiveness of Neoclassical Realism*. Cambridge, MA: MIT Press, 2003.

Scott, James. *Deciding to Intervene: The Reagan Doctrine and American Foreign Policy*. Durham, NC: Duke University Press, 1996.

Semple, Michael. *Reconciliation in Afghanistan*. Washington, DC: United States Institute for Peace, 2009.

Serra, Narcis, and Joseph E. Stiglitz. *The Washington Consensus Reconsidered: Towards a New Global Governance*. Oxford: Oxford University Press, 2008.

Skidmore, David. *Reversing Course: Carter's Foreign Policy, Domestic Politics, and the Failure of Reform*. Nashville: Vanderbilt University Press, 1996.

Tatum, Edward Howland. *The United States and Europe, 1815–1823: A Study in the Background of the Monroe Doctrine*. Berkeley: University of California Press, 1934.

Thompson, Robert. *Defeating Communist Insurgency: The Lessons of Malaya and Vietnam*. New York: Praeger, 1966.

Walt, Stephen. *Taming American Power: The Global Response to U.S. Primacy*. New York: W. W. Norton, 2005.

Waltz, Kenneth. *Theory of International Politics*. New York: McGraw, 1979.

Widenor, William. *Henry Cabot Lodge and the Search for an American Foreign Policy*. Berkeley: University of California Press, 1980.

Williams, William Appleman. *The Tragedy of American Diplomacy*. New York: Norton, 1988.

Woodward, Bob. *Obama's Wars*. New York: Simon & Schuster, 2010.

―――. *Plan of Attack*. New York: Simon & Schuster, 2004.

Zakaria, Fareed. *The Post-American World and the Rise of the Rest*. New York: Penguin Books, 2009.

Zysman, John, and Laura Tyson. *American Industry in International Competition: Government Policy and Corporate Strategies*. Ithaca, NY: Cornell University Press, 1983.

Articles

Agha, Hussein, and Robert Malley. "The Arab Counterrevolution." *The New York Review of Books*, September 29, 2011. Available at: http://www.nybooks.com/articles/archives/2011/sep/29/arab-counterrevolution/?pagination=false.

Albright, Madeleine, and Marwan Muasher. "Assad Deserves a Swift Trip to The Hague." *Carnegie Endowment for International Peace*, June 28, 2011. Available at: http://carnegieendowment.org/2011/06/28/assad-deserves-swift-trip-to-hague/b5a.

Alterman, Jon. "Middle East Notes and Comment: The Middle East Turns East." *Center for Strategic and International Studies*, May 17, 2011. Available at: http://csis.org/files/publication/0511_MENC.pdf.

Altman, Roger. "The Great Crash, 2008. A Geopolitical Setback for the West." *Foreign Affairs*, 88, no. 1, January-February 2009, 2–14.

Badran,Tony. "Obama's Options in Damascus: Why It's Time to Rein in Syria and Turkey." *Foreign Affairs*, August 16, 2011. Available at: http://www.foreignaffairs.com/articles/68129/tony-badran/obamas-options-in-damascus?page=show.

Baumgartner, Jody, Peter L. Francia, and Jonathan S. Morris. "A Clash of Civilizations? The Influence of Religion on Public Opinion of U.S Foreign Policy in the Middle East." *Political Research Quarterly*, 61, no. 2 (June 2008): 171–179.

Bhagwati, Jagdish. "America's Free Trade Abdication." *The American Interest*, October 6, 2011. Available at: http://blogs.the-american-interest.com/bhagwati.

———. "America's Threat to Trans-Pacific Trade." *Project Syndicate*, December 30, 2011. Available at: http://www.project-syndicate.org/commentary/bhagwati20/English.

Blix, Hans. "A Season for Disarmament." *The New York Times*, April 5, 2010.

Boukhars, Anouar, and Shadi Hamid. "Morocco's Moment of Reform." *The Brookings Institution*. June 28, 2011. Available at: http://www.brookings.edu/opinions/2011/0628_morocco_hamid_boukhars.aspx.

Brancati, Dawn, and Jack L. Snyder. "The Libyan Rebels and Electoral Democracy: Why Rushing to the Polls Could Reignite Civil War." *Foreign Affairs*, September 2, 2011. Available at: http://www.foreignaffairs.com/articles/68241/dawn-brancati-and-jack-l-snyder/the-libyan-rebels-and-electoral-democracy.

Brennan, John. "The Conundrum of Iran: Strengthening Moderates without Acquiescing to Belligerence." *The ANNALS of the American Academy of Political and Social Science*, 2008.

Brown, Nathan. "US. Policy and the Muslim Brotherhood." *Carnegie Endowment for International Peace*. April 13, 2011. Available at: http://carnegieendowment.org/files/0413_testimony_brown.pdf.

Brzezinski, Zbigniew. "From Hope to Audacity, Appraising Obama's Foreign Policy." *Foreign Affairs*, 89, no. 1 (January–February 2010): 16–30.

Byman, Daniel. "Beware the Perils of Libya after Qaddafi Has Gone." *The Brookings Institution*, June 2011. Available at: http://www.brookings.edu/articles/2011/0620_libya_byman.aspx.

Caporasso, James. "International Relations theory and Multilateralism: The Search for Foundations." *International Organization*, 46, no. 3 (1992): 599–632.

Casey, Steven. "Obama's Alliances." In *LSE Ideas Report: The United States after Unipolarity*, December 2011, 40–44. Available at: http://www2.lse.ac.uk/IDEAS/publications/reports/pdf/SR009/casey.pdf.

Cole, David. "After September 11: What We Still Don't Know." *The New York Review of Books*, September 29, 2011. Available at: http://www.nybooks.com/articles/archives/2011/sep/29/after-september-11-what-we-still-dont-know.

Cook, Steven. "The US Egyptian Breakup. Washington's Limited Options in Cairo." *Foreign Affairs*, February 2, 2011. Available at: http://www.foreignaffairs.com/articles/67347 /steven-a-cook/the-us-egyptian-breakup.

Cordesman, Anthony. "Iraq and the United States: Creating a Strategic Partnership." *Center for International and Strategic Studies*, June 2010. Available at: http://csis.org/files/publication /100622_Cordesman_IraqUSStrategicPartner_WEB.pdf.

———. "The Outcome of Invasion: US and Iranian Strategic Competition in Iraq." *Center for Strategic and International Studies*, November 28, 2011. Available at: http://csis.org/files /publication/111128_Iran_Chapter_6_Iraq.pdf.

———. "US Strategy in the Gulf." *Center for Strategic and International Studies*, April 14, 2011. Available at: http://csis.org/publication/us-strategy-gulf.

Cordesman, Anthony, B. Barfi, B. Haddad, and K. Mezran, "The Arab Uprisings and the US Policy: What Is the American National Interest?" *Middle East Policy Council*, April 28, 2011.

Daggett, Stephen. "Costs of Major U.S. War," *CRS Report for Congress*, June 29, 2010. Available at: http://www.fas.org/sgp/crs/natsec/RS22926.pdf.

Derviş, Kemal. "The Obama Administration and the Arab Spring." *The Brookings Institution*. April 1, 2011. Available at: http://www.brookings.edu/opinions/2011/0401_obama_arab _spring_dervis.aspx.

Destler, I. M. "Donilon to the Rescue? The Road Ahead for Obama's Next National Security Adviser." *Foreign Affairs*, October 13, 2010. Available at: http://www.foreignaffairs.com /articles/66772/i-m-destler/donilon-to-the-rescue.

———. "Will Obama's National Security Council Be 'Dramatically Different?'" *Foreign Affairs*, April 30, 2009. Available at: http://www.foreignaffairs.com/articles/65077/i-m-destler/jonestown.

Destler, I. M, and Ivo H. Daalder. "In the Shadow of the Oval Office: The Next National Security Advisor." *Foreign Affairs* 88, no. 01 (January–February 2009), 94–113. Available at:

Doha Brookings Center. "2011 Arab Public Opinion Poll." November 21, 2011. Available at:http:// www.brookings.edu/reports/2011/1121_arab_public_opinion_telhami.aspx.

Drezner, Daniel. "Bad Debts, Assessing China's Financial Influence in Great Power Politics." *International Security,* 34, no. 2 (Autumn 2009): 7–45.

———. "Does Obama Have a Grand Strategy? Why We Need Doctrines in Uncertain Times." *Foreign Affairs* 90, no. 4 (July–August 2011): 57–68. Available at: http://drezner.foreign policy.com/posts/2011/06/22/does_the_obama_administration_have_a_grand_strategy.

Edelman, Eric. "Fool Me Twice: How The United States Lost Lebanon—Again." *Center for Strategic and Budgetary Assessments (CSBA)*. June 1, 2011. Available at: http://www.csbaonline. org/2011/06/01/fool-me-twice-how-the-united-states-lost-lebanon%e2%80%94again/.

Fit, Brandon, and Anthony H. Cordesman. "U.S. and Iranian Strategic Competition." *Center for Strategic and International Studies*. August 11, 2011.

Forsberg, Carl. "Politics and Power in Kandahar." *Institute for the Study of War, Afghanistan Report 5*, April 2010. Available at: http://www.understandingwar.org/files/Politics_and _Power_in_Kandahar.pdf.

Fukuyama, Francis. "Political Order in Egypt." *The American Interest,* May-June 2011. Available at: http://www.the-american-interest.com/article.cfm?piece=953.

Futter, Andrew. "Obama's Nuclear Weapons Policy in a Changing World." In *LSE Ideas Report: The United States After Unipolarity*, December 2011, 13–17. Available at: http://www2.lse .ac.uk/IDEAS/publications/reports/pdf/SR009/futter.pdf.

Gates, Robert. "Balanced Strategy: Reprogramming the Pentagon for a New Age." *Foreign Affairs 88*, no. 1 (January-February 2009): 15–27. Available at: http://www2.lse.ac.uk/ IDEAS/publications/reports/pdf/SR009/futter.pdf.

Gausse, Gregory. "Rageless in Riyadh: Why the Al Saud Dynasty Will Remain." *Foreign Affairs*, March 16, 2011. Available at: http://www.foreignaffairs.com/articles/67660/f-gregory -gause-iii/rageless-in-riyadh.

Gershkoff, Amy, and Shana Kushner, "Shaping Public Opinion: The 9/11-Iraq Connection in the Bush Administration's Rhetoric." *Perspectives on Politics*, 3, no. 3 (September 2005): 525–537.

Goldman Sachs, "Dreaming with BRICs: The Path to 2050," *Global Economics Paper*, no. 99, October 2003. Available at: http://www2.goldmansachs.com/our- thinking/brics/brics -reports- pdfs/brics-dream.pdf.

Gourinchas, Pierre-Olivier, and Hélène Rey, *From World Banker to World Venture Capitalist: US External Adjustment and The Exorbitant Privilege*. NBER Working Papers Series, August 2005. Available at: http://www.nber.org/papers/w11563.pdf.

Gray, John. "A Shattering Moment in America's Fall from Power." *The Observer*, September 28, 2008.

Grimmett, Richard. "Instances of Use of United States Armed Forces Abroad, 1798–2009." *Congressional Research Service,* January 27, 2010. Available at: http://www.fas.org/sgp/crs /natsec/RL32170.pdf.

Gude, Ken, Ken Sofer, and Aaron Gurley. "Secretary Clinton Should Go to Yemen: US Should Openly Lend Diplomatic Support to Country's Vice President." *Center for American Progress.* July 12, 2011. Available at: http://www.americanprogress.org/issues/2011/07/secretary _clinton_yemen.html.

Haass, Richard. "The Age of Nonpolarity: What Will Follow U.S. Dominance," *Foreign Affairs,* May/June 2008. Available at: http://www.foreignaffairs.com/articles/63397/richard-n -haass/the-age-of- nonpolarity.

———. "Fatal Distraction: Bill Clinton's Foreign Policy." *Foreign Policy*, no. 108 (Autumn 1997): 112–123.

———. "The Restauration Doctrine." *The American Interest*, January/February 2012. Available at: http://www.the-american-interest.com/article.cfm?piece=1164.

Hassan, Oz. "American Democracy Promotion and the Arab Spring." *LSE Ideas Report: The United States after Unipolarity,* December 2011, 45–50. Available at: http://www2.lse.ac.uk /IDEAS/publications/reports/pdf/SR009/hassan.pdf.

Hastings, Michael. "The Runaway General." *The Rolling Stone*, June 22, 2010. Available at: http://www.rollingstone.com/politics/news/the-runaway-general-20100622.

Hiltermann, Joost. "Iraq: The Impasse." *The New York Review of Books*, August 19, 2010. Available at: http://www.nybooks.com/articles/archives/2010/aug/19/iraq-impasse/.

International Crisis Group. "Iraq after the Surge II: The Need for a New Political Strategy." *Middle East Report no. 75*, April 30, 2008. Available at: http://www.crisisgroup.org/~/media/Files /Middle%20East%20North%20Africa/Iraq%20Syria%20Lebanon/Iraq/75_iraq_after _the_surge_ii_the_need_for_a_new_political_strategy.ashx.

Jackson, James. "U.S. Direct Investment Abroad: Trends and Current Issues." *CRS Report for Congress*, July 28, 2010. Available at: http://www.fas.org/sgp/crs/misc/RS21118.pdf.

Jerome, Deborah. "Syria's Challenge to U.S. and E.U." *Council on Foreign Relations*, June 27, 2011. Available at: http://www.cfr.org/syria/syrias-challenge-us-eu/p25355.

Jervis, Robert. "Understanding the Bush Doctrine." *Political Science Quarterly*, 118, no. 3 (Autumn 2003): 365–388.

———. "Unipolarity. A Structural Perspective." *World Politics*, 61, no. 1 (January 2009): 188–213.

Jones, Bruce. "The West, the Rest, and the New Middle East: Obama in London." *The Brookings Institution*, May 27, 2011. Available at: http://www.brookings.edu/opinions/2011/0527 _global_order_jones.aspx.

Joyce, Joseph. "The United States and International Economic Governance." In *LSE Ideas Report: The United States After Unipolarity*, December 2011, 24–29. Available at: http://www2.lse.ac.uk/IDEAS/publications/reports/SR009.aspx.

Kahler, Miles. "Multilateralism with Small and Large Numbers." *International Organization*, 46, no. 3 (1992): 681–708.

Kaplan, Robert. "Man versus Afghanistan." *The Atlantic*, April 2010. Available at: http://www.theatlantic.com/magazine/archive/2010/03/man-versus-afghanistan/7983/1/.

Katzman, Kenneth. "Afghanistan: Politics, Elections, and Government Performance." *CRS Report for Congress*, June 29, 2010. Available at: http://www.fas.org/sgp/crs/row/RS21922.pdf.

———. "Iran's Activities and Influence in Iraq." *CRS Report for Congress*, June 4, 2009. Available at: http://www.fas.org/sgp/crs/mideast/RS22323.pdf.

———. "Iraq: Post-Saddam Governance and Security." *CRS Report for Congress*, October 28, 2009. Available at: http://www.fas.org/sgp/crs/mideast/RL31339.pdf.

Kelley, Robert. "Repairing the American Image, One Tweet at a Time." In *LSE Ideas Report: The United States after Unipolarity*, December 2011, 35–38. Available at: http://www2.lse.ac.uk/IDEAS/publications/reports/pdf/SR009/kelley.pdf.

Keohane, Robert. "Multilateralism: An Agenda for Research." *International Journal*, 45, no. 4 (1990): 731–764.

Kissinger, Henry. "The Age of Kennan." *The New York Times*, November 10, 2011. Available at: http://www.nytimes.com/2011/11/13/books/review/george-f-kennan-an-american-life-by-john-lewis-gaddis-book-review.html?pagewanted=all.

Krebs, Ronald, and Jennifer K. Lobasz. "Fixing the Meaning of 9/11: Hegemony, Coercion and the Road to War in Iraq." *Security Studies*, 16, no. 3 (July 2007): 409–451.

Kroenig, Matthew. "Time to Attack Iran." *Foreign Affairs*, January–February 2012. Available at: http://www.foreignaffairs.com/articles/136917/matthew-kroenig/time-to-attack-iran.

Kupchan, Charles. "Grand Strategy: The Four Pillars of the Future." *Democracy Journal*, Issue 23, Winter 2012. Available at: http://www.democracyjournal.org/23/grand-strategy-the-four-pillars-of-the-future.php?page=4.

Laïdi, Zaki. "The BRICS against the West?" *CERI Strategy Papers*, no. 11, November 2011. Available at: http://www.ceri-sciencespo.com/ressource/n11_112011.pdf.

———. "Europe as a Risk-Averse Power: A Hypothesis." *Garnet Policy Brief*, no. 11, February 2010. Available at: http://www.garneteu.org/fileadmin/documents/policy_briefs/Garnet_Policy_Brief_No_11.pdf.

Lake, Anthony. "Remarks: From Containment to Enlargement." *Johns Hopkins University School of Advanced International Studies, Washington D.C.*, September 21, 1993. Available at: http://www.mtholyoke.edu/acad/intrel/lakedoc.html.

Larson, Deborah, and Alexei Shevchenko. "Status Seekers: Chinese and Russian Responses to U.S. Primacy." *International Security*, 34, no. 4 (Spring 2010): 63–95.

Layne, Christopher. "The Unipolar Illusion Revisited: The Coming End of the United States' Unipolar Moment." *International Security*, 31, no. 2 (Autumn 2006): 7–41.

Lizza, Ryan. "The Consequentialist: How the Arab Spring Remade Obama's Foreign Policy." *The New Yorker*, May 2, 2011, 44–55. Available at: http://www.newyorker.com/reporting/2011/05/02/110502fa_fact_lizza?currentPage=1.

Lynch, Mark. "Obama's Arab Spring?" *Foreign Policy*, January 6, 2011. Available at: http://lynch.foreignpolicy.com/posts/2011/01/06/obamas_arab_spring.

Maloney, Suzanne. "Obama's Counterproductive New Iran Sanctions: How Washington Is Sliding toward Regime Change." *Foreign Affairs*, January 5, 2012. Available at: http://www.foreignaffairs.com/articles/137011/suzanne- maloney/obamas- counterproductive-new-iran-sanctions?page=2

Mason, Chuck R. "Status of Forces Agreement (SOFA): What Is It, and How Has It Been Utilized?" *CRS Report for Congress*, June 18, 2009. Available at: http://www.fas.org/sgp/crs /natsec/RL34531.pdf.

Mayer, Jane. "The Secret History: Can Leon Panetta Move the C.I.A. Forward without Confronting Its Past?" *The New Yorker*, June 22, 2009. Available at: http://www.newyorker .com/reporting/2009/06/22/090622fa_fact_mayer#ixzz0ubt8aj71.

Maynes, Charles William. "A Workable Clinton Doctrine." *Foreign Policy*, no. 93 (Winter 1993–1994): 3–22.

Miller, Aaron David. "For America, An Arab Winter." *Wilson Quarterly*, Summer 2011. Available at: http://www.wilsonquarterly.com/article.cfm?aid=1967.

Mix, Derek. "The United States and Europe: Current Issues." *CRS Report for Congress*, August 5, 2009. Available at: http://www.fas.org/sgp/crs/row/RS22163.pdf.

Monteiro, Nuno. "Unrest Assured: Why Unipolarity Is Not Peaceful." *International Security*, 36, no. 3 (Winter 2011/12): 9–40. Available at: http://www.nunomonteiro.org/wp-content /uploads/Nuno-Monteiro-Unrest-Assured.pdf.

Morgan, Iwan. "The American Economy and America's Global Power." In *LSE Ideas Report: The United States after Unipolarity,* December 2011, 30–34. Available at: http://www2.lse.ac.uk/IDEAS/publications/reports/pdf/SR009/morgan.pdf.

Nicholson, Michael. "Realism and Utopianism Revisited." *Review of International Studies*, 24, no. 5 (December 1998): 65–82.

O'Connor, Brendon. "American Foreign Policy Traditions: A Literature Review." *Working Paper*, October 2009. Available at: http://ussc.edu.au/s/media/docs/publications/0910 _oconnor_usforeignpolicy.pdf.

Packer, Georges. "Iran Reveals Us." *The New Yorker*, June 16, 2009. Available at: http://www .newyorker.com/online/blogs/georgepacker/2009/06/iran-reveals-us.html.

Perry, Mark. "The Petraeus Briefing: Biden's Embarrassment Is Not the Whole Story." *Foreign Policy,* March 13, 2010. Available at: http://mideast.foreignpolicy.com/posts/2010/03/14 /the_petraeus_briefing_biden_s_embarrassment_is_not_the_whole_story.

Potter, William. "India and the New Look in U.S. Non-Proliferation Policy." *Carnegie Endowment*, August 26, 2005. Available at: http://www.carnegieendowment.org/static /npp/2005conference/presentations/Potter.pdfhttp://cns.miis.edu/npr/pdfs/122potter.pdf.

Potter, William, Patricia Lewis, Gaukhar Mukhatzhanova, and Miles Pomper. "The 2010 NPT Review Conference: Deconstructing Consensus." *CNS Special Report*, June 17, 2010. Available at: http://cns.miis.edu/stories/pdfs/100617_npt_2010_summary.pdf.

Quinn, Adam. "Hard Power in Hard Times: Relative Military Power in an Era of Budgetary Constraint." In *LSE Ideas Report: The United States After Unipolarity*, December 2011, 8–12.

Rashid, Ahmed. "How Obama Lost Karzai: The Road of Afghanistan Runs through Two Presidents Who Just Don't Get Along." *Foreign Policy,* March/April 2011. Available at: http://www.foreignpolicy.com/articles/2011/02/22/how_obama_lost_karzai.

Russell, Gerard. "Foreign Policy, Staying for the Longer-Term in Iraq and Afghanistan?" *Foreign Policy,* August 16, 2010. Available at: http://afpak.foreignpolicy.com/posts/2010/08/16 /staying_for_the_longer_term_in_iraq_and_afghanistan.

Schaub, Gary, and James Forsyth Jr., "An Arsenal We Can All Live With." *The New York Times,* May 24, 2010.

SIGIR. "Hard Lessons: The Iraq Reconstruction Experience." February 2009. Available at: http://www.sigir.mil/files/HardLessons/Hard_Lessons_Report.pdf.

Simon, Steven. "The Price of the Surge: How U.S. Strategy is Hastening Iraq's Demise." *Foreign Affairs*, 87, no. 3 (May–June 2008): 57–76.

Slaughter, Anne-Marie. "Why the U.S Doesn't Need a Grand Strategy." *Belfer Center,* November 3, 2011. Available at: http://belfercenter.ksg.harvard.edu/publication/21482/dr_annemarie _slaughter.html?breadcrumb=%2Fproject%2F61%2Ffuture_of_diplomacy_project.

———. "Adapting U.S. Foreign Policy in a Changing International System," *The Atlantic,* September 19, 2011. Available at: http://www.theatlantic.com/international /archive/2011/09/adapting-us-policy-in-a-changing-international-system/245307/.

Stewart, Rory. "What Could Work," *The New York Review of Books,* January 14, 2010.

Tardelli, Luca. "Obama's Interventions: Afghanistan, Iraq, Libya." In *LSE Ideas Report: The United States after Unipolarity,* December 2011, 18–23. Available at: http://www2.lse.ac.uk /IDEAS/publications/reports/pdf/SR009/tardelli.pdf.

Telhami, Shibley. "The American Public and the Arab Awakening." *The Brookings Institution,* April 12, 2011. Available at: http://www.brookings.edu/~/media/Files/rc/ reports/2011/0412 _middle_east_poll_telhami/0412_middle_east_poll_telhami.pdf.

Waldman, Matt. "The Sun in the Sky: The Relationship Between Pakistan's ISI and Afghan Insurgents." *Crisis States Discussion Paper 18,* June 2010. Available at: http://www.crisisstates .com/download/dp/DP 18.pdf.

Walt, Stephen. "The End of the American Era." *The National Interest,* October 25, 2011. Available at: http://nationalinterest.org/article/the-end-the-american-era-6037.

———. "International Relations: One World, Many Theories." *Foreign Policy,* Spring 1998. Available at: http://www.columbia.edu/itc/sipa/S6800/courseworks/foreign_pol_walt.pdf.

———. "The Relationship between Theory and Policy in International Relations." *Annual Review of Political Science,* 8 (2005): 23–48.

———. "Why Attacking Iran Is Still a Bad Idea." *Foreign Policy,* December 27, 2010. Available at: http://walt.foreignpolicy.com/posts/2011/12/27/why_attacking_iran_is_still_a_bad_idea.

Waltz, Kenneth. "International Politics Is Not Foreign Policy." *Security Studies,* 6, no. 1 (1996): 54–57.

———. "Structural Realism after the Cold War." *Security Studies,* 25, no. 1 (Summer 2000): 5–41.

Witney, Nick, and Jeremy Shapiro. "Towards a Post-American Europe: A Power Audit of EU-US Relations." *ECFR,* November 2, 2009. Available at: http://ecfr.3cdn. net/05b80f1a80154dfc64_x1m6bgxc2.pdf.

Wohlforth, William. "Unipolarity, Status Competition and Great Power War." *World Politics,* 61, no. 1 (January 2009): 28–57.

Testimonies before Congress

Bowen, Stuart. "Oversight: Hard Lessons Learned In Iraq and Benchmarks for Future Reconstruction Efforts." *Comm. on Foreign Affairs,* 111th Cong. (February 24, 2010). Available at: http://www.sigir.mil/files/USOCO/SIGIR_Testimony_10–002T.pdf.

Craddock, John. "Oral Statement for the Senate Foreign Relations Committee." *Hearing on the NATO Strategic Concept* (October 22, 2009). Available at: http://foreign.senate.gov/imo /media/doc/CraddockTestimony091022a.pdf.

Graham, Thomas. "Transatlantic Security in the 21st Century: Do New Threats Require New Approaches?" *Hearing Before the Committee on Foreign Affairs,* 111th Cong. (March 17, 2010). Available at: http://www.internationalrelations.house.gov/111/55514.pdf.

Haqqani, Husain. "U.S. Policy Toward Pakistan." *Hearing Before the Subcommittee on the Middle East and South Asia Comm. on Foreign Affairs,* 110th Cong. (March 2007). Available at: http:// foreignaffairs.house.gov/110/34239.pdf.

Hormats, Robert. "On Strenghtening the Transatlantic Economy: Moving Beyond the Crisis." *The Senate Foreign Relations Comm. Subcommittee on European Affairs,* 111th Cong. (December 9, 2009). Available at: http://foreign.senate.gov/imo/media/doc /HormatsTestimony091209p(2).pdf.

Maloney, Suzanne. "Progress of the Obama Administration's Policy Toward Iran." *Testimony Before the House Subcommittee on National Security, Homeland Defense and Foreign Operations, Comm. on Oversight and Government Reform,* 112th Cong. (November 15, 2011). Available at: http://www.brookings.edu/testimony/2011/1115_iran_policy_maloney.aspx.

Prasad, Eswar. "The U.S-China Economic Relationship: Shifts and Twists in the Balance of Power," *Hearing on "U.S. Debt to China: Implications and Repercussions," U.S-China Economic and Security Review Commission,* March 10, 2010, 111th Cong. Available at: http://prasad .dyson.cornell.edu/doc/policy/USCESRCTestimony.Rev01Mar10.pd f.

Weinbaum, Marvin. "Bad Company: Lashkar E-Tayyiba and the Growing Ambition of Islamist Militancy in Pakistan." *Hearing Before the Subcommittee on the Middle East and South Asia of the Comm. on Foreign Affairs,* 111th Cong. (March 11, 2010). Available at: http://www.inter nationalrelations.house.gov/111/55399.pdf.

Wilson, Damon. "NATO Post-60: Institutional Challenges Moving Forward." *Hearing Before the Comm. on Foreign Relations,* 111th Cong. (May 6, 2009). Available at: http://foreign .senate.gov/imo/media/doc/WilsonTestimony090506p1.pdf.

Official documents

Albright, Madeleine, and Jeroen van der Veer. "NATO 2020: Assured Security, Dynamic Engagement: Analysis and Recommendations of the Group of Experts on a New Strategic Concept for NATO," Brussels, *NATO,* May 17, 2010. Available at: http://www.nato.int /nato_static/assets/pdf/pdf_2010_05/2010_05_D8B67F56A5CD4F44805365DB21B29108 _expertsreport_fr.pdfhttp://carnegieendowment.org/pdf/20100517_100517_expertsreport.pdf.

Department of Defense, Defense Guidance Review, 2012. Available at: http://www.defense.gov /news/Defense_Strategic_Guidance.pdf.

McChrystal, Stanley. "COMISAF's Initial Assessment." August 30, 2009. Available at: http:// www.washingtonpost.com/wpdyn/content/article/2009/09/21/AR2009092100110.html.

Text of the National Security Act of 1947. Available at: http://www.law.cornell.edu/uscode /html/uscode50/usc_sec_50_00000401 − − 000-notes.html.

U.S. Department of Defense, *Nuclear Posture Review Report,* April 2010. Available at: www. defense.gov/npr/docs/2010 Nuclear Posture Review Report.pdf.

U.S. Department of State, Bureau of Political-Military Affairs. "Counterinsurgency Guide: United States Government Interagency Counterinsurgency Initiative." January 2009. Available at: http://www.state.gov/documents/organization/119629.pdf.

The White House. National Security Strategy, 2002. Available at: http://georgewbush-white house.archives.gov/nsc/nss/2002/nss.pdf.

————. National Security Strategy, 2006. Available at: http://www.comw.org/qdr/fulltext /nss2006.pdf.

————. National Security Strategy, 2010. Available at: http://www.whitehouse.gov/sites /default/files/rss_viewer/national_security_strategy.pdf.

————. "White Paper of the Interagency Policy Group's Report on U.S. Policy toward Afghanistan and Pakistan." March 2009. Available at: http://www.whitehouse.gov/assets /documents/Afghanistan-Pakistan_White_Paper.pdf.

INDEX